TELEWORKING EXPLAINED

Mike Gray
BT, UK

Noel Hodson
SW2000, UK

Gil Gordon
Gil Gordon Associates, USA

JOHN WILEY & SONS
Chichester • New York • Brisbane • Toronto • Singapore

BT will donate the royalties for the sale of this book to the registered charity,
OUTSET. OUTSET develops technology-related employment opportunities
for disabled people—training some 400 people a year in computer and modern
office skills. OUTSET also provides a consultancy service covering all aspects of
disability and employment and runs a number of technology-based businesses
demonstrating the contribution made by disabled employees.

Other Wiley Editorial Offices

John Wiley & Sons, Inc., 605 Third Avenue,
New York, NY 10158-0012, USA

Jacaranda Wiley Ltd, G.P.O. Box 859, Brisbane,
Queensland 4001, Australia

John Wiley & Sons (Canada) Ltd, 22 Worcester Road,
Rexdale, Ontario M9W 1L1, Canada

John Wiley & Sons (SEA) Pte Ltd, 37 Jalan Pemimpin #05-04,
Block B, Union Industrial Building, Singapore 2057

Library of Congress Cataloging-in-Publication Data

Teleworking explained / Mike Gray, Noel Hodson, Gil Gordon.
    p.   cm.
    Includes bibliographical references and index.
    ISBN 0 471 93975 7
    1. Telecommuting.   I. Gray, Mike, 1946–   . II. Hodson, Noel.
III. Gordon, Gil.'
HD2333. T45   1993
331. 25—dc20   93–26459
                                                      CIP

British Library Cataloguing in Publication Data

A catalogue record for this book is available from the British Library

ISBN 0 471 93975 7

Typeset in 10/12pt Palatino from author's disks by Text Processing Department,
John Wiley & Sons Ltd, Chichester
Printed and bound in Great Britain by Bookcraft (Bath) Ltd

Contents

Foreword

Teleworking Explained adds a detailed, practical guide for organisational managers and for individuals to the growing body of teleworking literature. Variously termed as Home Working, Remote Working, Dispersed Working and Telecommuting, and carried on in households, telecentres and telecottages as well as from cars, commercial vehicles, ships, planes and hotel rooms, teleworking is growing as a way of life around the world. Telephone networks now transmit information around the globe with increasing speed and reliability. Clerical workers in Ireland are employed by American insurance companies as efficiently as if they were in the USA. Islands such as Jamaica, Hawaii and Majorca are establishing telecentres, working for mainland employers.

Wherever there is a functioning telephone, a local centre can be established. For the first time, regular work, of all grades of importance, is being brought to people without an absolute need for a modern physical transport infrastructure. While remote working is not new—in the 19th century hundred of thousands of families subsisted on piecework brought to their homes and collected by agents from the cities—electronics applications enable sophisticated, high-level remote working. Teleworking has been extended from being confined to electronics and computer experts to people of all ages, in most countries and all walks of life. Teleworking switches the focus of work from who you are to what you do, reducing bias and bigotry in employment. Through electronics, housebound people can become as effective and valued as the most mobile of executives.

Teleworking is trans-national and is recognised by all advanced economies as a boon to their populations' wealth and life styles. Singapore, with its determined policy to outstrip the USA on *per capita* income, possibly has the most complete home-wired network, closely followed by Japan, also publicly embracing teleworking. In the UK, every school had computers for children before most other countries. In the USA, President Bush promoted telecommuting, and the Clinton administration, announcing the 'Information Superhighway', endorses it. Teleworking offers a way to contain consumption of fuel with important implications for the oil industry and for the balance of payments of most economies.

Since the 1950s, when bookmakers would give 5000 to 1 against a human being reaching the Moon, commentators have predicted that electronics would change the way we live and work. They were right. Modern telecommunication networks, computer equipment, fax machines, mobile phones, and other peripherals, have been made available to every home and desk top. Neil Armstrong not only confounded the bookmakers when he stepped onto the moon but also became a pioneer teleworker.

Managers need to be alert to the human issues involved and to measure the results of increasing the numbers of teleworkers. Families need help to incorporate a modern office in the home and can help the teleworker make the transition to working in a sometimes isolated home. Colleagues in the central office are obliged to learn new communication skills and to support their invisible team mates.

Successful teleworking is not brought about by electronics and economics alone. Hence this book seeks to be a practical guide by also addressing other relevant areas. It contains sections to guide readers through the tangled maze of what to buy, what to learn, and what to keep for efficient teleworking. The authors who have contributed to this book planned to cover, and have covered, all the main teleworking issues for officers in corporations, companies and government bodies and for individuals. I commend the fruits of their labours to you.

Bruce Bond
Group Products & Services Director
BT

Contributors

Andy Ashmore (author) joined BT in 1981 as a trainee technician in the Inverness area. He was involved in the installation of telephone exchange and digital transmission equipment throughout the north of Scotland. In 1988 he was sponsored by BT through the University of Salford, Information Technology Institute, and in 1991 gained a BSc Honours degree in Information Technology. Andy joined the Teleworking Systems Group at BT Laboratories in 1991. Since then he has been investigating all aspects of teleworking and has gained considerable experience in setting up trials of teleworking with several major companies.

Clive Carrington (author) joined BT Laboratories in 1988 with a BSc in Electronic Engineering from Essex University. He has worked on the teleworking project since November 1989, working on the Inverness teleworking experiment as the design team leader responsible for hardware, communications and installation. He was part of the Martlesham support team for the experiment.

Angela Eden (author) works in BT as an organisational change consultant and supports managers who maintain international and local telecommunications networks. After gaining London University Diplomas in Education and Social Policy and Administration she worked in the public sector in social and economic development departments. She has initiated and managed national community projects, adult training and management workshops. She was trained as a consultant at the Tavistock Clinic in London, has consulted to public and private sector organisations, and contributed to teleworking seminars with SW2000 in Oxford.

Paul Foster (author) began his career with BT as a trainee technician apprentice in 1973, and with BT sponsorship gained a First Class Honours degree in Computer Science. He joined BT Laboratories in 1983 working on advanced Videotex systems for cable television networks. Later he played a major part in developing software for an operator-assisted Yellow Pages system (Talking Pages) and a videotex information services database. In 1990 he joined the Teleworking Systems Group where he was Project Leader for the homeworking experiment with Directory Assistance Operators in Inverness.

Mike Foxton (author) graduated in Electrical and Electronic Engineering from Heriott-Watt University in 1971 and joined BT. After an initial period studying circuit switched data networks he spent 10 years on the development of System X, working on the switching systems. In 1983 he joined a division studying how optical fibres can be used in the local loop. His present interests lie mainly in the evolution of the ISDN service.

Nick Good (author) joined BT in 1986, after gaining an Honours degree at Oxford Polytechnic. He has worked on the development of office automation systems, including work to integrate electronic mail systems. Other work has included the development of a race information distribution system, based on Telecom Gold, for the Whitbread Round the World Yacht Race. In 1991, he joined the Teleworking Systems Group, and was involved in the development and installation of the Directory Assistance teleworking experiment in Inverness.

Gil Gordon (author and editor) is founder of Gil Gordon Associates, a consulting firm specialising in telecommuting and other alternative work arrangements. Since 1982 he has worked with employers and governments in North America, Europe and the Pacific Rim to implement successful programmes. He is recognised worldwide as a leading authority on telecommuting. He edits the monthly newsletter *Telecommuting Review*, co-authored the book *Telecommuting, How to Make It Work for You and Your Company*, and has been a conference speaker across the USA and around the world. He has a BS in Business Administration from Northeastern University and an MS in Organizational Behaviour from Cornell University. Before starting his consulting business, he worked in Human Resources with Johnson & Johnson.

Mike Gray (author and editor) joined the Post Office Research Department, now BT Laboratories, in 1972 after obtaining an Honours degree in Electronic Engineering at Leeds University, on a Post Office scholarship. Worked initially on methods for assessing transmission performance of telephony products, including computer-controlled testing. Later work included the design of colour-graphics workstations for integrated circuit design, before managing projects on computerised geographic mapping systems and public service database enquiry systems. He has been involved in teleworking since 1988, as the Teleworking Systems Group `Technical Group Leader', managing a number of major teleworking projects. Within the overall aim of developing systems to support teleworking, the projects have included thorough studies of many of the issues impacting on teleworking, the setting up of a unique experiment in homeworking for BT's operators, and helping a number of teleworking trials get started both in BT and in other corporations.

Peter Harding (author) is an Electronic Security Project Manager with BT's Commercial Security Unit. He has some 26 years of IT experience ranging from mainframe computer operations to computer audit of datacentres and computing installations. He has been involved in computer/electronic security since 1986 and his experience ranges from the roll-out and implementation of a multi-site, national computer system, security reviews of business critical systems, virus detection and prevention, developing and implementing security policies and standards, throughout BT's global operations, to the introduction of ITSEC (Information Technology Security Evaluation Criteria) for the evaluation of new systems.

Neil Hendry (author) a personnel specialist in BT's personnel policy department. He has been with BT for 20 years and in the Personnel Policy Unit for the past 13 years. In 1992 he produced BT's *Teleworking: Guidelines for Managers*, setting out advice on the personnel, taxation and other factors for managers to be aware of when introducing homeworking.

Martin Hodges (author) received the degrees of BA, MSc and PhD from Essex University in 1976, 1977 and 1979 respectively. He joined BT Research Laboratories in 1980 to work on speech detectors for digital circuit multiplication systems. Since then he has worked on low rate speech coding, contributing to the CCITT standardisation of

G721, the 32 kbit/s ADPCM standard, and been actively involved in GSM radio studies, this latter activity involving work in the GSM standards arena and significant work with Cellnet on their GSM radio trials activity. He is currently a Technical Group Leader in the Cellular Radio Systems Section at BT Laboratories.

Noel Hodson (author and editor) in 1979, 10 years after founding the firm, left Blackstone Franks, Accountants, to work from home to see more of his children and avoid commuting. In 1983 he launched Morton Hodson & Co. Ltd, a teleworked business consultancy franchise, which operates 52 offices, 48 of which are at home. He formed SW2000 in 1988 which conducted workshops, in Oxford, on teleworking, with delegates from 120 major employers, some of whom set up teleworking pilot projects. In 1990 he published *Working Environment News* and in 1991 wrote *The Economics of Teleworking*. He researched teleworking in large UK organisations in 1989, 1990 and 1992. He is a leading teleworker consultant in the UK.

Pauline Hodson (author) is an Associate of the Tavistock Institute of Marital Studies and is in private practice as a marital psychotherapist. In 1988 she co-led workshops for the SW2000 Teleworking Studies on flexible and home working and is co-leading a therapy group for couples in Oxford. Her interest in teleworking is not only academic; she has worked at home for six years and has had first-hand experience since 1979, when her husband switched from commuting to teleworking when her two daughters were 8 and 12 years old.

Roy Hunter (author) graduated from the University of Manchester in 1968 and later received his PhD degree from the University of Salford. He joined the Post Office Research Department, now BT Laboratories, in 1971 and has been involved in the standardisation of telecommunication systems with respect to facsimile and the interchange of multimedia information between heterogeneous office systems. He has represented BT on various ISO and CCITT standards committees. Currently, he is involved in the integration of fax and computer applications and the development of information retrieval systems, in particular.

Alison Hutchins (author) joined BT Laboratories in 1989 as a Technical Officer to work on a major BT project investigating new products and services for personal and residential customers. Now a Professional Development Engineer, she has worked for the Teleworking Systems Group for the past three years. She has been involved in a number of teleworking projects including the development and installation of systems for the Inverness experiment as well as presenting and developing multimedia teleworking demonstrations. In 1992 she was one of the five finalists for the `Young Woman Engineer of the Year' award.

Douglas Jones (author) joined BT in 1987 as a sponsored student. He graduated in 1991 with a M.Eng. Honours degree from York University. After graduation he joined BT Laboratories as a member of the Teleworking Systems Group. Since that time he has been involved in the development and installation of systems for the teleworking experiment in Inverness, as well as research into the applications of video technology to teleworking.

Andrew McGrath (author and illustrator) trained at Glasgow School of Art and Manchester Polytechnic as an industrial and project designer gaining a BA Honours degree and an MA. He is involved in a number of teleworking projects for BT, in particular projects involving the design of teleworking spaces, furniture and equipment.

Ron Penny (author and project co-ordinator)   graduated from Robert Gordon's University in 1988 with an Honours degree in Electronic and Electrical Engineering . He joined BT Laboratories in the same year to work on the development of Local Area Network—Wide Area Network bridging. In 1989 he participated in a major BT project investigating new products and services for personal and residential customers. Since 1992 he has led BT's Teleworking Studies programme and been responsible for the development of a TeleServices Centre in the north of Scotland.

Alastair Rogers (author)   a Technical Advisor at BT Laboratories with a special interest in applications for multimedia and groupware. He is a member of a section within the Visual Applications Division concerned with the development of multimedia applications, particularly for major business customers. His previous experience includes work on telecommunication architectures and distributed systems.

Julian Stubbs (author)   after graduating from Oxford in 1971, worked in advertising for a leading London advertising agency and joined BT in 1975. He now leads a team of professional analysts in BT Group Products and Services Management involved *inter alia* in evaluating strategic options for developing and introducing appropriate competitive products and services for BT's volume markets (individuals, households, small businesses) in the UK and abroad. He is a member of the Chartered Institute of Marketing.

David Tucknutt (author)   graduated from Strathclyde University in 1985 with a BSc Honours degree in Computer Science. Joined BT Laboratories to work on Videotex research and development. He has been working in the area of teleworking since 1989. The work has involved leading studies of technical, managerial and social aspects of teleworking. At the time of writing, he has been initiating trials of teleworking, mainly within BT.

Chris Tuppen (author)   joined BT Laboratories in 1979 after completion of his BSc and PhD in Chemistry at Bristol University. Spent 12 years in semiconductor research before becoming BT's first Environment Manager in 1991. Current responsibilities include the coordination of environmental policy for the BT group, communicating progress to internal and external audiences and managing an environmental site auditing programme. He was directly responsible for the 1992 BT Environmental Performance Report which won the 1992 Chartered Association of Certified Accountants (ACCA) award for corporate environmental reporting. He has authored over 40 published papers, is a fellow of the Royal Society of Arts and a member of the Institute of Physics.

John Withnell (author)   graduated from the University of London in 1989 with a degree in Electronic Engineering and is currently a Senior Professional Development Engineer at BT Laboratories. He has been a member of the Teleworking Systems Group for four years. During this time he has worked closely both with customers and with other parts of BT, to explore the feasibility of introducing teleworking. Experience gained in the course of this work has been used to develop a process for capturing the technical and people requirements of a teleworking system.

Conversion Factors

'Billion' in this book follows the American convention, meaning one thousand million (one followed by nine zeros). The British convention was that one billion meant one million million (one followed by twelve zeros), being 1000 times more; this 12-zero number is 'trillion' in the USA, whose standards are used throughout the financial world. The abbreviation M is used for million and B for billion.

Money is converted at US\$1.42 = £1 sterling. Some comparative costs reflect price variations between the UK and USA.

30 miles per US gallon = 8 miles per litre
30 miles per UK gallon = 6.6 miles per litre

1 UK gallon (4.5460 litres) – 1.2 US gallons (3.785 litres)

1 UK ton (2240 lb) – 1.12 US tons (2000 lb)
1 UK ton – 1.016 metric tonnes = 1016 kg
1 US ton = 0.907 metric tonne = 907 kg.

1

Overview

'Flexible workplace policies will allow you to find and keep the best talent. And one of the most promising of these new business frontiers is telecommuting.'

George Bush 1990

1.1   INTRODUCTION

When George Bush made that statement in 1990, he used the word 'telecommuting', rather than 'teleworking', but the principle remains the same. Teleworking is *still* one of the most promising new business frontiers.

For several years, pundits have proclaimed that we are in the age of the 'Information Revolution', which will change the way we work as surely as the Industrial Revolution transformed the working lives of people in the 18th and 19th centuries. Not only will the way we work change, but *where* we work will also undergo a fundamental change. Indeed, the suggestion is that the Information Revolution will reverse the work-location trends of the Industrial Revolution.

Prior to the Industrial Revolution, people mostly lived and worked in villages. The shift of work to the factories meant that workers had to leave the countryside to live in the towns and villages near the factories. Following the Information Revolution, the majority of people will work with information rather than with physical objects. No longer will people be forced to travel to a factory or city-centre office to work. Modern communications networks are capable of carrying that information to wherever the people are—wherever they want to work. It has been predicted that huge numbers of people will choose to live and work in country areas. Some of these predictions may prove to be over-optimistic, but at least it is now possible for many to work remotely—the technology to allow it does exist (as we shall show in this book).

Teleworking Explained is aimed primarily at senior managers in medium and large corporations. For those managers who are considering whether their company should be investigating the use of teleworking, the book will explain the issues to be tackled, describe how to evaluate the costs and benefits and give practical advice on starting up a teleworking programme.

Although much of the book is concerned with the corporate view of teleworking, the individual's viewpoint is also important, and is given full coverage. There is advice, for example, on how to integrate working at home into the home environment, and into the rest of the family! Such advice will be of direct interest to individuals in persuading their organisations to let them work at home. It is also valuable to the corporate manager responsible for implementing a teleworking programme—it helps with briefing and training the potential teleworkers.

By giving corporate and individual advice, *Teleworking Explained* should help employees and employers understand the other's point of view.

1.2   TELEWORKING DEFINED

The first step in explaining teleworking is to define it. That is not as easy as it sounds. Most people will understand that the word itself implies 'working at a distance', but that is only the beginning.

Much of the trouble stems from the fact that there is no generally accepted definition of teleworking—different people use it with slightly different meanings, and even use a variety of other words meaning something similar. So as well as *teleworking*, a survey of the literature shows *telecommuting, networking, remote working, flexible working* and *homeworking* are all common. In the absence of consensus, we need our own definition for use in this book. Unfortunately, defining teleworking is no simple task, as it covers a variety of working practices.

Teleworking is a flexible way of working which covers a wide range of work activities, all of which entail working remotely from an employer, or from a traditional place of work, for a significant proportion of work time. Teleworking may be on either a full-time or a part-time basis. The work often involves electronic processing of information, and always involves using telecommunications to keep the remote employer and employee in contact with each other.

This definition excludes traditional 'outworkers', as well as people who work at home very occasionally, but includes:

- people working *at home* (e.g. programmers)
- people working *from home* (e.g. salespeople),
- people working at *work centres* (such as telecottages, or satellite offices).

Whatever form of words is used, it seems possible to think of a way of working which falls into a grey area, where it is not clear whether or not it counts as teleworking. A commonly accepted principle is that, to be classified as telework, the job must involve a new way of working.

A few more examples will help clarify the concept behind the definition.

Those teleworkers who are considered *full-time homeworkers* work at home nearly all their working hours (full- or part-time). They may visit an office for meetings or to pick up material from time to time. Although the visits may be regular, they are not likely to amount to more than a day or so a week on average. Into this category fit the computer programmers and analysts who have featured heavily in much that has been written on teleworking, the catalogue shopping telephone order agents who work for J. C. Penney in the USA, and data entry clerks, such as those employed by the London Borough of Enfield, to meet a peak workload caused by changes to local council taxing procedures.

The definition of teleworking excludes the traditional piecework homeworker, often an outworker for the textile industry, as such people make virtually no use of telecommunications or information technology as part of their work.

There are also *part-time homeworkers* who work in an office, but spend perhaps two or more days a week working at home. These tend to be managers and professionals—people with sufficient seniority in an organisation to justify the additional expenditure on information technology (IT) equipment at home as well as at work. The choice of two days at home is somewhat arbitrary, but we need to be able to distinguish between these homeworkers and the multitude of managers who take some work home for the occasional day to finish a report in peace and quiet, for example, or to work in the evening. These occasional homeworkers probably work at home on an entirely *ad hoc* basis (see Chapter 7.1). They have little need for the support technology described in this book, have a contract of employment which ignores the possibility of working at home, and have usually given little thought to the issues of working at home, such as security, safety, insurance and so on—issues which this book tackles.

Mobile teleworkers are those who spend most of their time out of the office, either 'on the road' or in customers' premises. These are typically salespeople, service engineers and consultants. The mobile teleworker's office, or base, may be at home or in a normal office building—or even occasionally in a vehicle. Mobile teleworking can also be thought of as 'location-independent working'.

Throughout the world, location-independent working defines one of the most populous and well-established group of teleworkers (Table 1.2 p25), although the majority of mobile teleworkers do not think of themselves as teleworkers at all! The distinguishing feature of mobile teleworkers is their use of communications and computing. A travelling salesperson who uses a lap-top PC to produce quotations and take orders on customers' premises and who uses cellular radio to get orders back to the head office immediately is a teleworker; the salesperson who collects a list of customers to visit from the office on a Monday morning and isn't in touch with the office again until Friday afternoon when the paper orders are handed in, is not a teleworker. Obviously, the definition is not watertight, and common sense has to be applied to each situation.

Another identifiable group of teleworkers is all those people who work in a *work centre*. Work centres vary widely from the rural telecentre (sometimes known as a telecottage) to a company satellite office. For the purposes of this book, a satellite office is a small office, remote from the company head office, which is not self-sufficient, i.e. it relies on good communications links with the head office. Desks and workstations in a work centre may be permanently allocated to an individual, or may be available on a short-term basis to a number of individuals. The full range of work centres are explained later in this book.

In teleworking terms, the work centre is a halfway house between the central office working situation and homeworking. Employees are more likely to be able to adapt to working in a centre than to working at home. Traditional employers find it easier to manage small groups of workers than dispersed individuals. However, there are some benefits of homeworking that would not be realised to the full in a work centre.

Because teleworking is essentially a flexible way of working, there are also working practices that may encompass two or more of the situations described. For example, it is possible to envisage a consultant who has a central office as a base. A large proportion of the consultant's time may be spent in customers' offices. To avoid interruptions, the consultant may write reports at home, or in a local work centre. The consultant's desk in the central office may be shared with a number of other consultants—since none of them are in the main office for more than a day or two a week. This process of sharing desks is often described as 'hot desking'.

1.3   TELEWORKING: BENEFITS ALL ROUND

What are the benefits of teleworking, and who are the beneficiaries? One of the attractions of teleworking is that almost everyone can benefit.

Companies adopting a teleworking programme can benefit in one or more of the following ways:

- Complying with environmental legislation aimed at reducing commuting

- Saving on overhead costs—city office accommodation, staff commuting costs (e.g. New York and London 'Loading' or 'Weighting')

- Flexibility—of staff working patterns, of ability to respond to new competitive challenges

- Skills retention—continuing to employ skilled staff who would otherwise leave

- Greater recruitment opportunities—people who live too far from the 'office' or who are housebound

- Increased productivity—teleworking programmes almost invariably show greater productivity from the teleworkers

● Resilience—against extreme weather conditions, terrorist activity, and public transportation system breakdowns

Individual teleworkers are also likely to benefit from some, if not all, of the following:

● Reduced commuting, leading to
    —saving money
    —saving time
    —less stress

● Flexibility—in many jobs, the teleworker is able to arrange working hours to suit personal needs

● Greater autonomy—people suitable for teleworking are likely to be self-reliant and enjoy the extra autonomy and responsibility that teleworking gives them

● Freedom—in many small ways: wearing 'comfortable' clothes, not having to sit next to someone you dislike, the ability to control your own working environment

The benefits of teleworking are much more widespread than just to those people involved in teleworking programmes, particularly through the reduction in commuting. Fewer commuting journeys means less pollution of the environment, and this is the major driver for the spread of telecommuting in the USA. However, once teleworking has grown so that significant numbers do not have to travel to city centres, road congestion is eased and the pressures on public transport will be reduced—bringing benefits to non-teleworkers as well.

Inevitably, there must be some losers. In particular, the losers will be those who provide facilities for office workers, but who are themselves location-dependent. Two examples are the builders of city-centre office blocks, and sandwich bars catering for office workers' lunchtime needs.

On balance, there are far greater benefits to be gained at the national and international level by the encouragement of mass teleworking than there will be losses.

1.4   WHAT THE BOOK COVERS

In this first chapter, teleworking is described for those perhaps not familiar with the many varieties of teleworking. This chapter includes a look back at how teleworking has evolved and a peep into the crystal ball to see what the future might hold.

The bulk of the book draws attention to the issues involved in teleworking programmes, and gives practical advice on the appropriate actions. The major sections of the book cover:

- The economics of teleworking—including guidance on how to balance costs against benefits from both the corporate and individual's point of view.

- Security aspects—one of the biggest worries for companies considering teleworking is the security of their information when the workforce is dispersed.

- The home perspective—teleworking from an individual's point of view, advising on tax and together with the impact of working at home on the rest of the family.

- Corporate and Human Resource Management issues—covering a number of subjects from selecting teleworkers to their management and support, together with advice on contracts of employment.

- Technology to enable and support teleworking forms the biggest section of the book—covering the different ways of keeping in touch (phones, fax, electronic mail, videophones, mobile phones), the pros and cons of the different types of telecommunications network that can be used, and the computer programs that can be used to help a dispersed team work together.

- The Bibliography suggests some sources of further information about the various aspects of teleworking. The editors would have liked to include it all in this book, but there isn't the space!

The book deals mainly with the USA and UK situations. There will be differences in legal and regulatory situations that make some advice (e.g. tax, safety) inappropriate in other countries, but most of the principles (training, support, management, communication, etc.) can be interpreted to fit local situations almost anywhere in the world.

The advice given is based on the most up-to-date expert opinion available at the time of writing. Some advice is less specific than ideal, because some issues are 'grey areas'. Particular examples are the tax liabilities of payments to homeworkers for additional expenses of running the home, whether or not part of the home is classified as a business for taxation purposes, the boundary of liability between employer and employee for safety in the home, and so on. Current legislation was not written with high-tech homeworking in mind. These situations are not likely to be resolved until the number of teleworkers has grown substantially.

Similarly, technology is changing rapidly. Competition and regulation in the telecommunications industry is bringing rapid changes worldwide. The rate of technological advance in the computing industry is staggering for the layman. By the time that this book is published, there will undoubtedly have been several announcements of new products or services that will aid teleworking.

In all areas, *Teleworking Explained* covers the bulk of the ground, and should give the basic knowledge needed to embark on a teleworking programme, but experts should be consulted for the most up-to-date information before taking any major decisions or making large purchases.

The existence of this book is largely the result of research and development work by BT since about 1988. Much of the work has been done by a multi-skilled team based at BT Laboratories, Martlesham Heath, near Ipswich, England. This team has been researching the teleworking scene to enable BT to develop the products, network services and network applications that will encourage and support teleworking. The team has experience of evaluating a wide range of teleworking situations both within the company and through dealings with a number of major UK companies in various market sectors. One of the problems with the production of this book has been the reduction of the information, already published in report form by the team, to fit it into the book.

The book also includes contributions from other specialist parts of BT, particularly from the Security, Training, Environmental and Personnel departments. The latter have had to tackle many of the thorny issues of teleworking (particularly working at home), such as tax, insurance, employment contracts, health, safety and so on, on behalf of BT's own teleworkers. Their experience has been incorporated into *Teleworking Explained*.

To add to the BT team's expertise, and to ensure that the BT authors did not have a blinkered view, external consultants have provided invaluable assistance. Significant sections of the book, on the issues of economics and tax, and the American dimension, have been the work of the consultants, as authors and co-editors.

A list of the authors and editors will be found at the front of the book. A description of how the contributors collaborated in the production of the book is given in Chapter 7.7.

1.5 ENABLING TECHNOLOGY

One of the reasons why teleworking is such a 'hot topic' at the moment is that the development of computing and communications technology has reached the stage to make remote working, but keeping in touch, a possibility. This point is not always appreciated, however, by those senior executives of companies who are the ones who will determine whether or not the company adopts flexible working practices as a policy.

A survey of attitudes to teleworking amongst senior decision makers in 27 large UK corporations was conducted in 1990 by BT. 'Telecomms and technology' was found to be the third largest *perceived* barrier to the adoption of teleworking, following closely behind 'Management attitudes' and 'Social isolation'. Note the word 'perceived': for those jobs which are suitable for teleworking—mostly information processing work—telecomms and technology were not a barrier to teleworking in 1990; they are even less so today, in 1993. Indeed, at the 'Telecommute 92' conference in Washington, DC, in a debate entitled 'Real Telecommuting Growth is Limited by Inadequate Technology', no-one argued that technology was a barrier to teleworking. The arguments were really about how it could be improved—and everyone wanted it, telecomms in particular, cheaper of course!

This all goes to show that, so far, the technologists have not made a good job of educating the world on just what is possible these days. Hopefully, for those of you sufficiently interested in teleworking to have picked up this book, the later chapters on technology will give you a good insight, so that you can see how telecommunications and technology would enable your job to be done remotely, or how some of the employees in your company could be adequately managed and supported in teleworking themselves.

That we are in this position is entirely due to the digital revolution. Today, you can carry round in your briefcase a notebook-sized computer that has the computing power of a 'supercomputer' of only a few years ago. The price/performance ratio of personal computers has been dropping by 30% a year or more. The costs of providing all the computing facilities that a teleworker would need at home, for example, are more than outweighed by the other advantages to the employer—as we shall see later in the book.

Although the digital revolution has not so far brought down the costs of telecommunications to the same degree as those of computers, the costs are reducing in real terms. Many companies introducing teleworking programmes will find that their telecommunications bill increases (hence the interest amongst all telecommunications companies in promoting teleworking), but as with the costs of computing equipment this will be outweighed by the other benefits to the company.

Digital exchanges and digital networks have brought other advantages for remote workers, too. Digital networks, while used for voice communications, are by their very nature suited to the transmission of data. The network known as ISDN (explained in Chapter 6.1) will reliably transmit data at 64 kbit/s in the UK[1] (56 kbit/s in the USA) for the same cost per minute as an ordinary telephone call on the analogue network—which is capable of transmitting data at 9.6 kbit/s (sometimes even 19.2 kbit/s) via a modem, but is usually restricted to 2.4 kbit/s or 4.8 kbit/s for reliability.

The digital exchanges can perform a number of 'tricks' that are useful for teleworkers: call diversion, conference calls, itemised billing, calling line identification, and so on.

There is no one set of computing/communications facilities that will provide support for all teleworkers. Each type of job needs to be examined individually and appropriate facilities provided. There is a wide range of facilities to choose from. This book is not large enough to detail them all, but the technology chapters will provide the basic knowledge to enable the layman to talk intelligently with the expert when seeking detailed advice.

In the meantime, the following are a few ideas to whet your appetite:

- Data transmission to and from the remote worker: modems for low-speed data over the traditional network; packet data networks for higher-

---

[1] kbit/s = kilobits per second. One kilobit is one thousand (actually 1024) binary digits. For normal transmission of data over a telephone line, one kilobit is roughly equal to 100 text characters.

speed, bulk, data (but not in real time); the digital (ISDN) network for real-time data, including multimedia; mobile data networks for the tele-worker on the move.

- Keeping in touch: telephones; audioconferencing; pagers, voice mail-boxes and cellphones for the mobile teleworker; desktop videophones; videoconferencing for larger groups; electronic mail; fax.

- Sharing information: electronic 'bulletin boards'; fax broadcasts; computer supported cooperative working (CSCW), also known as 'group-ware'; electronic 'whiteboards'; remote access to databases; wide area networks; bridges for local area networks.

Some of the enabling technology will have multiple uses in a teleworking programme. Take as an example videophones, which are now an affordable reality, with versions available for both the ordinary analogue network and the digital network. They have obvious uses as an enhancement in place of ordinary telephone conversations, with the added dimension of vision. Videophones can also be used for security, allowing users to 'log on' to sensitive databases only after contacting the database manager for visual identification. Two of the authors of this book have held an 'appraisement and counselling' session over a one-to-one video link. Videophones can also combat what is perceived by individuals (before they start teleworking) to be the biggest problem of remote working—isolation. Apart from 'official' communications, videophones can be used for social contact with other tele-workers and with office-based workers. While not a complete substitute for face-to-face, videophone conversations are much more 'natural' than audio-only talks.

Using packages that are combinations of the suggestions above, and other technological offerings, it is possible to provide solutions to many of the problems that arise from working remotely. The enabling technology is here now, with a wide choice of solutions, and with rapidly falling costs combined with increasing functionality.

1.6   TYPES OF TELEWORKING

1.6.1   Homework defined

The popular vision of a teleworker is of someone working at home, sitting comfortably in a cosy study or home-office. From a nearby window, there is a pleasant view of the countryside. For the lucky few teleworkers this vision may be a reality, but some work in less idyllic surroundings. Actually, as will be seen, excluding self-employed teleworkers (Table 1.2), the majority of full-time teleworkers are currently mobile, or 'nomadic', teleworkers—not homeworkers. But then, working at home is likely to be *the* main growth area for teleworking.

So who are the modern homeworkers? What sort of jobs do they do?

Unfortunately, there is no simple answer! By definition, teleworking involves using communications and information technology; homeworking teleworkers are therefore likely to be processing information, not physical objects. The infamous sweat-shops and pieceworkers, particularly well known in the textile industry in the past, are not related to teleworking.

In this context, homeworking covers a wide range of options, in many combinations:

- from senior executive to professional to clerical
- from full-time to part-time jobs
- from working at home almost full-time to occasionally spending a day at home
- from wholly employed through part-employed to self-employed

Typical examples include managers/professionals who spend a day or two a week at home, either as part of company policy to reduce commuting, or just because the peace and quiet of home means that concentration is uninterrupted. Some professionals, the best known being analysts and programmers in the IT industry, work at home all the time, visiting the main office infrequently. Increasingly, routine structured work like 'data entry' is being done remotely. So far, remote offices have mostly been used (like the American insurance claim forms for Massachusetts Mutual, Great Western Life and New York Life dealt with in Irish offices), but technology has now made it possible for more such work to be done at home.

The self-employed who work at home pose a problem when considering teleworking. Few people would argue against counting consultants, accountants, technical authors and the like as teleworkers—providing they use telecommunications to keep in touch with their various remote clients. But what of the novelist, or the one-man business run from home? They are homeworkers, but are they teleworkers? These examples are probably not, but they illustrate the difficulty in drawing the boundary around 'teleworking' when considering homeworking.

People who choose to work at home do so because of one or more of the possible benefits:

- saving time, money and stress by not commuting
- greater autonomy and flexibility of working hours
- not having to wear office clothes, or being forced to socialise!

Many people use the travelling time and costs saved to follow leisure pursuits. In BT's experiment with Directory Assistance operators working at home (of which more later), the operators even found that doing a household chore, like dealing with the washing, during their coffee breaks allowed them to put that time to better use at the end of their shifts.

The ability of some homeworkers to vary their work schedule might also allow time to fit in a hobby—like playing golf, which could otherwise be difficult in the dark after work! More seriously, the benefit for some homeworkers is being able to combine work with caring for children or elderly relatives. Contrary to popular belief, caring for children and working at home **cannot** be combined—**at the same time**. Anyone who needs child care facilities to go out to work will also need those facilities to work at home. Teleworking can be useful for parents, however, who are able to arrange their hours of work around periods of child care—such as the time immediately after school finishes for the day. There are examples of teenagers letting themselves quietly into their homes and getting on with homework while the parent works undisturbed. The teenager does not need 'care', but the teleworking parent is glad that the teenager is not left alone in the house.

The biggest problem that homeworkers face is that of isolation. There are many ways that the company teleworking programme can be designed to alleviate the problem, as discussed fully later on in this book, but the choice of where to work in the home should also be considered—not too cut off from the family and outside world, but not somewhere where work will be disrupted. A balance has to be struck.

For those for whom social isolation proves to be a big problem, working at a satellite office or telecentre rather than at home may be the solution.

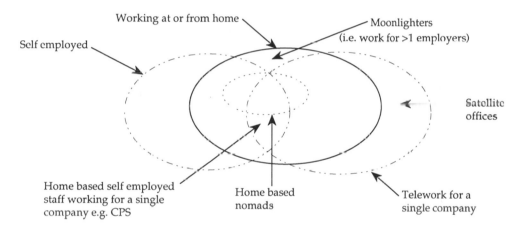

Figure 1.1   Overlapping sets of teleworkers

1.6.2 **Telecentres**

Telecentre is the generic term covering facilities which are shared and which provide telecommunications and office equipment to enable teleworking.

A telecentre will typically be easily accessible to a mixed working population, at low prices, and contain upwards of 10 well-designed and equipped work stations for teleworkers who might be self-employed or employed. The centre will usually have a manager to maintain the facility and perhaps to recruit work, operating the centre like an office service and temporary staff bureau.

Some telecentres take the initiative to provide training for teleworkers, usually cooperating with local public adult education, thus ensuring competence at using and caring for the equipment and in the quality and speed of work produced. Many initiatives exist to create jobs in depressed areas and as such offer low-priced keyboard skills from the centre to, in theory, anywhere on earth.

In practice, telecentres are generally limited to recruiting work in the tele-workers' own language, commercial terminology and culture and time zones. There are exceptions, however, where work is imported and returned over many thousands of miles, across time zones and across cultural and national boundaries. This trend is likely to grow in the near future, unless powerful protective legislation is introduced to ban it. It will in turn fuel the growth of telecommunication networks in third-world countries.

Rural telecentres in Europe are called telecottages. In Hereford and Worcester in the UK, the Chairperson of the 45-member Telecottages Association plans for 1994 an ideal 400-family televillage with cars banished to outer areas and shared telecentres across the village greens.

Where telecentres were first established is arguable but some of the earli-est are to be found, logically, in island communities, drawing work from the nearest mainland:

- *Gotland*:   In the Baltic Sea, off the Swedish mainland, started in 1986. It runs Informationsystem Gotland, a database of history, and employs 10 people on civil service salaries.

- *Jamaica Digiport*:   Founded in 1988, draws work at *circa* US $1 per hour, compared to $4.60 on the mainland. Via AT&T it plugs 10 operating busi-nesses employing some 600 teleworkers into the US network, and there-fore into the world.

- *Kyushu Island*:   South-west Japan, is home to The Kumamoto Prefecture project, two resort cottages converted in 1988 with 16 teleworkers from four major Tokyo employers.

- *Hawaii*:   The Hawaii Telework Centre Demonstration Project opened in 1989 in Oahu and is described as a 'neighbourhood office' with 17 tele-workers who previously commuted 2.5 hours a day to Honolulu.

- *Unst*:   The northernmost Shetland island, above Scotland in the North Sea. The telecentre, described as a telecroft, was established in 1991 with BT backing and run by two teleworkers as a local office bureau.

- *Majorca*:   In the Mediterranean, by Spain, from 1993 is developing a 'resort office' with teleworking facilities aimed at European travel agents and other teleworkers.

- *Ireland*:   A larger island than those above, but driven by similar factors, services several US corporations from offices and telecentres in Limerick, Galway and Kerry on its west (Atlantic) coast. Started in 1980 through the Irish Development Agency, the centres currently employ over 600 teleworkers. Employers include Travelers Insurance of Hartford, Connecticut, New York Life, and McGraw-Hill.

Mainland telecentres are now numerous, springing up in third-world countries, rural areas, and towns and cities accessible to commuters (or ex-commuters).

Rural:
- *Moorlands Telecottage (1989)* In Staffordshire, UK, in the Pennine Hills, it is managed by the local education authority, funded by BT. It has 10 workstations and 12 qualified teleworkers, with work for four full-time staff, and is growing rapidly. It is one of 45 UK telecottages in rural areas.

City:
- *Telebusiness Workcentres (October 1991)* In California, USA, started under the Inland Empire Economic Council Program, it provides 42 workstations in two locations 'close to housing' for ex-commuters into Los Angeles. $1 million of funding was provided equally by state and private investment. The centres are reported to be overbooked.

Telecentres generally have the following in common:

- Reduce commuting: saving time, money and improving air quality, health and family life.

- Import jobs: attracting work to rural, often low housing cost, areas and to inaccessible areas.

- Training: increasing local skills in information technology.

Figure 1.2   (a) View of Highlands Telecottage, California.

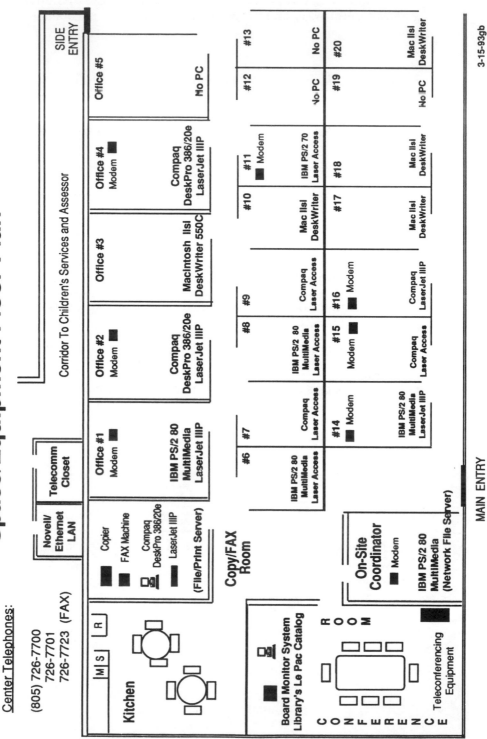

Figure 1.2 (b) Floor plan of Antelope Valley Telebusiness Center

- Community: teleworkers who fear isolation meet a broad range of fellow tele-non-commuters.

- Property efficient: workstations and the buildings can be used in theory for 24 hours a day by three shifts of teleworkers.

- Communications efficient: workstations may be better designed and equipped with more sophisticated telecommunications equipment than central offices.

- Serviced: cleaned, maintained, secured and stocked for work by the management.

- Accessible: away from jammed city centres, with parking for cars and bicycles. Often close enough to walk.

1.6.2.1 Funding

In Chapter 4.10 the costs of setting up a telecentre, telecottage or telecroft are examined in detail. The financial benefits to individuals and employers will pay back the capital of an equipped telecentre building in less than two years. The running costs vary, depending on local rates of pay, managers' expectations, owners' required standards and geographic locations.

The private sector can justify providing satellite offices or telecentres for existing employees who commute more than an hour each way. The public sector can justify funding to break even point (say three years) to provide education and jobs.

1.6.3 Nomadic teleworkers

Teleworking and telecommuting conjure up the image of high-tech home offices, economically and socially justified by substantial reductions in commuting and other travel. Other teleworkers, using the telephone and radio networks, grow in numbers as the technology becomes available at appropriate prices. Teleworking allows people, previously tethered to fixed location telephones and computers, to become nomadic, of no fixed abode, and yet to be as closely in touch with business and their families as before.

Teleworkers equipped with mobile and car telephones, fax machines, laptop computers, pagers and other message machines, now include:

- Home-office telecommuters, in the traditional image, who can be self-employed or employed, full-time or occasional homeworkers.

- Telecentre- and telecottage-based workers, usually dividing their time between home, a local telecentre and head office, as needs dictate.

- Customer- or client premises-based workers, including professionals carrying out long contracts at clients' sites, such as computer installation and support, audits, training courses and research.

- Vehicle-based workers, including most maintenance engineers, police, delivery services, taxis, travelling sales people, and site managers.

- Hotel-based workers, travelling by air and sea or long distances overland, including news reporters, financial researchers, diplomats, politicians and entertainers.

- Workaholics, often small business owners, vocational workers or captains of industry who take their portable computers and mobile phones, usually reliant on car-fitted systems, to villas, clubs, beaches, campsites, restaurants, hospitals, friends' houses and even to the theatre.

These latter five groups represent a fast-growing number of people who can keep in touch with head office day and night, who no longer rely on secretaries to present their work and to keep their diaries, and who have mastered sufficient of the new technologies to be confident of instant communications in most environments and from most parts of the world. They are true 'nomadic workers'.

Census reports have not even asked the questions which might enable researchers to arrive at the answers as to how many nomadic teleworkers there are. Industry and commerce statistics do not differentiate between types of office activity. The UK Chartered Institute of Marketing has 35 000 UK and 14 000 overseas members, but they may all do their work at fixed desks in tower block offices. Much selling is done by shop assistants, by mail order or by telephone and, while telephone sales people may be classed as teleworkers, their numbers give no clues as to how many sales people travel regularly.

Half of all jobs are desk jobs and Cornell University showed that over 40% of desks are unoccupied on any given work-day (Chapter 7.3.1). In the USA, 25% is 13.68 million empty desks, and in the UK 3.0 million. Holidays account for 6.25%, sickness for 2.9% and 1992 home-based teleworking numbers for 2.7%; *circa* 13% of the empty desks could be due to nomadic teleworking, representing 7.1 million US and 1.6 million UK office workers enabled by new technology to be nomadic.

In addition there are traditional mobile workers who have never had desks. Light commercial vehicles are 8% of all vehicles. Using an estimate of 25% linked to route planning computers and by mobile 'phones gives 3.6 million US and 480 000 UK commercial vehicle-based teleworkers. Car-based teleworkers are more difficult to estimate; these include major sales forces such as are found in financial services, and the traditional sales representatives, a fast disappearing breed as direct ordering replaces personal visits. The best estimate of 1993 figures is 300 000 for the USA and 60 000 for the UK.

Most heavy goods vehicles have mobile phones or radio phones but are not here classed as telework vehicles.

The number of hotel rooms occupied by and used for work by travelling business executives is excluded. Although legendary, workaholics with mobile phones on holiday beaches remain rare.

Table 1.1 Summary of estimates for nomadic teleworkers.

	USA	UK
Desk jobs now nomadic	7100 000	1600 000
Telelinked light commercial vehicles	3600 000	480 000
Car-based nomadic	300 000	60 000
Total nomadic	**11 000 000**	**2060 000**

1.7 PAST PRESENT AND FUTURE

1.7.1 Past and piecework

While teleworking is a phenomenon of the 20th century electronic era, working at home is as old as mankind. In Britain and in the early Pilgrim settlements in America in the 17th century, homes, great or small, were centred around the fire and most people's work took place within a few hundred yards of the house.

At the end of the 17th century, before the Industrial Revolution, when the majority lived on the land, people worked where they lived or lived where they worked. Henry Ford was yet to incarnate and invent 120 million American commuters. Human energy and ingenuity were applied to create tools, weapons and machines; hand looms and spinning wheels were as common then as televisions are today, making fabrics in every home. Most people grew food or tended animals, relying on the energy of the sun and hoping for predictable weather.

Communications were carried by horse, usually at 20 miles a day. Witherings, chief postmaster of Charles I (1625), marvelled that 'news which passed from Edinburgh to London [450 miles] in three days and nights by relays of horses, was outstripping thought'. These mounted postmen and Dick Turpin's ride to York were rare express information services, as was the famous relay bringing news of the Battle of Waterloo in 1815, from Belgium to Rothschild's Bank in London, 24 hours before the government received it—the equivalent of having a copy of tomorrow's *Wall Street Journal* to help decide which stocks to buy. The Pony Express, in 1860, could cover 250 miles a day on horseback carrying mail from Missouri to California. Today, information travels from California to Rome, Italy, in 1/30th of a second.

The Industrial Revolution speeded up the rhythms of 18th century life as irreversibly as the electronic revolution has accelerated the pace of 20th century living. In 1829 London's new Post Office, in St Martin's-le-Grand, distributed letters and parcels across the world in cast iron cases, soldered shut. Average mail shipments to Australia weighed 22 tons. The record daily posting in Britain, prior to the highly controversial 1 penny stamp being introduced in 1840 (proposed in 1680), was 90 000 items. After its introduction the number rocketed to 630 000 a day. By 1860 the US Postal Service adopted postage stamps. New Orleans and Nashville had their own and New Brunswick issued a 17 cent stamp depicting the Prince of Wales in a kilt. Volumes grew prodigiously, until today about one billion items are handled daily by the world's postal services. Reliable mass communications had arrived.

The British Empire, creating stable markets for raw materials and finished products, and new technology, such as Hargreaves' Spinning Jenny, Arkwright's Water Frame, Cartwright's Power Looms, Lister's Combing Machine and many other inventions, made the North of England, with its fast-running streams for both power and cleaning, the mass production centre of the world for textiles. Between 1730 and 1890 no nation could compete with the output of the 'dark satanic mills', importing raw cotton primarily from Louisiana and Georgia. The mills relied upon impoverished and insecure pools of 'outworkers' whose homes and handlooms became a flexible production facility to be switched on or off as market forces dictated.

Dr Duncan Bythell of Durham University (UK), in his seminal work *The Sweated Trades*, argues that, contrary to popular concepts, the factories and mills in England did not initially lure families from rural areas to the towns in huge numbers. The factories subcontracted to middlemen, journeymen and agents who in turn contracted with several hundred thousand cottage industry labourers, paid by the piece (the notorious 'piecework system') on such poor scales that an entire family working long hours could barely feed themselves. When the work ran out they starved. Piecework and cottage industries supported the wealth of the British middle classes for over 120 years. Homeworkers supplied a captive, flexible workforce for making textiles, lace, gloves, nails, chains, boxes, shoes and a host of other mass production items. American pieceworkers, mainly immigrant labour, caught up with the system after 1850, adding trades such as nut-shelling and light industrial assembly, ultimately enabling the USA to compete with the worldwide industrial dominance of Great Britain.

The outworkers bought or rented their own machines, equivalent to a teleworker's investment in a personal computer and printer, and would learn new trades as the market dictated. Even the most idealistic mill owners and traders grew rich, beyond the dreams of most modern entrepreneurs, with this limitless pool of part-time, self-employed, skilled labour. Children provided an even cheaper source of production, which the adult workers complained of both on humanitarian grounds and as unfair competition. A Royal Commission of 1860 heard: 'I have seen a boy, twelve years old, come home from winding at 8 or 9 o'clock, (at night) and then set to stitch three dozen fingers, i.e. the fingers of three dozen pairs of coarse gloves. He works a frame too, sometimes getting into his uncle's when he (the uncle) goes to dinner. I have heard him ask, "Am I big enough to be a sailor?".'

So scandalous were the conditions of homeworkers that reformers in 1890 were at last successful in having a resolution passed by the House of Commons, Sweating Committee to protect them, following pleas such as that of Clementina Black:

> ...[sweated work] in some shape or form, comes into every home in this country. Our potatoes and our flour are carried in sacks,

although not perhaps to our doors; our eggs are sold to us in boxes; our garments are fastened with buttons or with hooks, or perchance with safety pins; the gentleman's collar and tie and the lady's waist belt may probably be the handiwork of some half-starved home-worker whose life is being shortened by her poverty. Only ignorance can flatter itself... with the idea that none but cheap goods or cheap shops are tainted with sweating ... the taint is everywhere; there is no dweller in this country, however well intentioned, who can declare with certainty that he has no share in this oppression of the poorest and most helpless amongst his compatriots.

With such a fearful reputation, it is no wonder that Unions may even now react with horror at the concept of homeworking. To be accepted by all employees and their formal representatives, teleworking must never be tainted by or confused with Victorian pieceworking.

1.7.2 Teleworking today

The Industrial Revolution sowed the seeds of change that have led to the current interest in teleworking and its predicted growth. Out of the industrial process grew mass production. This led to automation and a reduced need for physical manipulation by people during the production process. To control the increasingly complex production processes, to manage the large corporations, even to influence national economies, information itself has become an ever more valuable commodity. Over the years, the mass of people who drifted initially from working the land into manufacturing industry have in turn drifted into 'information processing'.

Mass production and the accelerating rate of technological development have meant that computers and telecommunications have become widespread and affordable, particularly in the developed world. The international telecommunications network is the world's largest and most complex 'machine'. There are over 500 million telephone lines connected together worldwide. The computing power of 'personal computers' (PCs) is increasing rapidly, while costs are falling, giving a decrease in the price/performance ratio of PCs of 30% or more a year. There are few jobs in the information processing industry where there is not now a PC on every desk. More and more homes have a computer of some sort—even if buried inside a games machine!

Therefore the enabling technology is now in place for information processing to be done almost anywhere. The information worker is no longer tied to a desk in a city centre location.

At the same time, the Industrial Revolution has brought on many of the teleworking 'drivers'—the reasons why companies and individuals are showing an interest in various forms of remote working. The biggest of these drivers, as already discussed, is, of course, commuting. The daily travel of millions of people into central work locations wastes time, money and energy and causes pollution on an enormous scale. In Britain, the average commuter, living just over 7 miles from work, uses 525 litres of petrol travelling to work each year, producing nearly 1.2 tonnes of carbon dioxide—the main 'greenhouse effect' gas—in the process (see Chapter 4.2.1).

The real interest in teleworking started in the 1970s. Research was undertaken, predictions were made and books were written—probably the best known of the early books being Alvin Toffler's *The Third Wave*. However, many of the predictions have proved wide of the mark. (Predicting has always been a risky business: at the age of 10, Albert Einstein was told by his Munich schoolmaster, 'You will never amount to very much'!)

The number of teleworkers has not sky-rocketed, thanks to the worldwide recession, management attitudes and many other reasons which are covered later in the book. So many of the beneficial effects of mass teleworking have not (yet) been widely realised: less strain on the transport infrastructure, less pollution and other benefits. Neither has the countryside been overrun by mass exoduses from the urban areas. Thankfully, neither have most of the adverse predictions of the effects on individuals happened either. Teleworkers have not become exploited, the technological equivalent of the sweated labour of the past.

There are two types of teleworking: formal and informal. The informal, *ad hoc*, teleworking is, for example, when one person gets his or her manager's agreement to allow working at home to meet a particular domestic or personal need. Such teleworking has grown steadily as technology has made it easier for work to be done at home, but counting the numbers involved is almost impossible. Many senior managers do not even realise that tacit teleworking is going on in their companies; it is often a very local arrangement.

Formal teleworking, where it is introduced as part of a company policy, is easier to track. The early impetus for the adoption of teleworking was the environmental legislation introduced in the USA in the 1980s. Legislation specifically targeted at a reduction in commuting as a means of reducing pollution (and road congestion) was pioneered by California. Companies were forced to reduce the number of vehicle journeys to work made by their employees. Sharing cars, rather than travelling to work alone in the car, is one way of achieving the reduction. The alternative is not to travel to work at all. Work at home and avoid commuting. In this case 'telecommuting' is an appropriate term, even if the literal meaning—'travelling at a distance'—is a little suspect.

Many of these telecommuters only work at home a small percentage of their time, perhaps one day a week or less, and so would not be considered mainstream teleworkers. Pacific Bell, one of the leading examples of telecommuting companies in the USA, has over 3000 telecommuters, but included in this number are some who work at home only a day or two a month.

Further 'Clean Air' legislation in the USA should push up the numbers of telecommuters considerably. By 1996, in nine major cities, companies with over 100 employees will have to cut their employees commuting (in terms of the number of car journeys) by 25%. Europe, so far, has no comparable legislation to encourage teleworking.

However, avoidance of commuting is not the only driver for the adoption of teleworking. Many companies, on both sides of the Atlantic, have realised the other advantages of teleworking. The FI Group was set up to provide employment opportunities for mothers, computer professionals, who were not able to go out to work. American Express has introduced a programme to allow some of their travel agency staff to work at home as a way of stopping other travel agencies from 'poaching' their highly-trained agents. Examples can be found of companies adopting teleworking for all the reasons discussed in Chapter 4.3.

Although there is no 'Clean Air' legislation in force in Europe aimed at reducing commuting, the European Commission is taking an interest in teleworking. The Commission has established the 'European Commission Telework Forum', which provides some coordination for many of the European telework initiatives, particularly conferences. It is also part-funding a number of collaborative research projects investigating a wide range of topics related to teleworking. The projects are mainly aimed at developing employment opportunities for rural areas, but not exclusively so. Because of the rural aspect, the Commission is particularly interested in the development of telecentres.

Telecentres, also known as telecottages and by a variety of other names, were first established in Sweden. They provide communication and information technology services, usually in rural areas, for the local people—teleworkers, small businesses and 'students' of all ages. In the teleworking scene, telecentres can provide a half-way stage between normal office working and homeworking. The teleworker's journey to a centre will be much shorter than to the city office, the centre provides a meeting place, and more expensive equipment can be provided than at home. But the commuting journey is not entirely eliminated and other advantages to the company or to individuals may not be fully realised, e.g. overheads and lack of interruptions (see Chapter 4.10 and 4.11 for costings).

In Britain, there are now over 45 teleservice centres, with others being planned. Most of these have been set up with the aid of grants from the European Commission, local authorities, or large communications or IT companies. Few of them have yet proved their long-term business viability.

In all its forms, teleworking is growing; not as fast as some early predictions, perhaps, but growing nonetheless. Its expansion is being slowed by the worldwide recession, but companies are increasingly aware of the benefits of flexible working practices. With the increasing availability, and decreasing cost, of the enabling technology, the end of the recession could signal the start of the teleworking boom.

1.7.3 The future

The driving forces that have motivated teleworking are unlikely to go away. Traffic congestion will continue to increase, respect for the environment will become more important; companies will need to attract better staff, improve customer service and reduce costs. Based on these facts, the amount of teleworking is predicted to increase. Predictions for the number of teleworkers

Growth of teleworking

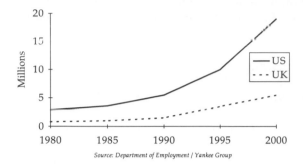

Source: Department of Employment / Yankee Group

Figure 1.3 Projected growth in teleworking (from Department of Employment/ Yankee Group)

vary widely, and to a large extent depend on the way teleworking is defined. But within our definition of teleworking, the predicted numbers of tele-workers in the year 2010 in the USA and UK are 33 million and 10 million respectively.

However, there will be no 'Teleworking Revolution'. What is more likely is an evolutionary change in working practices as a long-term result of the Information Technology Revolution. Teleworking will increasingly be absorbed into the mainstream of normal working practice. The current dis-tinctions between homeworking, telecentre working and office working will begin to blur. More flexible, location-independent working practices will emerge. It will become accepted practice for people to spend part of their time working outside the traditional office.

It is likely that full-time teleworkers will be outnumbered by occasional teleworkers who are otherwise office-based. The general consensus is that part-time home based working, in combination with telecentre working, will emerge as the predominant form of teleworking for employees within organisations.

The distinction between employment and self-employment is likely to become increasingly blurred. As large organisations concentrate on their 'core business' there will be an increase in outsourcing and subcontracting of secondary activities needed to perform their core work. This will lead to a growing number of individual freelancers and independent small busi-nesses. These people will make an organisation's secondary activity their primary business and should therefore do it better for less cost.

Examples of outsourced work include cleaning, catering, security, debt collecting, direct marketing, data processing and facilities management. Within this list are some obvious candidates for teleworking. Activities such as data processing and direct marketing are ideally suited to location-independent working. This can lead to teleworking across international boundaries. Examples from two insurance companies illustrate this: a UK insurance group, based in south-east England, flies clerical work to India, while a US firm, based in New Jersey, has a claims office in Ireland.

Organisations also require greater flexibility to expand and contract their services to meet customer demand. This means longer opening hours, and an ability to cope with peaks and troughs in demand. The flexibility is provided by using part-time and temporary workers. The result of this will be more flexible working contracts, including job sharing, school-time working and teleworking.

The factors underlying these changes in the structure of organisations are described by Charles Handy in his book *The Age of Unreason*. He outlines the development of the Shamrock Organisation, which will consist of three distinct categories of worker. The first is a central core of professionals and managers who work full-time for the organisation. The second group is the contractual fringe, to which work is outsourced. The third group is a flexible labour force, made up of temporary or part-time workers.

The concept of what constitutes an office is changing. Traditional offices will be used in a more flexible way and offices will be developed in which there is no individual ownership of desk space. People who work in the building will have access to shared resources such as telephone, terminal, meeting room, quiet room, or relaxation area. They will use these resources as appropriate when they are working in the office.

The continuation of this change will be supported, and at times driven, by advances in computer and communications technology. Centralised resources such as typing pools and clerical support are being replaced on the desktop by word processors, group editing and electronic mail. This removes a physical barrier to decentralisation. Workflow management tools and schedulers will allow teams to be formed from people working in different places at different times; while the increasing availability of video communications is also removing the barrier of not being able to 'see' the person at the other end of the phone.

The bandwidth of digital communication links will continue to increase, allowing more information to be transmitted more quickly from one place to another. At the same time, the cost of telecommunications is falling. Distance is becoming less of a factor in determining the cost of a telephone call. Information in transit is in effect weightless, in contrast to the weight and cost of transporting paper or people.

These developments in technology are allowing new types of organisations to be born—organisations that base their operations around the distance-independent nature of teleworking. Crossaig, in the Highlands of Scotland, is an example of just one such organisation. It uses the ISDN (Integrated Services Digital Network) (see Chapter 6.1) to link up a network of different categories of teleworker to process and add value to information.

This network of people forms a 'Virtual Organisation'. Many more organisations like this are developing, encouraged by the trends in outsourcing outlined earlier.

Virtual organisations will also be formed by rapid link-ups between two or more organisations for the purpose of fulfilling a specific customer requirement. The trends are already there in food retailing where major stores are linked electronically, via EDI (electronic data interchange), to their suppliers. 'Just in time' manufacturing techniques provide another example of close links between organisations.

As the nature of work and society continues to change, new places where work gets done will start to emerge. Rural areas are likely to see the development of 'televillages', communities in which people can both live and work in the information age. These televillages, growing from the concept of telecottages, will tackle the problems of housing and employment in rural areas, while making a positive contribution to the environment and to the quality of life.

Cities are likely to see the development of 'teleports', self-contained cities within cities acting as hubs of the global information network. These teleports, a logical extension of the intelligent building, will fully support an urban community of information workers. People will eat, sleep, and work within the secure walls of the teleport, away from the problems of the city environment.

Improved mobile communications and smaller, more powerful portable personal computers will make it easier to work wherever and whenever it suits—in the office, car, telecentre, hotel room, or at home. The office, with all its support systems, could be anywhere that the teleworker chooses.

No look at the future of work would be complete without mention of demographic trends. The dip in the birth-rate that followed the Baby Boom is now rippling through the age structure of the population and will result in a significant shortage of young employees through the 1990s. The consequence is that work will have to fit around people's evolving circumstances and commitments. More flexible working, including teleworking, is the only way that work can happen.

1.8   HOW MANY TELEWORKERS?

Teleworking most commonly occurs at home but the term also includes working in telecentres and telecottages, and working on the move, from airports, hotels, delivery vehicles and cars. The definitions and numbers of teleworkers are changing rapidly, making precise head-counts impossible, but there have been many brave attempts to hit this fast-moving target.

Teleworkers use telecommunications networks and peripherals to communicate with colleagues, customers and suppliers with the intention of reducing travel distance, time and costs and central office space and costs.

Table 1.2 shows the best estimates of the numbers of teleworkers on any single working day in the first quarter of 1993.

Table 1.2   Teleworker head-count (millions).

	USA	UK	Rest of Europe
Labour force (including unemployed)	121.60	27.4	168.0
1. Teleworkers who spend the majority of time at established home offices:			
Self-employed and small business sectors	2.88	0.57	N/A[a]
% of claimed total self-employed	29.0%	20.0%	
Employed in major organisations	0.25	0.06	N/A[a]
% of all claimed employees	0.23%	0.27%	
2. Teleworkers employed by major organisations who spend a minority of time at home offices	0.76	0.14	N/A[a]
% of all claimed employees[b]	0.75%	0.64%	
3. Mobile teleworkers on the road or in hotels	2.00	0.50	N/A[a]
% of all claimed employees[b]	1.81%	2.30%	
Total teleworkers	**5.89M**	**1.27M**	
% of workforce	4.8%	4.6%	
Populations	246.33	57.08	
Telephone lines	189.48M	15.40M	
	(77%)	(27%)	

Teleworkers on any one working day
[a] N/A = Figures not available.
[b] Including those currently unemployed.

1.9   ORGANISATIONS ADAPTING TO TELEWORKING

There are resistances within some organisations to officially embracing teleworking. The majority (75%) of large employers do practice tacit teleworking (see Chapter 7.1) and a large minority (17% USA and 43% UK) have formal programmes. Large employers are defined as employing more than 500 people and having one or more Personnel or HRM (Human Resource Management) departments. Large organisations employ some 40% of the workforce; in the USA there are 23 000 and in the UK some 7000 major employers.

The other 60% of the workforce operate in the 'small' and self-employed business sectors, the majority of units being less than 100 people, generally with only part-time personnel officers.

1.9.1   Corporate resistances to formal teleworking

One hundred and fifteen senior personnel managers from major UK organisations responded to a survey in March 1992 and, unprompted, gave their views of the corporate obstacles to increasing teleworking which are summarised in Table 1.3 and described in sections 1.9.1.1–1.9.1.7.

Note that these views of Personnel and HRM senior managers, who were not themselves teleworking at the time the research was carried out, do not accord with the views of personnel, of all grades, contemplating teleworking for themselves. Potential teleworkers are reported to regard 'Isolation' as the single greatest barrier to widespread teleworking. The opinions expressed below reflect the unprompted responses from corporate managers, from the employers' perspective. Just over 50% of the respondents said that they would personally like to telework.

Table 1.3   Corporate obstacles to increased teleworking.

1. Traditional methods; corporate identity	35.3%
2. Face to face with customers	21.0%
3. Difficulty in managing teleworkers	12.6%
4. Access to communications equipment	14.2%
5. Costs of setting up teleworking	11.7%
6. Isolation of teleworkers	2.5%
7. Security, selection and recession	2.7%
Total	100%

1.9.1.1   Corporate identity and tradition (35.3%)

As can be seen, the largest imagined obstacle was the perception that teleworking would threaten the corporate structure and identity. This perception has been confirmed by telecommuting and teleworking consultants, in the USA and the UK, from experience with client companies. In *The Economics of Teleworking* (BT, March 1992), corporate resistance to change was thought to be rooted in (a) traditional methods—if it works don't fix it; and (b) technophobia—senior managers' mistrust of technology.

Managing the change   Both these resistances, usually operated by older, experienced managers, are sensible balances to enthusiasm. To expand teleworking in any organisation, Management of Change strategies need to be employed, as for any innovation, and a product champion identified to carry the flag for teleworking (see Chapter 2.1). A more convincing case will be put by including the following in any presentation or discussion:

● The economic costs and benefits
● Case studies from other organisations

- A survey of unofficial tacit teleworking in the organisation (Chapter 7.5)
- Detailed costing of setting up a project
- Expert assurances on the technology applied
- Assurances that the plan follows proven methods

1.9.1.2   Face to face with customers (21.0%)

This is a compelling reason to work at the central premises, particularly in retailing. Manufacturing work often requires people interfacing with production lines and other machinery, although many production planning and management tasks are data-based and can be done remotely from the production facility, e.g. there are now more than 10 nationwide home- or telephone-banking services in the UK and at least as many in North America; retail banking is converting to teleworking, saving both staff and customers' travelling time and costs.

Where there is a tradition of serving clients and customers face to face, it is worth examining if the system might be out of date and in danger of being superseded by competitors. Just as in banking, more and more retail trade is converting to catalogue, mail order and telephone selling. In France and the USA, consumer goods are displayed and described on television with orders taken by telephone.

Saving customers a journey may leave them more time and money to consider, and to buy, the company's products.

1.9.1.3   Managing teleworkers (12.6%)

The *raison d'être* of teleworking and telecommuting is to reduce needless travel. Teleworkers achieve this by working at home, at clients (cutting out the intervening head office journey) and on the move. They communicate with the core team at head office from any of these remote locations or sites. From the traditional manager's point of view the teleworkers become invisible and therefore traditional and valued systems of management are threatened (see Chapter 2.11).The high percentage of managers (12.6%) who regard this as an obstacle might like to examine the results of teleworking when people are measured by 'effectiveness' rather than by attendance (see Chapter 4.3.3). This shows that greater productivity and welfare are normal amongst teleworkers and that teleworking managers not only get the best out of their teams but enjoy the benefits of teleworking themselves (Chapter 2.11).

Numerous well-managed and successful organisations depend on 'invisible', 'remote', 'nomadic', 'mobile' or home-based teleworkers. In the UK these include the giant Prudential Assurance, Allied Dunbar, the FI Group, CPS (Computer Programming Services), the Royal Automobile Club, the Automobile Association, many insurance, banking and financial services firms, and many firms which have adopted telephone selling, often from home-bases. In the USA, famous names include J. C. Penney, AT&T, GTE, Sears, American Express and Travelers Insurance.

Managing dispersed workers at a distance has operated since the Roman Empire, a reasonably robust and lasting organisation.

1.9.1.4   Access to communications equipment (14.2%)

The astonishing 14.2% of managers who regard equipment availability and reliability as an anti-teleworking issue underlines the technophobia which many managers suffer.

In writing this book, computers were linked via an ISDN (Integrated Services Digital Network) line and one of the 23 authors suffered a 'hung screen' (a frozen computer) on three occasions, requiring 10 hours of rewriting out of a total authors' time of *circa* 1000 hours. Such accidents or errors happen, but to imagine reverting to manual typewriters or pen and paper to get the job done would be a primitive reaction. Manual typewriters used to jam and their carriages failed. Pens leaked ink over papers and pages were lost or spoiled. Entire manuscripts were lost in the post.

Computer and communications equipment is as reliable as any office methods have ever been, is many times faster and therefore produces more and provides a flexibility and convenience which was unimaginable 20 years ago.

Like any phobia, technophobia is best tackled by exposure, reassurance and education. Technophobes could be:

● Trained in keyboard and equipment skills
● Involved for a day with youngsters and experienced users who take the technology for granted
● Enabled to work from a remote or mobile location
● Given a guided tour of manufacturers of equipment
● Asked to read the technology section of this book

1.9.1.5   Costs of setting up teleworking (11.7%)

The case studies in Chapter 4.3 show that setting up teleworking is not expensive and that the investment can be recovered within a few months. The Thorn EMI study of videoconferencing (Chapter 4.4) shows a 7-month payback followed by monthly profits, and the Lombard study (Chapter 4.8) shows an immediate 20% increase in productivity (falling off as the year progresses) which for an average office employee yields £9460 ($13 433) additional annual gross revenues for the company. Set-up costs are rarely more than half this figure.

Without proper planning, equipment, training and counselling, telework projects can lead to productivity dives and confusion. Some investment is required to get it right.

1.9.1.6   Isolation of teleworkers (2.5%)

Isolation is most often identified by commentators as the major potential obstacle to telecommuting and working at home. These corporate managers, however, rate it very low in the list of perceived problems. Studies in the early 1980s showed that a significant percentage of office workers feel threatened in a main office environment and are under considerable stress. A 1992 survey found that 68% of home-based telecommuters wanted to continue at home and that over 90% (including those who wished to return to the core team) were far more productive.

Isolation, in teleworking practice, is a real issue for a small number of people, but the majority of central office-based managers and home-based telecommuters do not find it a problem.

1.9.1.7   Security, selection, recession (2.7%)

Each of these categories scored 0.9%. Personnel and HRM managers on the whole do not rank them as significant problems. None of the three are major obstacles in the long term, but experts on the growth of teleworking see things differently from the managers interviewed.

Selection (see Chapters 2.3.1 and 2.10) With some advice and planning, selection for a successful teleworking project can be made rapidly and inexpensively. It poses no real obstacle.

Security (see Chapter 5) Adequate security is not difficult to put in place as the Lombard Bank study (Chapter 4.8) shows. It is, however, considered to be a major risk and difficulty for some organisations where confidentiality is mandatory or paramount. For example, the US Internal Revenue Service would be particularly concerned to maintain security on personal tax files being transmitted, as are the UK Inland Revenue and Social Security Department. The work of these three organisations is otherwise ideally suited to telecommuting and the security assurances are being worked on to enable it. As Lombard Bank state, 'Our teleworking offices are considered to be as secure as any other premises we operate', proving that with some additional measures, security is a soluble problem.

Recession The interviewed managers were entirely wrong in dismissing the impact of the recession on the growth of teleworking. The early 1990s recession has been the worst on record this century and has brought the world's major economies to a virtual standstill. Telecommuting and tele-working have bucked the trend but only just.

Reliable forecasts in 1988, just as the recession was being noticed by the public, predicted explosive growth, taking the number of UK teleworkers, and by implication in the USA also, up to 15% of the working population by December 1995. In early 1993, the figure was nearer 4% (see Chapters 4.1 and 7.1) and it seems unlikely that there is time left for the 15% prophecy to be fulfilled.

However, fast growth has occurred in the number of organisations launching telework projects, rising from 30% to 43% over the past two years, a massive 40% increase. When the recession does end and organisational down-sizing is replaced by competition for skilled people, the commercial efficiency of teleworking together with its value to the three R's of person-nel—Recruitment, Motivation and Retention—will fuel rapid worldwide growth in the numbers who telework.

1.9.2   A welcome change

The Finance Director of BICC said at the Royal Society in London in 1989 that 'Companies which do not adopt corporate networking will not survive the turn of the millennium'. Networking, linking all staff to the organisa-tion's computers to give them interactive access to the business plan, has proved to be highly profitable.

To echo the BICC forecast, reducing the traditional habit of commuting saves so much time and energy that organisations which fail to reap the ben-efits of teleworking will not survive. Change must be encompassed by all successful companies and the speed of change is accelerating with every improvement in communications technology.

2

Organisations and Employers

'In a country that has been moaning about low productivity and searching for new ways to increase it, the most anti-productive thing we can do is to ship millions of workers back and forth across the landscape every morning and evening'.

Alvin Toffler—Author, The Third Wave.

2.1 SETTING UP A PILOT

Once in a while, a company is set up based entirely on teleworking, such as the FI Group in Britain, but teleworking is usually introduced to companies who already have an existing 'traditional' workforce. In such circumstances, the introduction of any teleworking programmes may well start with a small-scale pilot trial—even if the 'vision' is to have most, or all, of the company working remotely in the long run. One day, teleworking may be so common a way of working that all the problems have been solved and trials are not necessary. Today, teleworking is still in its infancy (even if it was 'born' some 20–30 years ago) and every teleworking situation is different. It is therefore advisable to start small with a pilot. When that is running successfully, then it can be allowed to spread to a larger proportion of the workforce. Some organisations are bold enough to skip the 'pilot' and launch straight into the teleworking programme. The guidance given below can equally be used in those circumstances.

Setting up a pilot teleworking programme is not a trivial matter. There are many issues to consider and a number of steps to go through. This section of the book will help guide you through the process of getting the trial started. The necessary steps are:

- Identify business objectives
- Find a champion

- Plan the pilot
- Involve the people
- Identify jobs suitable for teleworking
- Decide on technical requirements
- Analyse costs vs benefits[*]
- Select the trial participants[*]
- Revise the contract of employment[*]
- Tackle the legal/regulatory issues[*]
- Train the people involved
- Install the system and go!
- Monitor the pilot
- Consider the roll-out

The steps that are marked above with an asterisk ([*]) are detailed elsewhere in the book; the remaining steps are developed below.

2.1.1   Identify business objectives

Why are you interested in teleworking? A simple enough question for an individual to answer—almost certainly because it would benefit that individual's personal circumstances—but that won't lead to a corporate pilot being set up. The first step in setting up a pilot is to get a clear idea of why a pilot is being considered.

There are enthusiasts for teleworking around, but one person's enthusiasm for the concept of teleworking is not a good enough reason for adopting the practice. There must be a sound business reason for wanting to introduce teleworking, or any other flexible working practice. Luckily, teleworking can provide a solution to a good many business problems. These are dealt with in detail elsewhere in the book, but in summary are:

- Reduced overhead costs, particularly office space

- Increased flexibility of working patterns

- Improved productivity, especially for knowledge workers

- Wider geographical catchment area for recruitment, and more competitive recruiting

- Retention of skilled staff, who move away for family reasons, or otherwise might have to resign

- Recruitment opportunities for disabled people and those with caring responsibility

- Increased employee satisfaction, through quality of life or working conditions

- Improved or extended customer service

- Compliance with local commuting reduction regulations (if applicable)

Whichever of these reasons are behind the company's interest in teleworking, the first step is to ensure that there is a clear statement of the business objectives of the company. Then, the business problem that it is hoped teleworking will alleviate should be clearly identified. In other words, you should have, from the outset, a clear view of the business benefit that teleworking is expected to deliver. Without this, the business case, to be developed later, will founder.

2.1.2 Choose the route: easy or hard

Companies now have to make a fundamental decision: whether to go it alone in setting up the trial, or to bring in a consultant to help. The choice will depend on circumstances within the company. There is no point in reinventing the wheel if it can be avoided. A consultant will undoubtedly shorten the time it takes to set up the trial, and should minimise the problems along the way, but employing a consultant will lead to external expenditure, which may be unwelcome news to the company accountants! If the company has within it the necessary experts in Human Resources, technology, etc., who have the time available, then a 'do it yourself' approach may be feasible. Whichever way is chosen, this book will be of help. It can provide guidance on the steps you should be taking, or it can show you what to expect from a consultant. You will only need to buy as much consultancy support as you need to get started; good consultants won't force you to choose from an 'all or nothing' menu of services.

There is no register of consultants at present, but finding one to assist should not be too difficult. The major telecommunications companies have an obvious interest in promoting all forms of remote and mobile working, and they are usually able to offer advice and sometimes provide consultancy. (Advice is free, consultancy costs!) Large corporations with experience of setting up their own programmes—largely corporations in the IT industry—also quite often are able to offer consultancy. Last, but by no means least, there are mushrooming numbers of independent consultants, individuals, small and large companies, who are willing to offer their services to get pilots started.

2.1.3 Find a champion

The facts of life are that it is very difficult for a first-line, or even middle, manager to implement a teleworking programme without the backing of a Senior Executive or Board Member. There are two major hurdles to overcome that make it imperative to have a high-level champion for the programme.

One is that it is not a simple task to start up a teleworking programme, particularly for the first time in a company. Although there are undoubted benefits all round to teleworking, significant effort (and hence cost) will have to be spent 'up-front' in order to get the programme off the ground, before any of the benefits can be realised. A far-sighted champion is needed to authorise that expenditure.

The other difficulty is the 'middle manager problem'. Some middle managers are set in their ways. They like to see staff sitting at their desks, and have difficulty conceiving how they could manage without that visibility. It needs the authority of a high-level champion behind the programme to ensure that it succeeds. The champion can sometimes usefully point out to middle managers who drag their heels that *good* managers do not need to see their staff. With workload and objectives clearly defined and agreed targets to meet, remote working is not really a problem.

Interestingly, the staff—the potential teleworkers—are not a major problem. Once a teleworking programme has been announced and clearly explained, most companies will find no shortage of volunteers. Indeed, a survey in Britain by the Henley Centre in 1986 found that over half of the (2000+) people questioned said that they would like to work at home if they were able to. To this proportion can be added those who might not like to be at home all day, but would welcome a short trip to a local telecentre instead of commuting to a city centre. Nonetheless, to have a senior manager backing the programme will increase people's confidence and make volunteering more likely. (Some countries are lucky in having a senior politician backing the concept, too—former President Bush, followed by Vice President Gore, are two good examples.)

2.1.4 Plan the pilot

Having made the decision to go ahead with the pilot, the next step is to plan the whole programme, just like any other major project. This may seem self-evident, but it is important to avoid treating the subject as just something of

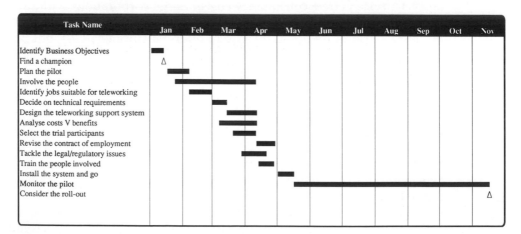

Figure 2.1   Steps to an efficient pilot project

interest that can be done as a background task. As will be seen, a large number of people will be involved in setting up the pilot. It is essential to get everyone's commitment to the project, and to be working to agreed deadlines. The remainder of this chapter will show you what needs to be in your plan. An example Gantt chart (Figure 2.1) is shown for your guidance. The 'time' scale on the chart is arbitrary; it will need to be fixed to suit your own company's particular circumstances.

2.1.5 Decide the 'success' factors

At this stage, it is worth considering how the success, or otherwise, of the pilot is to be measured. You should not expect perfection from the trial. Some things will not be right the first time around—a gap will be found in the support system, a pilot participant will leave the trial, a manager will find some part of the management role difficult. With revisions to the programme during the pilot, some of the teething problems will be ironed out. But when it comes to the end of the trial period, how will you know whether it has been a success—whether or not the pilot should be expanded into a full-scale teleworking programme?

The success factors, that should be defined now, need to be measurable against the business benefit that was expected from the trial, as far as possible. Some business benefits may still have to be predicted, rather than measured: where savings in office space are a driver for teleworking, it may be that the office desks have to be left vacant for the teleworkers in case the trial fails. So no actual saving is made during the trial. Once the decision has been made that the pilot has been in all other respects a success, only then can the space saving become a reality.

Measurement of the business benefit alone is not enough. The effect on the people concerned must also be taken into account. It is no good finding at the end of the pilot that, say, productivity has risen by 50% during the trial, but that all the teleworkers are on the point of resigning from the company because they are so fed up!

Whatever factors are chosen to measure success by, you will need a benchmark against which to judge the changes. This means that, in your plans, you should include an activity to measure those factors now, before the trial starts, and you should expect to measure these factors on a 'control group' of non-teleworkers during the pilot period, too. Measurement of the control group will enable you to make allowances for any factors which may affect the whole company (e.g. reorganisation, pay rises or new senior managers). It will also help you ensure that, while the teleworkers may be more productive, the introduction of the programme hasn't made the office-based workers' jobs more difficult and reduced their productivity.

2.1.6 Involve the people

Once the go-ahead for a pilot programme has been given, it is important to involve the people concerned at an early stage. Ignoring the fact that at an early stage of the pilot it will be necessary to study the way the people are working, rumours about such a project will start to spread anyway. Rumours will lead to wide-ranging fears about lack of job security, and general job dissatisfaction. Much better, then, to keep the staff well informed right from the start. Bear in mind that at least half of them are likely to welcome the possibility of working at home or locally. Involvement from the beginning will also help the workforce generally to 'own' the project, which will enhance its chances of success.

'Involving the people' entails three main elements: education, consultation and training.

Education should be an on-going process throughout the setting up of the pilot. Many of the workers (and managers) will have heard the term 'teleworking' or 'telecommuting', but not really understand what it involves. Many will fear that it means working at home full-time in isolation. By briefing the staff as the project progresses, by explaining how the remote workers will be supported, perhaps by using other companies' teleworking programmes as case studies, everyone can be shown the potential benefits to themselves and have their fears allayed.

The education process will probably reach a peak at the stage when people are about to be asked to volunteer to take part in the trial.

The purpose of *consultation* is to make sure that the system designed to allow people to work remotely meets the needs of everyone concerned. The major part of the consultation process will be during the 'requirements capture' phase of identifying the system requirements (detailed below). However, it should also involve noting any points raised during the briefings that are part of the education process.

Any relevant trade unions should also be consulted at an early stage. While some unions are dead set against any new working practices such as teleworking, many realise that more flexible working practices are inevitable—indeed their own members are demanding it. Bill Walsh, of the Manufacturing, Science, Finance union (MSF), put his union's point of view at the 'Teleworking 92' conference in Brighton, England. In trying to ensure that teleworking union members did not become like the infamously-exploited textile industry 'outworkers', the MSF has drawn up a list of requirements for teleworking (see Chapter 2.5). These requirements are entirely consistent with the views expressed in this book, and should cause no problems to any caring employer who values the workforce. So the points of view of those unions who are prepared to cooperate may well help to highlight all the issues that need to be resolved at an early stage.

The *training* element prepares the teleworkers, their managers and their families—especially for home-based teleworking—for the changes involved. This is discussed fully in Chapters 2.8 and 3.5.

2.1.7 Identify jobs

For each type of job that the teleworking pilot might involve, the ability of that job to be done remotely has to be evaluated. There are a wide range of jobs, at all levels in an organisational hierarchy, that are suitable for tele-working. A study for BT in 1990 identified 76 different areas of work that could be done remotely. A few examples of these are given in Table 2.1, divided into five broad categories, to illustrate the range of work.

Table 2.1 Areas of work suitable for teleworking.

On-line Professionals	Stockbroker
	Financial Analyst
Off-line Professionals	Computer Programmer
	Systems Analyst
	Manager
	Designer
	Accountant
	Translator
On-line Clerical	Telephone Enquiry Agent
	Telesales Operator
	Secretary
Off-line Clerical	Data Entry Operator
	Word Processor Operator
Nomadic	Sales Representative
	Journalist
	Auditor
	Service Engineer
	Surveyor

To evaluate any particular job's suitability, five characteristics need to be considered:

1. Degree of 'knowledge work'. Teleworking is suited to the processing of information rather than manual work.

2. Physical requirements. The fewer physical requirements (for example, face-to-face contact at a fixed location, manual handling, bulky equipment or storage requirements), the better.

3. Defined output. A teleworker needs his or her expected output to be well defined, so that there is no argument that the work has been done, and that performance can be measured.

4. Defined milestones. Not only does a teleworker need to know 'what' is expected, but also 'when'. This will help the teleworker plan the necessary hours of work, and will help the manager assess productivity.

5. Telecommunications needs. Whether the job currently entails a high or low level of communication with others (in or out of the office), a teleworker needs to be able to conduct (nearly) all communication over the telecommunications network. It will probably be necessary to involve the company's Communications or IT Manager (or a consultant) in the

decision as to whether the telecommunications requirements can be met.

These requirements are summarised in Table 2.2.

Table 2.2   Questionnaire to determine the suitablitiy of a job to teleworking.

Does the job involve the handling, processing or creation of information, rather than the production of a physical product?	Yes	No
Does the job have minimal physical requirement?	Yes	No
Is the output of the job well defined?	Yes	No
Can the work be broken up into defined milestones?	Yes	No
Can the majority of the teleworker's communication be carried out over the phone?	Yes	No

If the answer to all the questions in the table is 'yes', then there is a good chance that the job is suitable for teleworking. With one or perhaps two 'noes', the job may be suitable if the job content can be redesigned to change the answer to 'yes'. This could require the redesign of the business processes within the organisation.

It may be helpful in trying to decide which jobs are suitable for teleworking, and later in establishing the requirements of the job, if the company is surveyed for 'tacit teleworking'. Particularly in large corporations, many people will be found who already telework informally—perhaps without the knowledge of anyone except their immediate colleagues and supervisor. The experience of these tacit teleworkers can be invaluable to the team setting up the pilot.

From the jobs that are found to be suitable, either one job, or a small group of closely related jobs, should be selected for the pilot.

2.1.8   Decide technical requirements

Having chosen the category of job for the trial, the next step is to identify the requirements for the functionality of the teleworking system. The 'system' will be mainly the technology—the telecommunications and information technology—but will also include the manual processes that need to be established for the trial to function properly.

2.1.9   Decide type of teleworking

Before the system can be designed, the type of teleworking has to be chosen—homeworking, using satellite offices, working on the move, sharing space in a flexible office, and so on, or a mixture of these. The choice will depend on the reasons why the pilot is being set up, the type of work being done and the preferences of the individuals taking part in the trial.

2.1.10   Study 'at work' processes and interactions

Start the process of defining the functionality by studying the way that people in the job work at present. All the existing information flows and interactions with colleagues and their environment must be noted. This should include the informal as well as the formal, the social as well as the work-related interactions. It is important to remember that much of people's job satisfaction comes from contacts that are not directly part of doing the job. These elements of 'work' must not be overlooked when it comes to planning the pilot.

All the relevant points of view must be taken into account. The teleworking system must allow for the needs of the teleworkers, their colleagues in

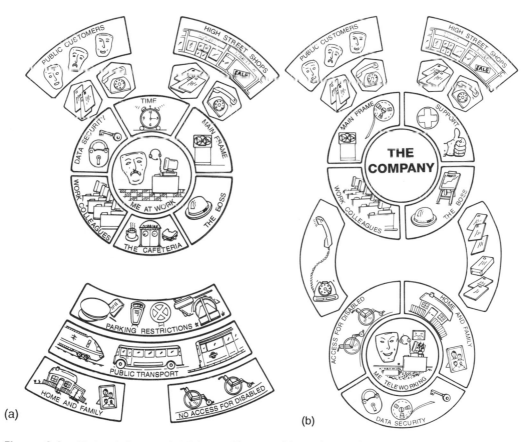

Figure 2.2   Rich pictures of (a) key office working elements and (b) key teleworking elements

the office, their managers, the training, safety and security departments, and so on. The requirements of the instigators of the trial must not be forgotten. Overall, a very complex picture will emerge. It may help to understand and analyse the situation if a diagram, or series of diagrams, is used. Simplified examples, of the type known as 'rich pictures', are shown in Figure 2.2.

2.1.11   Design the teleworking support system

From the functional specification, the teleworking system can be designed. The design process involves matching each requirement against one or more proposed solutions. For example, a requirement to enable a teleworker to book a holiday period could be satisfied by using electronic mail to the line manager, by giving the teleworker access to an electronic shared calendar or by phoning the line manager who would enter the holiday manually on a chart.

Advice on some of the technology available to support teleworking is given in Chapter 6, but not all requirements need a technological solution, In some cases, the answer may be a simple manual process. Each requirement will probably have more than one possible solution. A good way to comprehend the overall situation is to use a matrix, like the example in Figure 2.3

FUNCTIONAL REQUIREMENTS	MEANS OF IMPLEMENTATION				
	Visit Office	Video phone	E - Mail	Bulletin board	Other utilities
Access to office performance statistics				✓	✓
"Sign-on" at start of duty		✓			✓
Select scheduled annual leave	✓	✓			
Exchange scheduled leave with colleagues	✓	✓	✓	✓	
Apply for special leave	✓	✓	✓		
Report-in sick		✓	✓		
Arrange to swap duties	✓	✓	✓	✓	
Claim overtime	✓		✓		
Receive notification of time for regular training		✓	✓		
Report a hazard		✓	✓		✓
Communicate with colleagues informally	✓	✓	✓	✓	

Figure 2.3   Alternative solution matrix

From the matrix, pick out a set of solutions that will meet all requirements. Where there is more than one suitable set, comparing the costs should help to make the choice.

2.1.12   Install the system and go!

When all the previous steps have been completed, it's time to get the systems installed and the trial under way. This is likely to be a time of excitement and enthusiasm for those involved. Your company now has the option of publicising the pilot.

As we have already discussed, organised (rather than *ad hoc*) teleworking programmes are still relatively rare. This fact together with the continued current interest by the press and TV in the subject gives your company an excellent opportunity to get media 'editorial' coverage. If all the ground-work has been thoroughly done, then only positive publicity can result—showing the company as being a progressive, flexible employer.

If it is decided to publicise the trial, give the teleworkers a couple of weeks to settle into the new routine—and give the support system time for any oversights or errors to become apparent—before inviting the press to come and take a look. You may decide on a formal press conference, but the media are most likely to be looking for the 'human interest' angle and will proba-bly want to interview individual teleworkers (and maybe even their man-ager!). None of the teleworkers should be forced into talking to reporters; even less should the media be allowed into the homes of homeworkers unless they are themselves totally happy with the idea. The chance of brief fame is enough to persuade a few volunteers, usually.

Two warnings about publicity: once the existence of the trial is well known, the company is likely to receive further requests from the press for updates from time to time; and students on wide-ranging courses are likely to ask for questionnaires to be completed or to interview the teleworking team to help with their own theses or dissertations. Teleworking is currently a popular subject for student projects! There is no harm in this interest in itself, but the teleworkers' manager will have to ensure that the interrup-tions do not become so frequent as to intrude on the work in hand.

2.1.13   Monitor the pilot

Once the trial is up and running, the plan previously made for monitoring it can be put into action. Monitoring the pilot can have three benefits. It can:

- Confirm the benefits
- Validate the selection process
- Allow revision of the support system as necessary

The trial should be monitored for at least six months, or longer if the pro-gramme is breaking new ground. For the first month or two—the honey-moon period—all the volunteers are likely to be delighted with the opportunity to telework. This will be reflected in a better standard of work and general happiness. It is too early at this stage to try to make any judge-ments about the success, or otherwise, of the pilot.

After a few months, the novelty will wear off, and the teleworkers will begin to realise the little things they are missing out on by not being in the office. How strong this effect will be is inversely proportional to the quality of the training and the support being given to the teleworkers. In most cases, the teleworkers soon come to terms with the new way of working, perhaps devising their own ways of overcoming minor problems.

During this period, it has been found that a useful way of bringing to light any problem issues, and of highlighting the benefits, is to get the telework-ers together for 'discussion groups' every month or two (see Chapters 2.11.2 and 3.5.8). The teleworkers welcome the opportunity to talk through how they are getting on with each other. It helps them realise that their reactions to the situation are normal—all the others are in the same boat! In the early stages, it is important to have a skilled discussion leader who can set the tone and draw out the responses. Later on, the meeting may develop into more of a 'self-help' group, with the teleworkers preferring to hold a more informal meeting, perhaps as part of a social gathering.

Experience has shown that, in most circumstances, three to four months is long enough for most people to have adapted to the new way of work and to have settled into new routines. For the remaining months of the trial, real evidence will be available to enable judgements to be made about the suc-cess of the trial.

2.1.14   Consider the roll-out

At the end of the monitoring period, if the trial has been a success, the roll-out of teleworking to more employees can be planned. Doubtless there will be lessons that have been learned during the pilot, and changes to the sup-port system can be made before making the offer to more employees. The 'Terms and Conditions' of employment may need to be reviewed in the light of experience. For example, an allowance for heating and lighting costs may have been given to those taking part in the trial. The level of the allowance can now be looked at again based on the actual expenses incurred by the teleworkers.

The benefits experienced by the individuals who took part in the trial, such as the reduced stress from commuting, can be used to 'sell' teleworking to other employees. The organisational benefits, such as increased produc-tivity, can, once proved, be used to win over the doubting middle manager.

With more and more employees taking up the teleworking option, many of the monitoring functions for the trial will become part of the routine man-agement task. However, the company should remember that each new group of teleworkers need helping into their new working situations much as did the original trial group. They need the same level of training and of support—just because teleworking becomes more commonplace, managers should not assume that any less attention needs to be paid to the remote workers.

2.2   COSTING A TELEWORKING PILOT PROJECT

2.2.1   Unrecognised teleworking

The first step in setting up a pilot project is to research the incidence of exist-ing teleworking in your organisation. This can take several forms:

- Tacit teleworking (see Chapter 7.1)—the number of unofficial days staff spend working at home or remotely.

- Mobile teleworking (see Chapter 1.6.3)—people who rely on telecommunications while travelling on business.

- Telecommuting—some departments may already have formal projects underway which have not been publicised.

- Site working—travelling direct to clients' premises and working there.

Remember that teleworking is identified by the use of telecommunications to reduce journeys and to reduce office space. The incidence in any organisation is usually greater than managers recognise.

Conduct an unused desk count on two or three working days and analyse why the desks are empty (see Chapter 7.1).

Costs Ideally all personnel should receive a questionnaire, carefully designed to ask the right questions and to define the terms. The answers need collating and analysing. Design, paper, distribution, collection, collation and analysis will cost not less than $1.50 (£1) per head. Assuming 500 people in the office, the total cost of this exercise divided between 20 proposed teleworkers will be about $40 (£25) each.

Benefits Enables identification of existing activity which can be subjected to cost/benefit analysis prior to any new projects. Identifies equipment used by the individuals and the organisation, and its perceived efficiency. Identifies personnel with existing home offices or mobile facilities. Looks for time savings and increased 'effectiveness' (see Chapter 4.3.3).

2.2.2   Cost/benefit analysis of identifying teleworkers

Costs Will occupy not less than three professional work-days at inter-departmental cost of $1200 (£900). External professional costs are *circa* $4000 (£3000).The internal costs between 20 teleworkers gives $60 (£45) each.

Benefits Collates all the factors including the contribution to meeting mandatory environmental standards (BS 7750 for 1994) or USA Clean Air standards. Enables budgets to be approved and short, medium and long term productivity and financial targets to be set.

2.2.3   Selection of proposed teleworkers

Costs Requires drawing up and application of 'Personality ProFile' (PPF) or similar tests to, say, three volunteers to every one selected. External professional selection psychologists would spend some two hours per volunteer or six hours per successful selection, costing between $500 (£350) and $1000 (£750) per final selection.

Benefits Employers are not in the R&D business in setting up teleworking. They are planning to succeed and to benefit from reduced employment costs and increased productivity. Some industrial psychologists feel that professional selection increases the likelihood of a successful pilot project, though no such tests have yet been applied to any projects studied to date.

2.2.4   Training the teleworker

Costs Many volunteers will have some experience of working at home and will feel confident about using the equipment required. However, courses in personal communications are recommended (see Chapter 3.5.1) for both the dispersed and core teams. Three half-day sessions may suffice at an internal cost of three trainer days, including preparation—say—$1200 (£900) per batch of 20 employees or $60 (£45) each. Professional external trainers will have prepared and designed specialised courses and charge only the 1.5 training days, which may be more economic.

Benefits Teleworkers and core team colleagues will be more likely to achieve all the targets set and will understand the costs of communications in time terms and line charges. Team building will have been assisted.

2.2.5   Training the managers

Managers may remain in the central office core team or become dispersed teleworkers themselves. One manager per 20 teleworkers might be trained in remote communication and communications equipment skills.

Costs Two training days; costs depend on numbers. Estimate at $500 (£300) per head.

Benefits Most managers have residual fears of managing 'invisible' workers (see Chapter 4.8). Training will reduce these fears and add valuable knowledge concerning the equipment.

2.2.6   Involving the households

Negotiations for space and facilities and support are important for most teleworkers (see Chapter 3.4).

Costs Family members should be consulted. An average household of three persons per teleworker, plus the teleworker, makes four persons;

family workshops of not more than 20 persons are recommended. For 20 proposed teleworkers, four workshops of, say, one day each are required. Costs depend on location, but if held at existing premises will incur four days of group leaders' time plus two days to set up, i.e. six days totalling $3000 (£1800) or $150 (£90) per teleworker.

Benefits Short circuits settling-in problems and time which can cause productivity dives. If teleworkers achieve an instant 20% increase in deliverables, the benefits are *circa* $11 000 (£9 000) per head.

2.2.7   Designing home offices

It is recommended to design from scratch using existing designs as guides. Design-in the security requirements at the same time (see Chapters 5 and 6.12).

Costs Architect or office ergonomics professional with advice from Information Technology, Health and Safety, Security, and Office Systems experts. Perhaps two weeks' work to specify furniture, equipment, lighting and space—say—$7500 (£5000), which divided by 20 teleworkers gives $375 (£250) each.

Benefits Assists the employers to meet their legal obligations and reassure labour unions. Provides teleworkers with guidelines for laying out their personal workstation and making it safe for (and from) family and friends.

2.2.8   Furniture and equipment

Teleworkers require the same as they have at central office, plus access to shared facilities such as a copier bureau. An additional 'business' telephone line is needed, and ISDN (Integrated Services Digital Network, see Chapter 6.1) should be considered when installing new lines.
   A survey of teleworkers in the UK in 1992 found that they initially underestimated the amount of shelf or storage space required. A planned office stationery starter pack is useful.

Costs Vary widely depending on status, area furnished and telecommunication and office equipment supplied. Long-term, telework experienced, senior managers will eventually accumulate up to $12 000 (£10 000) worth of equipment including soft furnishings and heating/cooling appliances. Most pilot projects studied cost *circa* $5000 (£4000) to equip middle managers, some of which consists of the cost of transferring existing office equipment.

Benefits Well-equipped teleworkers not only achieve the targets set for the project but become multi-skilled (see Chapter 3.5.1), thus increasing their value to the employer.

2.2.9   Legal contracts

None of the projects studied have employed external lawyers but all have
varied the existing contract of employment and/or issued detailed guidelines (see Chapters 2.3.14 and 2.5).

Costs Say, three interdepartmental professional days or $1200 (£900);
divided over 20 teleworkers this gives $60 (£45) per head.

Benefits Enables negotiations between employers and teleworkers and
removes ambiguity from the relationship. Allows labour unions to see that
terms and conditions of employment have not deteriorated.

2.2.10   Measuring and monitoring

A pilot project must be evaluated to decide whether to expand it. Measuring
productivity and effectiveness against costs needs to be set up from the start
and to be continued throughout the first year (see Chapters 2.1 and 4.3.3).

Costs Several forms and reports need to be designed. A base for measurables (work done) has to be set before the project commences and a control
group in the core team needs to be identified and measured to compare with
the teleworkers. Care needs to be taken to avoid the observers affecting the
experiment. SW2000, Oxford, UK, supply a detailed checklist which identifies the forms needed. Because few organisations measure work in offices,
this may be a new and therefore slow process. Allow 2–3 weeks of cost
accountant's time to set up and two manager's days a month to collect, col-
late and analyse information: say 36 professional days at an internal cost of
$18 000 (£10 800); external professionals may have existing formats. For 20
teleworkers this amounts to $900 (£540) each.

Benefits The major financial benefit of teleworking is an increase in output
and 'effectiveness' (Chapter 4.3.3) from teleworkers. Lower travelling costs
and reuse of office space are major benefits. These fine details must be collated and compared to traditional costs and results, to convince the organisation that teleworking is profitable for them.

2.2.11   Cost summary

Table 2.3 summarises the costs and benefits calculated above.

This example of net benefits from a pilot project assumes that increased
productivity is priced at the ACTGR (Average Contribution to Gross
Revenue) output rate and not at the, lower, cost of employment rate.

Continuing 'effectiveness' (output × cost × quality) might be improved by
60% and remain at this level, the rationale being that 4 days a week tele-

Table 2.3   Costs and benefits for experimental pilot project involving 20
senior teleworkers.

	Year One Costs/benefits per head			
Costs				
Identifying existing teleworking	$	40	£	25
Projected cost/benefit analysis	$	60	£	45
Selections	$	1 000	£	750
Training teleworkers	$	60	£	45
Training managers	$	25	£	15
Counselling households	$	150	£	90
Designing offices	$	375	£	250
Furniture and equipment	$	5 000	£	4 000
Legal costs	$	60	£	45
Measuring and monitoring	$	900	£	540
Subtotal	$	7 670	£	5 805
Additional energy allowance	$	400	£	250
Teleworkers' preparation time	$	2 250	£	1 350
Total costs per head	$	10 320	£	7 405
Benefits				
Increased output—say 20% ACTGR	$	11 000	£	9 000
Reduced central office space costs	$	5 000	£	5 000
Reduced travel/city loading allowance	$	Nil	£	1 500
Total benefits per head	$	16 000	£	15 500
Net benefit to employers	$	**5 680**	£	**8 095**

workers may save 12 hours a week commuting (30%), some 6 hours a week
office politics (15%) and half the sick leave (2%), totalling 47% of the hours of
a normal working week. Part of this liberated time applied to the task
accounts for increased output. Costs of mature teleworking projects are less,
by percentages of salary—by New York or London loading or weighting
(5%), by reduced commuting costs and/or extended car life (10%), by
reduced office space costs (10%) and by reduced staff support costs (10%),
totalling an equivalent of 35% of the salary level. Quality of work is generally reported as improved by teleworking, resulting in lower management
costs, greater job satisfaction and therefore better retention of expensively
trained operatives. (The nature of professional costs has been outlined in
Chapter 2.1.)

2.3   TELEWORKING GUIDELINES FOR MANAGERS

This section gives a guide to managers to commence and successfully operate a homeworking arrangement. There are fewer issues to be considered for

other forms of teleworking, which are also covered here. Employers may wish to produce their own homeworking policy and supporting guidelines to guarantee consistency of application and ensure legal requirements are being met.

2.3.1 Selecting the homeworker

The success of a homeworking arrangement is largely dependent on the manager and the homeworker. It is important, therefore, that both are enthusiastic about homeworking, aware of potential benefits and disadvantages and how the arrangement will operate. A checklist of the pros and cons of the arrangements is shown below.

It is recommended that a set of 'questions and answers' is produced for the potential homeworker, and/or they are asked to complete a self-assessment of whether they meet the job, personal and home-related criteria (detailed below). This will encourage enquiries from people who have given homeworking serious thought.

It is the responsibility of the employer to check that the potential teleworker is aware of all the implications of homeworking and their responsibilities before an arrangement is introduced. It is important to ensure that the job, the individual and their home environment are suitable. A cost analysis should be undertaken to assess the benefits and costs of the changes. Managers also need to be aware of what will be required from them for the arrangement to work effectively.

2.3.2 Job requirements

Characteristics of suitable homeworking jobs include:

- A degree of autonomy—or non-autonomous where there is an easy way of supervising and monitoring the job holder (e.g. a job involves use of computer facilities which can be used to help monitor or supervise work)

- Intrinsically satisfying; not dependent solely on external feedback for rewards

- Routine communications needs which can be met by existing communications systems

- Agreed work programmes and time scales which are easily defined both quantitatively and qualitatively

- Does not require any large business equipment which could not easily be fitted into the home

- Involves a good deal of travelling

- Career development prospects depend as much on the development of the individual's skills as on a good knowledge of Company culture

- Work requiring long periods of quiet concentration

2.3.3 Personal requirements

Not everyone will be an ideal homeworker. If a homeworking arrangement is to be a success it is important that the potential homeworker has the following personal qualities commensurate with working unsupervised or being supervised remotely:

- Self-motivated
- Self-disciplined
- Committed to homeworking
- Capable of working with minimum supervision
- Safety conscious
- Adaptable (e.g. it may be necessary for the homeworker to be trained on new equipment or take on new work such as that previously undertaken by administrative support functions in the office base, like purchase of stationery, photocopying, typing, etc.)
- Well organised
- Good communicators
- Able to cope with minimal social contact
- Able to balance work with domestic responsibilities
- Not a 'workaholic'
- Willing to travel to attend meetings, courses, etc., when required

2.3.4 Home environment

The home office must be a suitable workplace. Items which should be considered are:

- Noise levels
- Likelihood of being disturbed by other occupants
- Security: the home, work and equipment need to be secure
- The home must meet any statutory business health and safety requirements
- Whether there is suitable storage space for equipment
- If there is a suitable room which can be used as an office

2.3.5 Cost analysis

Most companies expect a teleworking arrangement to be cost-effective and require managers of potential teleworkers to produce a detailed business case justifying the proposal. The following items should be included:

- Office costs
- Equipment

- Power
- Terms and conditions
- Communications costs
- Administrative costs
- Work output

2.3.6   Management responsibilities

Managers must consider the impact of the introduction of a homeworking arrangement on their job and the jobs of others:

- Make regular visits to the homeworker's home to check the home is safe and secure and maintain face-to-face contact with the homeworker

- Check the impact of the homeworker's absence on the work of other office-based employees. Check whether some of the responsibilities of the potential homeworker have to be passed to other employees, or vice-versa; make any necessary changes to the job descriptions, and discuss with the affected employees

- Brief other affected employees

- Establish working, reporting and communication arrangements between the homeworker, management and other colleagues. The attendance arrangements of the homeworker must be agreed, as well as contact times, i.e. times when the homeworker can contact the manager and vice-versa

Procedures are required for:

- Emergency contact arrangements

- How sickness and accidents will be reported

- How expenses will be claimed

- How faults with equipment are reported (e.g. direct to the company holding the maintenance contract or via a company contact point)

- Ensuring that the homeworker does not become isolated from the Company and colleagues, and watching for any adverse personality changes. To avoid isolation homeworkers should attend team meetings and any Company social events. They should be sent the same work-related literature which they would have received in the office (eg. in-house journals) and be given the same opportunities as other employees to apply for other jobs in the Company, which might entail a move back to central office

- Monitoring the performance of the homeworker, against a central office team member, to ensure that there is no deterioration in quantity and quality of delivered work

- Ensuring that the homeworker attends any necessary training courses (e.g. new equipment)

- Learning how to use new communications technology

- Ensuring that the homeworker is counselled on the position regarding career development

2.3.7 Equipment

The homeworkers will have to be provided with whatever equipment (e.g. PC, facsimile, phone) they need to carry out their job effectively at home. Office furniture should also be provided. It may be sensible to use existing Company stock for this purpose as this will ensure that the equipment/furniture is ergonomically suitable. Arrangements for the transportation and installation of equipment will have to be made. Existing maintenance (and where appropriate rental) contracts will need to be examined and, if appropriate, changed.

Where Company equipment is supplied, an asset register is needed for Company equipment held at home. The homeworker should sign for equipment held at home.

2.3.8 Insurance

The impact of homeworking on any of the individual's or Company's insurance policies needs to be explored and the policies changed where required.

2.3.9 Pay, conditions and other entitlements

The pay and conditions of the homeworker need to be established taking account of Company policy and any statutory regulations. In many cases there will be few, if any, changes.

The position regarding additional home expenses incurred as a result of homeworking needs to be established (e.g. whether the Company is prepared to meet extra electricity/gas usage and mail charges) and the homeworker informed of the outcome. The position regarding the payment of travelling expenses (e.g. to attend meetings) also needs consideration.

Claims for additional expenses must be backed with supporting documentation. Where there are likely to be a large number of homeworkers doing the same sort of work and using the equipment, it saves administrative costs to pay an allowance instead of the additional expenses. A written variation in terms of employment will have to be agreed by the homeworker.

2.3.10 Taxation

There are a number of potential pitfalls awaiting the unwary. So ensure that you know about any national and local taxes which could affect the

Company or the homeworker. In the UK, areas which need particular attention are additional home expenses, travelling expenses, use of business equipment for private use, and use of a room solely for business purposes (see Chapter 3.1).

2.3.11 Other issues

Establish if the owner of the home is someone other than the homeworker. If so, check that there are no difficulties commencing the homeworking arrangement in their property. Similarly establish if there are any local by-laws preventing homeworking.

2.3.12 Review mechanism

Most teleworking starts on a trial basis. Review and termination arrangements should be agreed before the trial or pilot arrangement is introduced.

A review after one year enables initial problems to be resolved.

The vast majority of homeworking arrangements will be successful and of a permanent nature. In some circumstances, however, an individual may wish to cease homeworking or the employer might find it necessary to terminate an arrangement. To make a termination easier to implement it is recommended that there is a provision in the contract specifying adequate notice and terms. Managers must establish the precise terms.

2.3.13 Pros and cons of homeworking

The basic pros and cons of homeworking need to be clearly understood by both the manager and the homeworker. Potential benefits for individuals include:

- Saving in travelling time and expenses
- Fresher (because of less travelling)
- More free time (less travelling)
- Can improve productivity and earn more money
- Saving in home expenses (e.g. child minder)
- Enables continued working instead of retiring or relocating
- Greater flexibility in working hours

Potential disadvantages for individuals include:

- Missing the social contact of work
- Difficult to balance work and domestic commitments
- Lack of office support means time wasted on menial tasks

Advantages to employers include:

- Savings in office costs
- Productivity increases
- Saving in pay and conditions
- Avoiding the need to pay relocation costs following a move
- Retention of quality employees who would otherwise have to relocate

Potential disadvantages for organisations include:

- Effort to set up and administer
- Increased costs (e.g. home expenses)
- Need to buy new equipment
- Damaging to teamwork
- Lack of 'hands-on' management control
- Communications difficulties

2.3.15   Employment contracts

Contract variations depend on the nature of the changes, the wording of the existing contact and contract law requirements. Items to be included are:

- the commitment to work from home rather than an office base
- the homeworking arrangement may be terminated by the employer at any time
- any change to employment conditions (e.g. pay, hours of work, holiday entitlement) or a statement to the effect that these arrangements will be unchanged
- a statement about the provision and use or non-use of Company equipment for private purposes
- a commitment from the homeworker to return Company equipment when they cease homeworking
- insurance arrangements
- a commitment from the homeworker which ensures that they are aware of their safety responsibilities
- a statement about any expenses which may or may not be reimbursed

2.4   COMMUNICATING DAILY

For all remote workers, keeping in touch is important. Individual teleworkers are widely reported as finding social isolation their biggest problem. In 1991, BT conducted a survey of senior managers in large corporations. The survey found that two-thirds of the managers interviewed thought that isolation was a major barrier to the introduction of teleworking. As a barrier, it was second only to 'management attitudes'. A study of 500 medium- to large-sized companies conducted by the NCC in 1992 corroborated the view that isolation is a perceived problem. Over three-quarters of these companies felt that loss of face-to-face contact was a significant problem for teleworkers, while over half of the companies thought that it was the most significant problem.

Teleworkers who routinely work in a central office are unlikely to be unduly worried by such problems. The situation for employees based at a teleservice centre will depend largely on the type of centre they work at. If it is a one-company satellite office, then there should be few problems for individuals (although as a group they may suffer from lack of contact with the rest of the company). A teleworker making use of a rural telecottage may not be lonely, but still may miss the contact with colleagues and the company.

Lack of contact will impact on other potential problem areas for teleworkers, too. An employee who has not heard from his or her company for days, even weeks, will feel forgotten, or ignored. In such circumstances morale will be affected, reducing productivity. The 'out-of-sight, out-of-mind' feeling will increase worries over promotion prospects. And the company senior managers might well wonder what the supervisor is doing if there is so little contact between worker and manager!

So what can be done, particularly for individual teleworkers, to keep them in touch and content?

Firstly, the company needs to recognise that there is a problem, and then to put in place procedures to improve the situation. Teleworkers, not wishing to be left out in the cold, may initiate some procedures themselves, but it is much better not to leave such developments to chance and plan the procedures right from the start of any teleworking programme. Trade unions recognise the problems, and are keen that issues are tackled formally (see Chapter 2.5). There are various types of communication that routinely take place in an office environment that should be considered:

- Company news
- Peer assistance
- Training (giving/receiving)
- Assessment/counselling
- Management control/supervision
- Office gossip/team banter
- General socialising

All of these are essential to the efficient functioning of a team. Where the team is dispersed, methods other than face-to-face contact have to be used instead.

Telecommunications can offer a variety of ways of keeping in touch, from 'POTS' (the Plain Old Telephone Service), through audio conferencing, fax,

	Same Time	Different Time
Different Place	*Remote Meetings* Audio conferencing Video conferencing Screen sharing Spontaneous electronic meetings	*Messaging* Voice and electronic messaging Computer conferencing Shared calendars Group writing Shared databases Workflow
Same Place	*Face-to-Face Meetings* Electronic white boards PC screen projectors Electronically supported meeting rooms	*Team Coordination* Electronic medical record Currency portfolio management Factory control room

Figure 2.4   Place and time matrix

electronic mail, bulletin boards and pagers, to videophones, video conferencing and computer-supported co-operative working. These vary in their usefulness in two ways. The first is in the 'quality' of the communication. For example, in the BT operator homeworking experiment in Inverness, the operators usually started work by 'checking-in' with their supervisor over the videophone. After about six months, for operational reasons, the operators were asked to 'check-in' with an audio phone instead for a week or two. During this time, the operators' morale took a distinct downward dip. The second view of usefulness is in the simultaneity of the communication, i.e. whether all the people taking part in the communication are present at the same time. A useful way of illustrating the point is through the place/time matrix (see Figure 2.4) although in this case our real interest is only in the 'Different Places' half of the matrix.

Whilst videophones are an improvement over audio phones for keeping people in touch, there is no denying that most people prefer face-to-face meetings. In some teleworking situations, it may be possible to have sufficient personal meetings that little else is needed. In the USA, for example, the catalogue shopping company J. C. Penney have 200 part-time teleworkers taking orders over the phone. They all live near to the local call centre and can visit it easily. They visit the centre for a variety of reasons (including picking up their pay!) and so are in the call centre on average once a week. This provides enough opportunity for communications of all types that there is little need for additional telecommunications.

Many teleworking programmes will start with existing employees who are likely to live near enough to the office where they formerly worked that regular visits are no great problem. However, as time progresses, the workforce will become more and more distributed, making telecommunications more and more significant. For some people, social contact with work-mates is very important. Since the well-being of its personnel must be of concern to a company, the planners of teleworking programmes should consider allowing teleworkers to socialise over the corporate telecommunications network, at the company's expense.

There is no golden rule that will provide the solution to all communication problems, but the planners of teleworking initiatives should try to ensure that the procedures give teleworkers contact with colleagues or managers at least once a day. Where face-to-face meetings cannot be frequent, the company should make sure that some occasions for meeting are provided. Teleworkers should be invited into the 'office' for a day now and then—for company briefings, counselling sessions, refresher training, brainstorming meetings and team-building events (see also Chapters 2.11 and 3.5.2). Companies may even consider financial inducements for remote employees to travel in to the centre to join in company social events. Particularly while teleworking programmes are in their early years, it is beneficial to arrange discussion groups for the teleworkers. These enable the teleworkers to talk about any problems they may have amongst themselves, and share solutions. A skilled discussion leader will set the right tone and draw out the responses.

In summary, it is essential that remote workers are kept in touch with the rest of the company. The ways of doing this, appropriate to the situation, should be planned into the teleworking programme right from the start. In most cases, telecommunications are likely to be essential—and new developments like the videophone and CSCW promise to be extremely useful. Feedback from the teleworkers will alert their managers to the sufficiency, or otherwise, of the communication methods being used.

2.5   UNIONS: STATEMENTS OF PRACTICE

Pioneer teleworkers were mostly self-employed people and not usually members of labour/labor or clerical unions. Employed teleworkers, who have joined the quiet revolution over the past decade or so, tend to work for large organisations and generally have union representation. The unions' offices, in both the UK and the USA, deal with enquiries about teleworking or telecommuting via units set up to study 'homeworking'. Homeworking still conjures up images of little barefoot match girls, Victorian sweatshops and heavily exploited, elderly widows working all hours, in miserable conditions, for very little pay (see Chapter 1.7.1).

Telephone calls to most union headquarters elicit that there are few official acknowledgements of high-technology teleworking and fewer completed studies. This is unsurprising given the recent provision of desktop technology at 'family' affordable prices, allowing previously high-priced and precious equipment to be taken home from the office or bought from a local store for family use. Large scale teleworking is as recent as the accessibility of the enabling technology, and unions are as aware as most employers about the emerging trends.

The Communications Workers of America (CWA) union initially resisted initiatives from AT&T and regional Bell operating companies but, as understanding about teleworking spread, the local union offices reduced their opposition. *Telecommuting Review*, produced by Gil Gordon, New Jersey, cited reports from the Bureau of National Affairs in March and October 1992, saying that the CWA had agreed to limited experiments in telecommuting, despite earlier refusals to cooperate with Bell Atlantic's plans for a pilot project. The union had issued guidelines to protect teleworkers, requiring:

1. Equal pay and benefits

2. Two days a week at the central office

3. Managers visits to homes no more than twice a month

4. Proper equipment and furniture supplied by employers, reimbursement of all costs, and union rights to inspect home workstations

5. Equal promotion information and opportunities, with union contacts given daily on teleworkers' computer screens

6. Limitations on monitoring of teleworkers

7. No preferential treatment for teleworkers

8. Equal training and extra training if the equipment provided demands it

9. Recruitment of teleworkers only from existing personnel—no direct hiring from the job market

10. No conversion of status from employee to subcontractor or 'outsourcing supplier'

The legitimate anxieties of the union are apparent from these 10 rules.

In the UK, the Banking, Insurance and Finance Union (BIFU) (see Chapter 4.8) demanded in 1990 that:

11. All teleworkers must be volunteers

12. There must be an automatic right to return to the core team

These two (additional) demands were made in response to discovering 'secret' proposed or actual teleworking projects at Centre-File, with five home-teleworkers; at Lombard North Central, advised by ICL, contemplating 214 home-teleworkers (detailed in Chapter 4.8); and at Bradford Pennine Insurance who put their motor engineers onto computer calculated customer call lists, with the engineers travelling from their homes. BIFU reported in November 1990 their strong 'unease' at these working conditions changes, without union consultation.

In the UK, the TUC (Trades Union Congress) referred teleworking enquiries to the Labour Research Unit (071-928 3649) where Stephanie Peck was aware of the issues and suggested that the Civil Service unions had made progress on a policy statement. Twenty or more telephone calls to different unions produced only the BIFU paper detailed above.

It seems that many unions are no more advanced in their thinking about teleworking than are many senior managers in large organisations and, like some of those managers, initially regard the movement as a threat to the status quo.

The Manufacturing, Science, Finance union (MSF) add further points to the demands:

13. Teleworkers' workstations in a separate room in the home

14. Regular meetings between teleworkers and with core team personnel

15. Rights to use equipment to communicate with colleagues (reducing isolation)

16. Specified 'mentor' manager for each teleworker (see Chapter 3.5.4)

17. Specific Health and Safety Officer visits and reports, with teleworkers represented on Health and Safety committees

18. Union access to teleworkers via electronic networks

19. The setting up of a homeworker inspectorate

20. Legal rights for teleworkers to see levels of pay of core team and other teleworkers

21. Legal right of refusal to work from home

Note that the list of 21 union demands, above, does not represent the demands of one union but the demands of the three unions, accumulated into one list. Each union separately produced a list and the three lists overlapped in many respects. Equally, not all the points were raised by all three unions but in the main these 21 points accurately represent the matters raised, providing an unofficial 'Statement of Practice'.

Bill Walsh, speaking on teleworking for the MSF in September 1992, said, on opportunities being made available to the home-based worker, **'The alternative to taking a positive stance on these potential developments, is to try to sustain the unsatisfactory and unpopular employment status-quo for many people who want to opt for change'** . . . **'For these reasons, MSF is campaigning to ensure that home-based working is a genuine extension of freedom for people at work . . . The union wants to see a wide range of employment opportunities being made available to the home-based worker . . .'**

President Clinton's announcement in March 1993 of a $100–400 billion 'Information Superhighway', and the investigation into every UK Ministry's policy, due for publication between June and December 1993, perhaps mark the coming of age of teleworking and may precipitate the crystallisation of union policy in Europe and America.

2.6 EMPLOYMENT CONTRACTS

As teleworking has grown over the years, there has been a realisation that most telework arrangements would benefit from a formal document that describes the terms and conditions of employment for the teleworker. This document, often called a 'telework agreement', is separate from (and does not take the place of) any other employment contract that may exist between the worker and the employer. (In the USA, the shift toward 'employment at will' conditions of work has caused employers to expressly avoid any document or personnel policy manual language that could imply a long-term contract relationship. 'Employment at will' means that the employer has the right to terminate employment for virtually any reason, and not necessarily limited to a specific cause. Thus, any telework agreement used in 'employment at will' States should contain similar definitive language.)

2.6.1 Purpose and contents of the agreement

The purpose of the telework agreement is to spell out the unique characteristics of the employer–worker relationship that arise due to the telework arrangement, and in particular the work-at-home form of telework. This agreement should serve three functions:

- To clearly identify what is (and is not) different about the work relationship as it occurs with telework

- To clearly state the unique responsibilities of both parties, especially as they differ from standard office-based work

- Most important, to reduce the likelihood of misunderstandings in the event of problems during the telework period. The goal should be to avoid the laborious 'I thought' syndrome, i.e., the employee says, 'I thought that the company would pay for repairs to my PC', and the Company says, 'We thought you knew that you would pay, since it is your own PC', and so on

Here are two such agreements that demonstrate these principles. The first was created by Gil Gordon Associates of Monmouth Junction, New Jersey, USA, for a telework (or 'telecommuting,' as it is often called in the US) trial in the systems division of a large US insurance company, identified here as the ABC Company. This is typical of telework agreements that are in use today:

The purpose of this agreement is to clarify the issues involved in a telecommuting pilot program sponsored by ABC Company for some of its employees. Because telecommuting is a relatively new way of working, certain policies and procedures in place to cover work in the office may not apply, or have to be changed. Also, there are new conditions that arise that were never intended to be covered by ABC Company policies.

Please read this carefully and discuss it with your manager or your Human Resources representative if you have questions, and also, perhaps, with your spouse or family members if applicable.

The telecommuting pilot at ABC Company is an experiment to see how well the work-at-home concept works for the company and its employees. We do not know if it will be a permanent arrangement and it may be discontinued at any time.

It is not an employee benefit intended to be available to the general ABC Company population. The company is optimistic about its chances for success but is not guaranteeing how long it will run. It is intended to continue for approximately six months, but this is subject to change depending on how well the pilot progresses, department workload and other factors.

Similarly, as a telecommuter you are volunteering for this pilot based on having been given thorough information about the pilot and the pros and cons of telecommuting. You, like ABC Company, have every reason to believe it will work out. However, if you find that telecommuting is not to your liking and want to return to your office work location full-time you can do so by notifying your manager.

When the pilot ends, or if it is terminated before the expected end date, you will be expected to return to your job at your office location. Also, if your work performance suffers and your manager decides that it will be in your best long-term interest to return to the office full-time, you will be expected to return to the office. If you choose not to return on the expected date, this will be considered to be a voluntary resignation and will be treated as such under standard policies.

Your salary, job responsibilities, and benefits will not change because of your involvement in the pilot, except as they might have changed had you stayed in the office full-time, e.g., regular salary reviews will occur as scheduled, and you will be entitled to any company-wide benefits changes that may be implemented. You agree to comply with all existing job requirements as now are in effect in the office.

Your total number of work hours are not expected to change during the pilot, and you will be responsible for providing information for the weekly time sheet according to standard ABC Company policy. In the event that you expect to work more than the standard number of hours, this must be discussed and approved in advance by your supervisor, just as any overtime scheduling would normally have to be approved.

Your daily work schedule is subject to negotiation with and approval by your supervisor. To the extent that your job duties allow it and your supervisor feels a change would not impair your ability to be in contact with co-workers, you are free to vary your hours to suit your preference. Your manager may require that you work certain 'core hours' and to be accessible by telephone during those hours.

You will be expected to come to your office location at ABC Company a minimum of one day per week and up to three days per week, depending on scheduling and workload considerations. This schedule will be worked out weekly in advance with your manager.

In addition, there may be times when you will be requested to come into the office on a day that would normally be spent at home. ABC Company and your supervisor will try to minimize these unplanned office visits, but we ask that you recognize the need for them and agree to come in when requested. Similarly, there may be weeks when you have to spend more time than planned (up to the full five days) in the office when the nature of the workload requires it. It will be your responsibility to come into the office as requested during these times.

ABC Company will provide the necessary computer, modem, software, and other equipment needed for you to do your job. All of these items remain the property of ABC Company and must be returned to ABC Company upon request, in case of an extended illness, upon your resignation or termination, or when the pilot ends. When they are to be returned, you agree to return them yourself or to allow ABC Company to arrange to pick them up from your home.

ABC Company will reimburse you for the cost of installation and monthly service on a telephone line to be installed for your use during the pilot. This is intended for ABC Company purposes only and not for personal use. ABC Company will reimburse you for business use of this telephone line when you submit a reimbursement request. It will be your responsibility to insure that no one else has access to the phone.

Office supplies as needed will be provided by ABC Company; your out-of-pocket expenses for other supplies will not be reimbursed unless by prior approval of your manager. Also, ABC Company will not reimburse you for travel expenses to and from the office on days when you come into the office, nor for any home-related expenses such as heat, light, or electricity.

The computer, modem, software, and any other equipment or supplies provided by ABC Company are for use primarily on ABC Company assignments. However, you can use these items for reasonable personal purposes as long as these do not create any conflict of interest with your job. The equipment should not be used by other household members or anyone else. Company-owned software may not be duplicated except as formally authorized, and you agree to comply with terms of software licensing agreements. Also, the company will provide virus-check software to be used every time you start up your computer. Further, you agree that you will not connect your computer to any unauthorized bulletin boards or computer networks, or install any software not provided by the company, as reasonable precautions against computer viruses.

The security of company property in your home is as important as it is in the office. You are expected to take reasonable precautions to protect the equipment from theft, damage, or misuse. You are required to contact your homeowner's insurance carrier to determine to what extent this property is covered under your homeowner's policy. If ABC Company property is NOT covered, you agree to notify your manager and, if requested, take out additional coverage at the company's expense to cover the property.

Any ABC Company materials taken home should be kept in your designated work area at home and not be made accessible to others. In no case will you take proprietary or confidential materials home except with the approval of your supervisor.

ABC Company is interested in your health and safety while working at home just as it is while you work in the office. For this reason, you are required to maintain a separate, designated work area at home. ABC Company has the right to visit your home work area to see if it meets company safety standards; such visits will be scheduled in advance.

Any equipment provided should be placed where it is adequately supported and there is no danger of it falling. It should be connected to a properly-grounded electrical outlet and all wires kept out of walkways. If you have any questions about the adequacy/safety of your home work area, ABC Company will help you in this regard and will arrange for an inspection of this area at your request.

ABC Company will be responsible for any work-related injuries under state Workers Compensation laws, but this liability will be limited to injuries resulting directly from your work and only if the injury occurs in your designated work area.

Telecommuting is not to be viewed as a substitute for child care. ABC Company expects that you will make arrangements for someone to care for your children (if applicable) if needed. The company recognizes that one advantage of working at home is the opportunity to have more time with children, but it is your responsibility to insure that you are fully able to complete your work assignments on time.

It will be your responsibility to determine any income tax implications of maintaining a home office area. ABC Company will not provide tax guidance nor will the company assume any additional tax liabilities. You are encouraged to consult with a qualified tax professional to discuss income tax implications.

I accept the conditions of this agreement.

EMPLOYEE SIGNATURE _____ DATE ____

COMPANY REPRESENTATIVE SIGNATURE _____ DATE ____

This second example comes from a UK company:

CONTRACT VARIATION FOR TELEWORKING

NAME:
GRADE:

JOB TITLE:

Further to our discussions on working from home, I am now offering you a variation of contract on the following terms and conditions:

From [date] you will be working from home. This arrangement may be terminated at any stage by UK Company plc.

There will be no change to pay, hours of work, annual leave entitlement, superannuation arrangements or other employment conditions unless detailed below. Details for your grade of [job grade] are given in the Employee Terms and Conditions publication.

UK Company plc will supply you with the necessary equipment that may be reasonably required to enable the contract to be performed from home. All equipment shall at all times remain the property of UK Company plc, not be used for private purposes and be returned by you when you cease working from home. All equipment supplied by UK Company plc for use at home will be insured by the Company.

UK Company plc will provide a telephone line for business use which will be paid for by the Company.

You should note that you have a responsibility for your own safety in your home and to ensure that at all times you work in a safe condition. You will accordingly be required to comply with all relevant safety guidelines/instructions and to satisfy UK Company plc that you have done so.

PERSONNEL MANAGER

I agree to the Teleworking Contract on the terms and conditions stated.

Signed _____

Date _____

2.6.2 Considerations for designing the agreement

There are several points to note in these agreements. Some of the clauses will vary according to company preferences. For example:

- Does the company or the employee provide the equipment?
- Does the company or the employee provide the phone line?
- Does the company want to restrict the use of the equipment for other purposes?

These and other sections of the agreement should be carefully studied to determine their suitability in a given situation.

This agreement is written between the employee and the company. In cases where the teleworkers are represented by a union, the union may prefer that the agreement be prepared as an adjunct to the existing contract. Or, the union might prefer that the employee not sign the agreement at all (since that might constitute an implied contract not wanted by the union); in this case, the supervisor would sign the agreement to note that it had in fact been reviewed by and discussed with the employee, or simply send it in the form of a letter to the teleworker.

Some organisations (prompted by their legal advisors) have chosen not to use an agreement such as this. The rationale is that such an agreement might actually create more problems than it avoids. For example, one item addresses workplace injury issues; some lawyers would say that a site visit by the employer to 'certify' the home office as safe could be problematic if an injury subsequently occurs, and that the liability could be greater than if no such inspection had been made. This position could be argued in either direction, and employers are thus advised to carefully consider both possibilities before selecting the wording of the agreement.

Because it is important for everyone to fully understand the agreement, it should be written in plain English and with a minimum of legal terminology and format. The objective should be to balance the legal requirements of precise language with the practical objective of having an agreement that is clear and easily readable.

2.6.3 Suggestions for explaining and using the agreement

Experience has shown that this kind of agreement is well received by the potential teleworkers and their managers. The teleworkers value it because it takes away some of the uncertainty about the telework arrangement, and the managers like it because it puts on paper the answers to many of their questions and concerns.

It is suggested that the employees considering telework be given the agreement long before their telework begins. They should have an opportunity to review it carefully by themselves and with their manager, spouse, or other advisors. Above all, it should not be thrust at them at the last moment just before telework begins, at a time when they might feel they are signing it under duress. When it is distributed early in the planning process, the employer will have an opportunity to explain the rationale behind the agreement in general and each clause in particular.

Some organisations will choose to attach to the agreement a copy of related policies or documents. These might include confidentiality or proprietary information policies (including, perhaps, the requirement to keep important papers in a fireproof cabinet), and software licences. These are especially useful if the employer wants to remind the teleworkers of their continuing obligations about issues such as privacy of company documents or the penalties for making unauthorised copies of commercial software.

In summary, the teleworker's agreement is a true preventive step that will help establish the telework relationship on a positive note, and should greatly reduce the likelihood of troublesome problems later on. A clearly-written agreement that will demonstrate to the teleworkers that this alternative work style is, in fact, serious business demonstrates mutual obligations for the teleworker and the employer and will strengthen the telework programme.

2.7   SAFETY AT WORK

Teleworkers who work at home, and their employers, must comply with statutory Health and Safety requirements. In the UK, both employer and teleworker must ensure that the conditions of the Health and Safety at Work Act 1974 have been met. In the case of homeworking, this places joint legal responsibility on the Company and the teleworker to ensure that the part of the home and the equipment and furnishings used are maintained in a safe condition.

It is advisable for the manager or another Company employee with responsibility for safety to visit (with prior notice) the home workplace to ensure that it, any equipment, systems of work, the work environment and facilities are safe. Visits and safety checks should continue on a regular basis to ensure that the home workplace remains safe. Potential teleworkers should be made fully aware of their safety responsibilities and the terms of any legislation.

It is important for the employer to be satisfied that any furniture and equipment to be used by the teleworker complies with any statutory legislation and that it is ergonomically suitable, thereby preventing back strains and other injuries. Where it is suitable and available, existing Company stock could be used. Where equipment is to be used, the teleworker must be provided with whatever information, instruction and training may be necessary in order to ensure that they know how to operate and maintain it. More complex equipment should, however, be regularly maintained or serviced by properly qualified service technicians in accordance with the manufacturer's instructions.

Other occupants of the home and visitors to the home workplace should be informed of any potential dangers of the equipment. There should also be a suitable, safe, storage space for equipment. The home-based teleworker will need to ensure that children, pets and food are kept away from the equipment.

It is important for the employer to emphasise that teleworkers should take sufficient rest and meal breaks and do not work excessively long hours, and that they should comply with any statutory legislation. For example, VDU/VDT operators should have frequent breaks. A sensible approach would be to tell people moving from an office to homeworking to continue with the same work pattern. For many, homeworking will be a new experience and, despite all the checks built into the selection process, and an individual's certainty that homeworking is for them, it may be that they are unable to cope with the isolation from colleagues. The teleworker's manager must be alert to this and ensure that the teleworker remains part of the team, by speaking to and seeing the teleworker regularly. Where a teleworker is a member of a team it is recommended that he or she attends team meetings regularly.

A method of reporting accidents or potential hazards needs to be adopted; wherever possible it is recommended that this follows existing Company accident/hazard reporting arrangements.

2.7.1   Insurance

The employer needs to ensure that any statutory obligations are met. Generally this would mean that the individual would have to be insured by the Company while homeworking. Indeed, European Community legislation gives the employee the same rights at home as they would have at work. The employer will, therefore, need to establish the impact of homeworking on the existing insurance policies and ensure these are changed when required.

2.7.2   Health and safety checklist for employers of homeworkers

- Does it comply with statutory Health and Safety legislation?
- Is furniture and equipment suitable?
- Is there suitable storage for equipment when not in use?
- Set up a method for reporting accidents and hazards
- Establish the position on insurance
- Check the safety at the home workstation
- Inform the homeworker about:
  —Health and Safety legislation as it affects them
  —Rest breaks
  —Insurance
  —Advising other occupants about the equipment
  —Keeping children, pets, etc. away from equipment

It is advisable to consider the health and safety of teleworking employees when formulating or changing the contract of employment (see Chapters 2.3.14 and 2.6) and when designing the home workstation or office (see Chapters 6.0 and 6.13). A home visit as performed by Lombard Bank officers (see Chapter 4.8) is also advisable but remember the advice concerning employers' possible liabilities, should claims arise.

Chapter 5 details the insurance issues should deliberate or accidental damage to persons or property occur and also in the case of theft.

2.8   TRAINING

2.8.1   Core team to dispersed team to core team

The value of training in telework programs has been clearly demonstrated. It makes the difference between trial-and-error and trial-and-success. The training is especially important for work-at-home telework because the work setting and supervision (and related communication and work organisation methods) are significantly different from what is typical for the head office.

2.8.2   Content of the training

A suggested approach for training is a series of three consecutive sessions, one for the teleworkers, one their managers, and then one for both together. Among the topics covered for the teleworkers are:

- Where and how to set up a home office
- Planning for security, safety and ergonomics in the home office
- Setting up the optimal schedule and work plans at home
- Dealing with family, friends and neighbours
- Taking on the 'deliverables' mentality, i.e., emphasising the work product
- Staying in touch with clients and co-workers in the office
- Managing your career from a distance

Among the topics covered for the managers are:

- Managing by results instead of by observation
- Fine-tuning skills for setting performance standards
- Giving ongoing performance feedback
- Keeping teleworkers connected into the social and information networks in the office
- Career management issues for teleworkers
- Spotting problems early and dealing with them effectively

Among the topics covered in the joint discussion session are:

- Details of schedule, availability, phone coverage, and office days
- Planning the first few weeks of teleworking
- Minimising effects on department workflow
- Making sure that co-workers are not required to take on extra work that would normally have been done by the teleworkers
- Providing technical (equipment) support as needed
- Dealing with system shutdowns and other problems

The training plan for satellite office or telecottage teleworkers is essentially the same; the biggest difference is that the teleworker training would omit the sections on working and living under the same roof, e.g., setting up the home office and dealing with family members. All the other issues are the same, since the common thread is the need to learn how to manage and be managed at a distance.

A relatively few organisations also provide training for the family members of the teleworkers, on the assumption that their support and ability to coexist with the teleworker at home are vital. Most organisations have opted to leave this 'training' to the teleworkers themselves, believing that there might be something slightly 'Big Brother'-like in having the employer intervene in these household matters. The teleworker training outline noted above includes tips for the teleworker on how to hold a productive planning discussion with family members, covering topics such as use of space in the home, allowable interruptions, and expectations for chores to be done (or avoided) by the teleworkers. Perhaps these matters are better left to the family to discuss.

2.8.3 What is—and isn't—new about telework training

With the exception of the specific work-at-home topics, all the rest of the training is virtually indistinguishable from what would be covered in a thorough management skills curriculum. That is the irony of telework: managing at a distance is not necessarily different from managing on site. The challenge is to convince managers to shift away from practising 'eyeball management' (in which they observe activity) to managing for results (in which they concentrate on the results of that activity).

Thus, the essence of good remote management for any form of telework revolves around the basic managerial principles of setting performance expectations, tracking progress, giving corrective feedback, and providing coaching or other resources as needed to help the employee achieve the desired results. While most managers know these principles, they often fail to practice them as well or as often as they should, because they have the luxury of frequent, close contact with their staff in the office.

Quite remarkably, it is very common to hear a manager of teleworkers report that the practice of managing from a distance (using those tried-and-true managerial principles) results not only in good results from the teleworkers, but also in good results with the staff in the office. The manager typically adopts these same practices for all the staff members no matter where they work; when this happens, the results from everyone are improved. This is a hidden benefit of telework programmes.

2.9 TAX TREATMENT FOR EMPLOYERS AND EMPLOYEES

The main section on tax for teleworkers is Chapter 3.1.

Substantial tax costs or benefits stem from teleworking. Individuals can gain advantages as set out in Chapter 3.1 but need advice from the outset to get it right. Employers should buy the best professional advice and pass it on to their teleworkers. For 100 teleworkers there can be $1m of tax deductible expenses, which at a tax rate of 30% comes to $300 000 a year. This figure is doubled to calculate the actual cash benefit to individuals (see Table 3.1). Taking a 15 year view some $4.5m of tax is at stake.

The UK Inland Revenue and the US Internal Revenue Service have not yet issued guidelines on teleworking. However, mobile and homeworking are not new and precedents do exist to base tax planning on. The major tax issues include:

- The home office—heat, light, and overheads
- Assistants at home—child care facilities and baby care
- Equipment supplied—deductible or benefit in kind
- Building a home office—interest and VAT or Sales Tax
- Telephone calls—private element
- Depreciation—furniture, decorating, equipment
- Home office as branch office—tax status
- Car expenses—commuting to head office, private use
- Capital Gains Tax on selling the home
- Office in hotel rooms—level of claims
- Who pays the bills, who claims, who reclaims?

Arguments in favour of teleworking tax breaks, at a national level, must include the environmental benefits of less exhaust gas.

2.9.1 Case law

2.9.1.1 Travel costs

There are no cases precisely matching employed teleworkers with home offices. Guidelines indicate that for journeys between home and central office to qualify for relief, the teleworker must be *required* to work at home, which must be the main place of work; in such circumstances the costs will be allowed. Prudential Assurance in the UK employed an area manager in Nottingham who claimed to work from home and claimed journeys between the Nottingham office and home. The claim did not succeed. Coincidental cases involving medical doctors have been reported in both the USA and the UK.

In the case of IRS-*v*-Dr Nader Soliman, th USA Supreme Court found Dr Soliman (anesthesiologist) could not deduct journeys between his home office and the three hospitals he serviced, none of which provided office space. That it took from 1983 to 1991 for the decision demonstrates the legal confusion and debate over this issue.

In the UK, the case of Pook-*v*-Owen, in the Appeal Court in 1970, found that a self-employed doctor (obstetrician and anaesthetist) who practised at home and was also employed (salaried) by a hospital 15 miles away which paid part of his commuting costs, could deduct the full travel costs.

Dr Parikh (UK), a self-employed general practitioner established at home with three salaried hospital posts, appealing in the UK Chancery Division in 1988, was denied the deduction of travel between the four locations.

To avoid every teleworking employee having to hire professionals to fight such contradictory issues, the employer should take the responsibility on their behalf. Computerised legal and taxation expert systems do exist and can be consulted but it will be decades before such systems replace any accountants, lawyers or judges in this very grey area of debate. The tax authorities tend to interpret written tax law to the Treasury's advantage and the taxpayers argue for an interpretation in their own favour. Indispensable professional advisors sit in between the protagonists and nod wisely in both directions, demonstrating again and again the immense difficulty of accurately communicating via the written word.

2.9.1.2   Home offices

To establish home office expenses as deductible, arguments will start with an examination of the basic contract of employment (see Chapter 2.6). Some costs, such as records of business calls, can now be accurately and indisputably listed, thanks to new technology and telephone services (Chapter 6.11). The *requirement* to work at home may be critical in disputes, but so far there are no published cases in either the USA or the UK to give reliable guidance.

2.9.1.3   Capital gains

On selling a home where an office has been claimed (see Chapter 3.1.9).

For further guidance, see tax references in the Bibliography and consult professional tax experts.

2.10   SELECTION

2.10.1   Planned, not accidental

The most important message about selecting teleworkers is that they must be selected. One common myth about how teleworkers emerge is that a manager goes to the workgroup, asks 'Who wants to work at home?', and then points those who raised their hand in the direction of the door so they can head for home. This strategy is a prescription for failure.

Above all else that has been learned about telework in the last 10 years is the fact that it is not for every person or every job. The matter of which jobs are suited to telework is covered in Chapter 2.3.2, so this section will concentrate on choosing the right people.

It is best to think of telework as a specific job assignment; like all assignments, some people are interested in it and suited for it, and others are not. The key challenge in selecting teleworkers is to help prospective teleworkers to make an informed decision about whether they want to be considered for selection, and then to have management choose from among these informed volunteers. Comments on helping employees make this informed decision will be found in Chapter 2.3.

2.10.2   Essential criteria: teleworkers as quasi-entrepreneurs

In many ways, teleworkers are like entrepreneurs—at least for the days when they are working away from the head office. They make more of their own decisions, they solve more of their own problems, and they rely more on their own judgment. And, they do all this with a sense of independence and without the feeling that they must discuss every action with a co-worker or supervisor.

Any employee selection decision is a prediction about future performance; the question to be answered is, 'How well will this person perform this task in the future?' Since we are all creatures of habit, the best way to answer this question is to look at how well the person performed the same (or a similar) task in the past. This is the single most important reason why employers are generally advised to select teleworkers from among current staff members instead of hiring them 'off the street' with no work history in the organisation. The current employees have a record of performance that can be examined to see how and whether they have shown these quasi-entrepreneurial traits in the past, even when working in the office.

Let's consider what these traits are:

- *Decision-making*   Good teleworkers make sound decisions in a short time, know where to get the information needed for the decision, and know when they are out of their element and in need of counsel from a co-worker or the manager.

- *Problem-solving*   Good teleworkers must be able to (and find it satisfying to) solve their own problems instead of immediately calling on someone else for guidance, and they need to have a relatively disciplined approach for analysing the true causes of the problem so they come up with the appropriate solution.

- *Self-management*   Good teleworkers are their own bosses; to a large degree they can motivate themselves, manage their own time, evaluate and correct their own work (as opposed to frequently needing external feedback and praise), and, above all, put all these skills together so they can consistently deliver quality work products on time.

Managers looking to choose teleworkers should have information about the person's performance in these areas readily at hand. It can come from formal sources like performance evaluations, or, more likely, from the accumulated observations by the manager over time. This may seem to be an unscientific approach, and some managers might instead prefer a kind of assessment instrument to help them make the decision. To date, no reliable survey or questionnaire has been developed for this purpose; it is perhaps just as well, because there are plenty of other observational data sources available for making the selection decision.

2.10.3   Additional considerations

Here are some points to keep in mind.

- *Don't confuse selection decisions with administration*. If you are concerned that three of your best people all want to telework and your department would be missing its core of expertise if they all are away, control this by setting guidelines for how many days each can telework. The correct selection decision might be to choose them all; the correct administration decision might be to stagger their telework days.

- *Be wary of the 'cure of telework'*. Some employees might tell you their performance, quality, or attendance problems might be solved if you would only let them telework. This will probably go against your instinct because you will be inclined to reject their request due to their substandard performance in the office. Follow your instinct; it's rare that someone working away from the office will magically fix problems that couldn't be fixed while they were working in the office.

- *Nothing is forever*. Most telework programs give the manager the right to extend the telework privilege—and to withdraw it if necessary. No matter how diligently you make your selections, some teleworkers simply might not be able to succeed. If you're on the fence about an individual who could well be successful, give it a try and then monitor performance. These are revocable selections, not permanent ones. Remember, too, that no one will be as interested in making telework succeed as the teleworker; this high motivation to retain the telework privilege is a strong incentive to produce what is expected.

- *Watch out for social butterflies.* Some of the people most likely to succeed as teleworkers based on their work habits might be most likely to fail based on their high needs for socialising and being the hub of the social network in the office. All forms of telework have fewer opportunities for socialising than exist in the normal office; the social butterfly might be better off in a satellite office, or perhaps should limit the work-at-home days to no more than one or two per week. Sometimes these people aren't even aware of their own tendencies to be such strong socialisers (which is not inherently bad unless it interferes with office productivity); the manager sees them as they cannot see themselves, and must use this information in the selection process.

- *Direct vs indirect supervision* This entire section presumes that the form of telework being considered is one with little direct control and supervision; the teleworkers are physically apart and relatively independent from the organisation and its supervision. There are some forms of telework (e.g. satellite offices or telework centres) which are more similar to the head office than to work-at-home telework, in terms of the amount of latitude and independence allowed. In these remote-office settings, it is less important (but not unimportant) to find people with the quasi-entrepreneurial traits described above.

- *Ignoring the irrelevant.* Finally, it is worth noting what criteria should *not* be considered when choosing teleworkers. These include age, sex, race, physical characteristics, sexual preference, family status, or religion, to name a few. Just as these are not legitimate selection criteria for work *in* the office, they are not legitimate or relevant for work *outside* the office.

There is an old joke about a doctor talking to a patient about his medical problem: 'Mr. Jones, I can tell you that half the people your age with this problem will get worse, and the other half will get better. Unfortunately, I can't tell you which half you belong to.' Contrary to the problem faced by this doctor, most managers can quite simply tell whether an employee is likely to succeed as a teleworker—or at least able to make a reasonably good guess that can be verified in the early stages of telework.

Choosing good teleworkers isn't a matter of high science or mysticism; it's simply a matter of good common sense and good managerial judgment, with plenty of reliance on work histories and work samples in the office. The manager who is familiar with the work of his or her staff, and has seen them perform on a variety of tasks, should not find it difficult to identify those most likely to be successful, productive, happy teleworkers.

2.11 TEAM BUILDING

One of the objections raised about telework is that it makes true teamwork difficult to achieve. 'If the team isn't located in the same place, how can they work together, share ideas, and develop the sense of joint effort' ask the sceptics. This is a reasonable question that is becoming even more important

in today's flattened organisations where self-managed teams and empowered employees are becoming the norm.

2.11.1   Myths vs realities of teams

As we answer this question, let us note two of the myths about teams and
teamwork that stand in the way of team building for a dispersed workforce:

- 'If they aren't working in the same place, they aren't working together'.
  The reality is that plenty of work teams are not co-located, yet they share
  common goals, common objectives, and jointly contribute to results. The
  best and oldest examples are in field sales organisations; more recent
  examples are in multinational project teams for global organisations that
  divide up work to be done by individuals or small groups spread around
  the world. Extra effort is required, to be sure, but these are workable
  arrangements.

- 'Good teamwork means that everyone shares ideas and can draw upon
  the resources of the entire team to solve problems'. The reality is that
  only a portion of what team members produce demands this kind of collaboration. The very mundane truth of day-to-day organisational life is
  that most team members spend the majority of their time working as
  individual contributors; they do not spend every working moment chatting over the cubicle walls or exchanging brilliant insights. In fact, too
  much of this kind of interchange can lead to diminished team results
  because not enough time is spent on the specific tasks that need to be
  done.

2.11.2   Tips for building strong (dispersed) teams

Here are some do's and don'ts about effective collaboration across distances:

- DO make sure the team has the time and opportunity to form as a team;
  disperse them too early and the critical mass will not exist. Also, provide
  some time periodically for the team to assess its performance and study
  its work processes. This is analogous to a sports team that views the
  videotape of a recent game to learn how team performance can improve.

- DO over-communicate; fast and full information flow is the 'glue' that
  holds a dispersed work group together.

- DO provide plenty of opportunities for the team to collaborate (in person
  or electronically) on matters of importance to the team, i.e., objective-set-
  ting, scheduling, resource allocation, and also to get together on a social
  basis whenever possible. There's no end to the amount of real collaboration that can happen over a beer or pizza, or on a playing field.

- DON'T allow a two-tier workforce to evolve, in which either the head office group or the dispersed workers become the 'prima donnas' at the expense of the others. Neither group should have an undue share of either the prized assignments or the more mundane ones.

- DON'T shortchange the team by over-economising on technology that facilitates collaboration, e.g., e-mail, voice mail, computer conferencing, and selective use of audio- or even videoconferencing.

- DON'T be inflexible about work location changes; there's no reason why today's head office workers can't be tomorrow's teleworkers, and vice versa. This kind of 'location rotation' gives everyone a stake in making sure the team continues to function well as a team.

2.11.3   A few words on the changing role of the manager

If we are to believe the business press reports about trends in self-managed teams, then we can expect to see the manager's role shifting from being a 'sage on the stage' to a 'guide on the side'. As this happens, the team

Figure 2.5   Managing a dispersed team: keeping in touch

members (no matter where they are located) will begin to turn to each other more and more for support and guidance. As they do so, the responsibility for keeping a dispersed workforce united will shift from the manager to the workers—leading to more ownership of the team building process by the members themselves, instead of having this responsibility fall on the manager's shoulders.

2.12   MANAGING DISPERSED TEAMS

Managers facing the prospect of managing a team of remote workers are sometimes troubled by the idea. They are not sure how they will adapt their standard ways of dealing with staff to a long-distance mode, and they are concerned about the risks of losing a sense of team belonging and loyalty. These are legitimate concerns, and in this section we will offer some proven tips for addressing them.

2.12.1   What, when, and how to communicate

These are the three issues the manager must tackle: what kind of information gets exchanged with (and among) teleworkers, when is it best exchanged, and how can it be done efficiently and simply?

2.12.1.1   What kind of information?

This is best answered by asking the manager to stand in the shoes of the teleworkers and imagine what they need or want to know so they can do their jobs and continue to feel part of the organisation. Examples include project status, production results, corporate announcements, and updates on the results generated or the problems encountered by head-office co-workers. This last item is especially important because it is precisely the type of information that normally passes from cubicle to cubicle when everyone is in the office, but can be missed by teleworkers who are remote. Also important is the 'soft' information, such as tidbits picked up in meetings, over lunch, or in a casual hallway contact with a fellow manager from another department. The importance of some of these seemingly small news items is often much greater than would seem likely, e.g., a fellow manager's casual comment that she is thinking about increasing her advertising budget by 20% could have a major impact on a teleworker whose job is to develop market research studies to assess the 'pull' of various ads. The teleworker's manager has to play the role of the town crier or village gossip, in the sense of being the information conduit to reach those not directly privy to those pieces of information.

Conversely, the manager must look to pick up information from the teleworkers that is valuable to others in the office, though the manager need not pass on these facts himself or herself. It is essential that the manager strongly encourages the teleworkers to take the responsibility themselves to pass along this information, perhaps via a quick phone call or e-mail message, or to be sure to drop in to chat briefly with a co-worker when the teleworker next visits the office.

2.12.1.2 When is information best exchanged?

Many managers of remote workers have learned to discriminate between that which is truly urgent and that which can wait. This is a good skill to learn, compared with what normally happens in most offices—a constant flow of information that leads to unending interruptions for the receiver, all in the name of 'good communications'.

Managers of teleworkers have at least five time and mode choices available:

- Calling on the phone to speak in real time
- Sending an e-mail or voice mail message or fax
- Waiting for a scheduled phone call with the teleworker
- Waiting until the teleworker next returns to the office to talk to the teleworker
- Writing out a short note that will be in the teleworker's in-box upon his or her return

There is a direct relationship between the timeliness and the 'interruption value' of these five; calling the teleworker on the phone is most timely and creates the worst kind of interruption (and should be reserved for truly urgent items), while leaving a note in the in-box has the least urgency and is the least intrusive on the teleworker. It is incumbent on the manager to begin making some conscious choices about the timing of the communication, keeping the balance between urgency and effect in mind.

By minimising the number of real-time interruptions, the teleworker can enjoy the benefits of longer uninterrupted periods of concentration—and the manager will also find that his or her work day is also less hectic—an unexpected benefit of telework.

Managers of remote workers might keep a log of the number and types of contacts they have with their teleworkers on days when they are working away from the office. If this is done for even a few weeks, it might show whether the manager is doing a balanced job of communicating with every teleworker—and not just with those who are more talkative, more comfortable with telework, or involved in the day's 'hot' project.

2.12.1.3 How is information exchanged?

Real-time contacts (i.e., picking up the phone to make an unexpected call) should be limited, to avoid undue interruptions. Of course, there's no reason why the manager or even a co-worker can't pick up the phone just for a social chat—as long as these calls are kept short and infrequent. Overall, e-mail, answering machines, and voice mail tend to be the communications lifelines for many teleworkers—but they are useful only if the teleworker unfailingly checks for incoming messages at least twice each day. Nothing will frustrate message-senders more than teleworkers who 'hide' from their messages in the name of working uninterruptedly; this is a serious performance problem for teleworkers, and should be dealt with promptly by the manager.

The advantage of most e-mail, voice mail, and fax systems is that they are relatively easy to learn and use. The days of keyboard phobia among corporate executives seem to be fading away, and those phobics who remain can rely on voice mail or even the standard answering machine. Interestingly, many managers who were reluctant e-mail users became more comfortable with the technology as a result of using it with teleworkers, and then go on to use it (often with great benefits) for in-office contacts as well. While the use of these electronic tools is being suggested quite strongly, they are not being offered as a complete replacement for real-time (and, when possible, face-to-face) communications. We do all need to maintain the human element in communications—but the fact remains that telework will suffer if managers fail to make good use of those electronic methods.

2.12.2   A word about conferencing tools

All of the methods cited above are effective for one-to-one interactions, but they are not adequate for one-to-many or many-to-many exchanges such as meetings. Also, they lack a visual element (except for fax or PC transmission of photos or graphics, neither of which is always widely available and/or fully satisfactory).

Audioconferencing, computer conferencing, and videoconferencing are tools that can be considered for certain telework applications. Some points to consider about each are as follows.

Audioconferencing (better known as a 'conference call') is vastly underused in most telework settings; this is unfortunate because it is a powerful tool when used correctly, and is relatively inexpensive. It lets teleworkers 'attend' meetings remotely, get involved in *ad hoc* problem-solving discussions, and, most important, gain time flexibility by being able to 'meet' with a group without being limited to the schedule of in-office days.

Computer conferencing (a kind of glorified and more powerful e-mail) is an effective tool for helping work groups collaborate and share ideas when they are dispersed in location and time. They can approximate the kind of ongoing discussions that often occur in an office, and they have the added benefit of having a written record of those interchanges. A new software category called 'groupware' includes many tools for collaborative work, one well-known example of which is Lotus Notes.

Videoconferencing has long been touted as the ultimate resource for telework, but the current state of the art leaves a few things to be desired. First, though costs for the equipment (and the equipment size) have been shrinking, they are still beyond the reach of many users; the cost trend is positive, though, and the market will keep growing. Second, the video signal cannot yet travel over standard voice-grade phone lines, thus requiring higher-bandwidth (and more costly) phone services; the wider deployment of ISDN (Integrated Services Digital Network) will help address this. Third, today's adults who grew up with television expect videoconferencing to look like the evening news on television—sharp picture, bright colour, and full motion. This does not describe most videoconferencing in use today, though the technology is improving very rapidly (see Chapter 4.4 for a discussion of the costs of this technology).

It should be noted that the videoconferencing units themselves are becoming smaller and more portable. They no longer require specially equipped rooms, and even the more recent rollabout units are being chased down the technology curve by desktop units. These can be used as pairs of small videophones that comfortably fit on a desk, or by opening up a video 'window' on a PC so that two remote users can look at their PC screens and at each other while they are conversing.

Despite these welcome technical advances, it is still prudent to recognise there is a risk that videoconferencing is being sought for telework for all the wrong reasons. Managers who want it so they can see their remote workers might be looking for a kind of long-distance pseudo-supervision; this is a costly and inappropriate way to manage from a distance. The best uses for video in telework are for jobs that require a visual element, e.g., a design engineer working at home who needs to see the flaw in the widget that just came off the assembly line. It is also useful for those meetings where face-to-face contact would be helpful if not essential, and which otherwise would have to be delayed until the teleworker's next day in the office.

See the detailed advice and information on the above equipment contained in Chapter 6.7.

2.12.3 Final advice for managing at a distance

Managers new to telework need not worry about having to learn an entirely new set of skills or methods. Rather, they must learn to adapt what they currently do to the remote-work environment. This means paying more attention to ensuring a good flow of information to and from the teleworkers, and not leaving it to chance or expecting that such exchanges will occur through casual contact as they often do in the office. (As an aside, managers who assume that information always flows freely and accurately when everyone is in the office are, unfortunately, mistaken.)

Many of these adaptations will flow naturally from the kinds of training that are discussed in Chapters 2.8 and 3.5.1. Also, some organisations favour the idea of the managers themselves being among the first teleworkers. The rationale is that the managers will then experience first-hand what it's like to work remotely, and thus will become much more sensitive to these communication needs addressed in this section. This idea is workable only if the managers' jobs are themselves suited for telework—something that tends to be the exception, given their responsibilities for training and coaching staff, attending many more meetings, and otherwise being more 'office-bound' than their subordinates might be.

The cumulative effect of just a bit of extra effort by the manager in directing and keeping in touch with the teleworkers will be:

- Maintained or enhanced performance by the teleworkers, who will be 'kept in the loop' about their work and the goings-on in the office

- A continued sense of belonging and loyalty among the teleworkers, who won't feel they have been cast adrift and excluded from the office

- Quite possibly, a less hectic and more manageable work-day for the manager who attempts to get control of (instead of being controlled by) the constant stream of information. This can lead to better time management for the manager—not an unimportant benefit in today's downsized organisations where everyone has to make do with less.

2.13   TOO YOUNG/TOO OLD FOR TELEWORKING

Given the opportunity, many office workers would jump at the chance to telework and thus escape the rigours of the daily commute. After all, what's not to like? Telework offers flexibility, comfort, a better balanced lifestyle, and a chance to concentrate on the tasks at hand. As appealing as it is, though, it's not for everyone; one key challenge in successful telework is to give prospective teleworkers enough guidance so they decide for themselves whether they're really suited for this unique work style.

Here are some important questions that would-be teleworkers should ask themselves as they consider the options:

CAN YOU—AND WILL YOU—MANAGE YOURSELF?
Time management, problem-solving, etc. are handled by the teleworker—you must have and be willing to use these skills. This includes your comfort with using a PC and other equipment that might be needed; you'll be relying more on yourself to figure out how to get all those microchips to do what you want.

CAN YOU—AND WILL YOU—MOTIVATE YOURSELF?
No cues from the office (or manager) to get you started and keep you going; self-starting is essential.

ARE YOU WILLING TO BE HELD ACCOUNTABLE FOR 'DELIVERABLES'?
This is a results-oriented concept—product takes preference over process in most cases.

DO YOU HAVE A GOOD WORKING RELATIONSHIP WITH YOUR MANAGER?
It's harder to manage and be managed from a distance—be sure you're starting off with a good foundation.

DO YOU HAVE A SUITABLE, 'DEDICATED' WORK AREA AT HOME?
You need space that's just for work—a (semi) private, quiet area that's comfortable and encourages productivity.

CAN YOU AVOID DISTRACTIONS FROM FAMILY MEMBERS?
You don't have to be a hermit, but you must stay out of the mainstream of family life—and be willing/able to co-exist with your spouse if he/she will be at home during your work hours.

HAVE YOU MADE DEPENDENT CARE ARRANGEMENTS (IF NEEDED)?
You can't do two important jobs at once—don't try to do your job and take care of a child or elder at the same time.

CAN YOU AVOID TEMPTATIONS?
If you're prone to the lure of various distractions at home (e.g., everything from the sack of potato chips (crisps) to the television), will you be able to block them out when working?

CAN YOU GET ALONG WITHOUT DAILY OFFICE SOCIALIZING?
If you thrive on office contacts, telework may not be for you.

CAN YOU VARY YOUR WORK SCHEDULE AND WORK LOCATION?
Be prepared to be flexible—you're going to be shifting between two work sites on different schedules.

© Gil Gordon Associates

Office workers who are contemplating telework should go through these questions more than once, and preferably with the help of the manager, the spouse or family members, and even a trusted co-worker. These seemingly simple questions require careful thought to lessen the chances that the wrong person becomes a teleworker.

There is no single correct score for these 10 questions, but would-be teleworkers should be able to answer at least seven of them with a resounding 'yes'—and it's much better if 9 or even all 10 get the same answer. Keep in mind that corporate telework programmes aren't scientific trials done for the sake of experimentation. They are meant to be well-planned job assignments in which every effort should be taken to ensure success. The first step is to make sure that the workers are making an informed decision when they volunteer for consideration. After that, it's up to management to make the final selection.

2.13.1   Timing is everything

The selection questions listed above are relevant for everyone considering telework at any time. However, there are some additional factors to consider about the 'life cycle' of telework, relative to the employee's life stages and career stages. Here are some guidelines:

The best ages for telework Contrary to popular belief about telework being most suitable for working parents with young children (which it generally is *not*), we have seen that there is no single 'best' time in one's life to telework.

There are fewer teleworkers in their early to mid 20s, but that is because many in this age group are single, and for them, the office is a prime source of social contact. They often see enough of the four walls of their apartment or flat, and genuinely look forward to being a member of the office team. Also, we see fewer teleworkers above age 55 or 60, perhaps because many people at this age have reached a managerial position which is less suited to telework. This does not imply that people in either age group are not suited for telework; it is a description, not a prescription.

Flexibility is an asset   One of the reasons why we see teleworkers at many ages is because telework helps employees cope with life events that otherwise would interfere with or make it impossible for them to work in the office. Examples include the teleworker with a teenager who would benefit from more time with the parent a few days after school, or the teleworker who needs to be home to help an older relative recovering from surgery. In neither case is the teleworker's full-time attention required, and both are episodes of finite length. The teleworker might choose to telework only for the duration of these episodes, or might continue beyond them. These episodes can occur for workers in their 20s or their 60s, and every age group in between.

Core vs dispersed team   Another age-related decision is to select the optimal career stages for telework. This relates in part to degree of experience. One more reason why we see few teleworkers in their early 20s is that this is a prime learning period at the start of one's career; most of the coaching and mentoring that occurs will happen more easily as part of the office-based team.

As people move into managerial jobs, it becomes somewhat more difficult to telework. Most managerial jobs are less predictable, require more meetings, and include coaching and training duties that are difficult to execute at a distance. As a result, most managers who telework will do so on an *ad hoc* basis—a day here and there, but nothing scheduled.

One large concentration of telework is in the ranks of professionals who are individual contributors—and in many organisations with a so-called 'technical ladder' in which professionals can progress without moving into supervisory roles, telework can be feasible at all career stages. It may be quite common for these teleworkers to rotate in and out of the office as their assignments change; new assignments may mean a stint in the office to get started, and then back out to telework once the routine has been established on the project.

To sum up, telework works best when it is tailored to the person's life stages, the nature of the task, the preferences of the manager, and the available technology. As with all good tailoring, a 'one size fits all' approach does not, in fact, fit anyone very well. Getting the best fit for telework calls for flexibility, a willingness to try something on for size, and an ability to adjust the fit as job conditions (like waistlines) change over time.

3

Individual Teleworkers and Home-based Offices

'A typical 20-minute round trip commute to work over the
course of a year adds up to two very stressful 40-hour weeks
lost on the road. But if only five percent of the commuters in
L.A. County telecommuted one day a week, they'd save 205
million miles of travel each year—and keep 47 000 tons of
pollutants from entering the atmosphere. So telecommuting
means saving energy, improving air quality, and quality
of life. Not a bad deal.'

President George Bush—March 1990.

3.1   TAX DEDUCTIONS

The only two certainties in life are death and taxation. These common experiences link mankind across the earth and, while a teleworking manual is
unlikely to issue guidelines on dying, it must give advice on taxation. Tax
officers come in all shapes, sizes, colours, denominations and nationalities.
They speak and write in as many diverse languages as there are countries in
the world and yet a tax return form is as instantly recognisable in Beijing as
it is in Washington. With a worldwide tax form design and with double taxation agreements operating between most nations, taxpayers might start to
fantasise about an international conspiracy of tax bureaucrats. They would
be right. There is no escape.

There may, however, be valuable tax breaks for teleworkers who work
with the system. As a new method of working, telecommuting or teleworking has not yet made any impact on the tax system. The advice set out below
is based on current practices which may change if millions of teleworkers
make tax claims for home offices and other expenses.

3.1.1   National tax regimes

While tax rates vary throughout the western world economies, the statutory rules tend to be similar and the overall direct and indirect tax collections, as a percentage of income, are also similar. From studying the tax allowances for deductible expenses it can be seen whether a nation is encouraging or discouraging teleworking, or whether it has no policy.

Taxes, worldwide, tend to fall into familiar categories:

- Withholding Payroll taxes—Pay As You Earn, deducted at source from wages and salaries after various fixed allowances, usually monthly

- Social Security and Medicare or National Health (Insurance) contributions—usually a percentage of salary paid part by employers and part by employees

- Income taxes—reported by the taxpayer as a self-calculation of income and tax deductible expenses, usually annually

- Benefits taxes—reported by the giver or receiver, usually payable by the recipient, on non-cash benefits such as free cars, free accommodation and interest free loans

- Sales Taxes or Value Added Taxes—indirect taxes added to the price of goods and services; often recoverable by business consumers but not by private individuals

- Capital taxes—levied on gains or profits from sales of assets and investments including property; rarely levied on nominal increases in value in the absence of a sale

- Property rates or local taxes—usually calculated as a percentage of the values of property and collected by the local state, county or town authority

- Interest on business loans and residential mortgages—not a tax but the tax relief on interest payable on such loans or mortgages is a major tax consideration for teleworkers with offices at home or in second homes.

3.1.2   Who can claim and who pays

Rule 1 He who pays the piper calls the tune. The person or organisation who pays the expense is the one who is entitled to claim the tax relief or deduction.

Rule 2 Any benefit to an individual is taxable. If an employer pays part of your home office expenses either directly by, for example, sending a payment to the electricity company, or indirectly by paying the money to you, then you have received a benefit which must be reported and you must claim the original invoice as an allowable business expense, to offset the tax on the benefit received.

Rule 3 Tax laws can be contradictory and confusing. Tax officers are paid to collect tax. If you ask their opinions on whether an expense is allowable, they are likely to say no. Check with a tax advisor.

Rule 4 Tax laws may not have caught up with teleworking. Argue your case for tax allowances and persuade your employer to argue the case for you. Keep in touch with and consult other teleworkers on their tax claims. Don't be isolated and don't try to fight City Hall with your own resources.

Rule 5 You cannot get tax relief on costs you have not paid. There must be an invoice or claim from a third party and you must have paid or will pay that invoice or claim, to apply for tax relief.

3.1.3   Why bother—what's at stake?

There is a great deal of money at stake in tax claims for teleworkers, whether they are based at home, are travelling, are using telecentres, are employed or self-employed.

Any expense you pay, for example a home office heating bill of $500, costs *several times* more without tax relief than with (assuming a shift or partial shift from full time employment to self-employment).

Table 3.1   Effect of tax relief.

Electricity bill	Tax rate	From taxed income	With Tax relief	Factor
$500	10%	$555	$450	1.2
$500	15%	$588	$425	1.4
$500	20%	$625	$400	1.5
$500	25%	$666	$375	1.8
$500	30%	$714	$350	2.0
$500	35%	$769	$325	2.3
$500	40%	$833	$300	2.8
$500	45%	$909	$275	3.3
$500	50%	$1000	$250	4.0
$500	55%	$1111	$225	4.9
$500	60%	$1250	$200	6.2

Table 3.1 shows that the higher the rate of tax you pay, the more valuable it is to make the claims. For example, at a 60% tax rate, as in the last line of the table, to bring home enough money to pay a $500 bill requires pre-tax earnings of $1250. But, if $500 is deductible at 60% rate, the net cost is $200 or 6.2 *times* less than paying the same bill out of taxed income.

If the days of 60% income tax rates return to America, teleworkers will have to learn to love their tax advisors as much as their tax advisors will love the Treasury.

In the USA, social security taxes increase the effective rate of tax for employees without conferring the right to claim allowances at the full rate. This also occurs in the UK.

In the UK, higher paid executives are in effect taxed at 60%. The higher tax rate is 40% and they pay *circa* 10% for National Insurance. The employer also pays *circa* 10% National Insurance, effectively coming out of the executives package. But the maximum income tax rate claimable on expenses, remains at 40% (National Insurance is not reclaimable). Thus the Treasury levy up to 60% tax rate while restricting relief to 40%.

3.1.4   What can a teleworker claim?

While different authorities allow different expenses, the following list gives the main items which you should consider claiming; though not all may apply in your case.

3.1.4.1   An office or workshop at home

If you use your home as your main place of business then those expenses which would be incurred in commercial premises can be claimed:

- Heat, light and power
- Telephone call charges
- Depreciation of furniture
- Depreciation of carpets or floor coverings
- Depreciation of fixtures and fittings
- Extra power points and telephone sockets
- Office equipment and stationery
- Postages and copying
- Cleaning including window cleaning
- Coffee, milk, sugar for meetings
- Assistants' wages
- Refurbishing or redecorating the area
- Extra security measures including guard dogs
- Business insurances
- Professional fees
- Entrance and gardens improvements and maintenance
- Extra parking, garage or storage area
- Interest on property improvement loans or mortgages

- Local property taxes or rates
- Protective clothing
- Child care and creches (see below)

See Capital Gains Taxes in Chapter 3.1.9 for apportioning expenses.

To draw up a list of expenses, imagine moving to a commercial area and renting a space. All the expenses which such premises would incur may be incurred at your home office and, providing they are necessary for you to perform your work or business, may be claimed. Claims may not be agreed, however, and professional advice should be sought, particularly in the first year when precedents may be established for many years to come. Keep detailed records of what you buy and why the work needs that particular expense.

Child care facilities It is virtually impossible to be a primary carer for children or others and do a professional teleworking job at home. But UK tax authorities are deeply confused about liberating parents and carers for full commercial employment.

You, or your employers, may hire a secretary or assistant for part of the week at home, to help with your work, and their wages would be a valid tax claim. But UK child carer's wages are not deductible. Balance baby on your knee, exposed to keyboard skills, and be grateful for the right to vote.

In the USA, an employer can pay up to $5000 a year for an employee's child care costs, as a tax-free benefit. Remember to pay their social security and Medicare taxes, unless you employ your own (older) child under 21 where this is not required.

3.1.4.2 Other teleworking locations

A teleworker may work from a mobile home or a road vehicle, use a telecentre, work from hotel rooms, or may live and work on a boat. For tax expense claims the same basic logic applies.

Is it your primary place of work or business, your business address? Is it known to be your place of work or business (printed cards, letterheads)? Has the expense been incurred as a necessary part of your work or business (would your work be curtailed or made impossible without the expenditure)?

What expenses would be incurred and allowed for tax if you were to hire or rent or buy the same facilities commercially, to enable you to do your work? Any expense, paid or to be paid, which meets the above criteria, can be claimed by a teleworker, wherever they choose to live and work.

3.1.4.3 More than one office

Generally an employed teleworker will find it difficult to justify claiming expenses for more than one office, though such claims may not be impossible.

For example, an employed engineer may establish an office or workshop at home, then go on a field trip leaving a member of the family to handle communications with central office and customers. If the engineer used the family's holiday home as a secondary base in the field, then expenses might also be claimed for that 'use of home as office' while still claiming expenses for the original home base. It would need to be demonstrated that two offices had to be in operation to enable the work to be done.

There is no difference in principle in tax law between the claims of a corporation needing more than one property for business and those of an individual. It is, however, more difficult to prove the need in the case of an individual who necessarily leaves one office empty when using the other.

A self-employed teleworker, in tax terms, has the advantages of being treated as a 'business' with the disadvantages of being a sole operator. The self-employed may be more successful than employed teleworkers in proving a case for two locations.

3.1.5   How much can a teleworker claim?

The level of claims depends on the type of work performed and the accepted style of working environment required to carry out that work. For example, a chief executive working at home and seeing colleagues, suppliers and customers there, can argue for a more expensive (and therefore credible) environment than a clerical worker needs.

3.1.6   Interest on loans for home offices

Borrowing to build an office onto your home creates a mortgage or loan, the interest on which may be tax deductible. In the USA the claim is restricted by capitalised interest on qualified real property. The UK restricts tax-deductible interest to a total mortgage of £30 000 on your home unless a commercial/domestic planning permission (which would probably be refused) has been obtained, splitting out the office cost and the borrowing; the commercial part will attract potential Capital Gains Tax on any profit on sale, but this may be less than the value of claiming the interest annually (see Chapter 3.1.9). If your employer were to advance a loan for the purpose and waive or reduce interest, you could be taxed on the notional interest as a benefit, as long as you are the owner of the property.

At present, tax law has not properly and fully addressed teleworking and home offices, making it difficult to rely on relief if you build an office in your home. But ask your tax advisor if there are ways round the obstacles.

3.1.7   Working overseas

It is beyond the scope of this book to advise on the complexities of foreign residency and expatriate working, involving double-taxation agreements between nations. Teleworking does, however, allow people to work far from their central offices. In principle the costs incurred in working remotely are allowable for tax purposes. Such costs would include the communication system and call charges, videoconferencing, teleconferencing, necessary travel between locations, and mailing costs.

Teleworking is a relatively new activity but as it grows some teleworkers will choose to work from foreign countries. Their residence for tax purposes will depend on the laws of both their host nation and their home nation. Double-tax agreements have been in place for years to deal with such cases. They work, in principle, by taxing the income twice (though this rarely happens in actuality), recording it on tax returns in both countries. Depending upon the tax residence status of the individual, one country receives the tax and the other credits the amount paid.

For example, if the tax residence remains in the home nation (USA), then the annual tax payable is calculated as normal, the tax paid to the host nation is credited and the taxpayer pays or is refunded any balance. Thus the taxpayer pays the rates of tax of his home nation.

As teleworking grows, it is not unlikely that wealthier 'home' nations will review their double-taxation agreements and definitions of residency to ensure they do not lose income tax revenues while supplying jobs.

3.1.8 Travel costs

Telecommuting confers one of the greatest benefits of teleworking. It saves time, money and personal stress. If the home or local telecentre is established as the usual place of business, then the costs of travelling from that location rank as tax deductions.

Generally, the cost of commuting from home to a central location is not tax allowable. The majority of employees in the UK and the USA have to pay the costs of commuting from after-tax income. The real costs of paying from taxed income are set out in Table 3.1 above. An example is given in Table 3.2.

Table 3.2 Example of travel cost savings.

Commute costs pre-teleworking:	
Say 20 cents/mile for 6000 miles p.a.	= $1200
Tax at 30% makes pre-tax cost	= $1714
Commute costs post-teleworking say 1/5th	= $ 240
Tax relief at 30% gives net cost	= $ 168
Annual benefit to telecommuter = $1714 − $168	= $1546

3.1.8.1 Motoring costs and private use

There is a general rule that no expenses tax claims can succeed if based on estimated or composite figures which do not relate to actual invoices or cash paid. Tax officers usually will not accept claims based on published composite rates such as the AA rate or the AAA rate. An exception to this rule appears below.

3.1.8.2   Own car

In the UK, where an employer pays a high composite rate per mile, including interest and depreciation, to reimburse an individual, the Inland Revenue assumes and taxes a benefit, multiplying the claimed mileage by a composite rate of benefit. For the tax year ending 5 April 1993, the rates vary by engine size and by mileage; for example, cars over 2000 cc are rated at 51 pence for the first 4000 miles and 27 pence for each mile thereafter.

For example, if an employee's (over 2000 cc engine) car travels 8000 business miles in a year and is reimbursed by the employer at the AA rate, the employee will be taxed on a benefit of 51 pence on the first 4000 miles = £2040 and 27 pence on the second 4000 miles = £1080, a total benefit of £3120 @ 25% tax = £780. The individual can opt to submit a (very) detailed account of expenses reimbursed less actual costs and be taxed on any difference. Few elect to go through the process.

3.1.8.3   Company car

Where a company car (over 2000 cc engine) is supplied in the UK to an employee it may typically generate a taxable benefit on its value of £4440. In addition an assumed fuel benefit of £940 is likely (the figures vary by size of engine, value and age of car). The two combined give a tax bill at 25% of £1345 per annum.

Sedentary UK teleworkers beware! Where a teleworker shows less than 2500 business miles a year on a company car, the car value benefit will increase by a half to £6660, the fuel benefit remains at £940 and, if the tax rate is 40%, will pay tax of £3040. The company will pay a further £790 National Insurance (Social Security) tax. For the time being, until the regime changes to perhaps include a carbon tax to discourage motoring, it pays UK teleworkers to travel more than 2500 business miles a year.

The home base benefit—managers' journeys As calculated above, teleworkers who establish their main office at home, and can therefore claim journeys to central office as business miles, benefit, at 40% tax rate, by a factor of 2.7 on their costs of getting to central office and back. Clearly, a manager of dispersed teleworkers who travels to see them at their home or local bases can also claim the journeys as business miles.

3.1.9   Capital gains on the home office

A Capital Gain on office use at home may only arise if you have made claims for business expenses. If you work at home but make no expense claims then the tax discussed here should not apply to you.

The US Internal Revenue Service and the UK Inland Revenue may levy a Capital Gains Tax on that part of a residence which has been claimed for business use. This potential tax worries many home based teleworkers but its impact may be less serious than is feared.

Claiming expenses for using part of your home for work indicates that the office is a business 'asset'. Having enjoyed tax relief on related expenses for the space, the Revenue view a sale as being separate from the normal non-taxable event of selling your prime residence or main home. The tax authorities are not interested in the zoning or planning status of your home and office (see Chapter 3.6.3).

In the UK, a precedent has existed for decades that if a home area has been claimed for business *but not exclusively*, i.e. it is also used by the family from time to time, then no Capital Gain would attach to that part of the property. This leads to subtle arguments over the size of annual expense claims, which are generally reduced by reference to time and space occupied for work in any one year.

1. Any Capital Gains Tax (CGT) may be payable only if the house changes ownership, on a sale or death for example.

2. In calculating a potential profit, the *area* previously claimed for business use modified by the *time* for which it was claimed are divided into the total profit.

3. The total profit on transfer of the house is the difference between the cost and the sale price (or the cost may be replaced by the *value* at March 1982).

4. The total profit is reduced by a process known as indexation, which sets aside the increase in value in the property as a result of inflation. The Revenue indexes are below the real levels of inflation but do account for much of the increase.

5. The total profit is further reduced by sale expenses, including agents and legal fees and in some cases vital repairs.

6. Expenses specific to the business area may be deducted from the business portion of the profit.

7. Substantial retirement relief on the sale of business assets is available in the USA and the UK to over 55s. In most cases this relief will cover any likely taxable gain.

8. UK Roll-over relief or USA Postponement relief is available and will negate the profit if you purchase another residence and home office. While you may not be allowed to postpone a gain on a home office under 'Selling Your Home' rules, such right may be available under 'Small Business' rules.

9. Personal annual exemption on Capital Gains is £5000 in the UK and an equivalent allowance may apply in the USA to Capital Gains on homes.

3.1.10   Home offices tax summary

The tax laws on Capital Gains on home offices are generally flexible enough to postpone any gain until retirement, at which point retirement or age relief will generally wipe it out. Cases of people actually paying Capital Gains Tax on selling their homes are rare.

However, before deciding to overwhelm the Revenue offices with claims for use of home as office, calculate the economic balance between annual Income Tax relief and a possible future Capital Gains Bax bill. The most efficient strategy is to claim high annual expenses for a very small home office, not used all the time for business. Table 3.3 gives an example (using an average tax rate of 30%).

Table 3.3   Example of net Capital Gains.

Income Tax	
Annual expenses claimed and allowed	$10 000
Annual value to teleworker (see Table 3.1)	$20 000
Value over 15 years teleworking	$300 000
Assume cash is saved (or not borrowed):	———
Plus interest at 2.5%	$358 000
Capital Gains	
House Cost	$400 000
Sale 15 years later	$800 000
Gain	$400 000
Gain on space claimed as offices, say 1/10th	$40 000
Capital Gains Tax @ 30%	$12 000
Benefit to teleworker	$346 000

This calculation assumes that none of the nine possible reductions of the capital gain, as listed in the previous section, apply.

Readers should refer to Chapter 4.10.13 for more information, and check the indexes, sources and references at the back of this book for publications which may be helpful.

3.2   EQUIPPED FOR EFFICIENCY

One of the drivers for teleworking is the promise of improved efficiency. Maximum benefit will only be gained if the teleworker is equipped with the appropriate tools. Elsewhere in this book we have described the various products and services which are available to assist the teleworker. The key to efficient teleworking is packaging these products and services to meet an individual's requirements. In some cases this extends to designing the home office as discussed in Chapter 6.13 (see also Chapter 6.0.2).

There is no single package that covers the whole range of teleworking tasks but some equipment such as the telephone, answering machine and fax are likely to be essential tools for most teleworkers. The following examples suggest the equipment required for efficient teleworking by teleworkers who are managers teleworking on a part-time basis, full-time home-based teleworkers, and nomadic teleworkers.

3.2.1   Part-time telework for managers

This is the sort of person who takes time out of a busy schedule to work at home in the evenings or for a few days each month. It is likely that this person will require a Personal Computer, which may be a portable, and transfers files using floppy disks. It may be useful to have a home fax machine, perhaps one of the low cost phone/faxes now on the market. Depending on the amount of time spent at home, it may be useful to have call forwarding to enable office calls to be redirected to the home phone and a chargecard to allow business calls from home to be billed to the office account.

3.2.2   Full-time teleworkers

This type of teleworker requires a comprehensive office in the home which, given the length of time it is occupied, should ideally be set out according to the guidelines in Chapter 6.12. The teleworker will need to perform tasks normally undertaken in the office and so will require similar equipment such as a PC, printer and fax. Access to company databases, file servers and mail systems will often be required so a communications link, utilising a modem or ISDN (Integrated Services Digital Network) card, will be needed. Usually a second telephone line, other than the domestic line into the home, or ISDN 2 where appropriate, would be used. Appropriate use of network services on the telephone line such as those described in Chapters 6.1 and 6.11 helps to maximise the efficiency of telephone-based communications. The use of videotelephony to replace face-to-face contact such as team meetings will become increasingly widespread.

3.2.3   Nomadic teleworkers

Nomadic teleworkers, such as insurance salespeople, travel extensively in their jobs and spend only a small proportion of their time at an office desk. Indeed, much of the work carried out at the office could just as easily be done at home, or in a car, thus avoiding non-essential journeys. Being based at home, the nomadic teleworker requires access to many of the facilities that he or she would have at a central office such as telephones, fax machines, PCs and printers. In addition, a mobile phone to make outgoing calls while on the move is commonplace. Many have voice messaging services linked to a pager to ensure incoming calls are dealt with promptly but without the need to have the mobile phone on all the time, saving battery power. Of the network services, Call Diversion is particularly useful as it gives the teleworker the flexibility to direct calls to home or mobile phones or to a voice messaging service whichever is most appropriate. In the home a fax machine to supply quotes, return sales information and receive briefing material is useful.

Efficient equipment, with technical descriptions, and the design of home workstations are fully covered in Chapter 6.

3.3   DISTANCE LIMITATIONS

Modern telecommunications undoubtedly make the resources of remote communities more accessible and make it possible for people to work remotely. Areas such as the Highlands and Islands of Scotland have, in the past, suffered as a result of their distance from the main urban centres and lack of a high quality telecommunications infrastructure. In many areas this situation is changing as a result of improvements to the telecommunications network, funded by government agencies and the telecom companies. The Scottish Highlands and Islands, for example, now enjoy telecom services which are second to none in Europe. As a result people living in the area now have the work brought to them by wire rather than having to relocate or commute to the cities.

For example, one ICL employee now works from his farmstead home on the island of Orkney, and via computers in Manchester, 500 miles away, maintains the dock traffic system of Hong Kong harbour, 6000 miles away.

Elsewhere, individuals and telecentres are also undertaking work for customers hundreds, or even thousands, of miles away. In Northern Ireland, Dataprep provide word processing and audiotyping for customers in London. Other centres in Ireland undertake work from the USA.

Based on these and other examples it would be easy to proclaim that distance was no longer a consideration in this information age. However, a more practical analysis reveals that distance, or rather location, factors continue to have a bearing on the success of teleworking. Even those people who do not commute to work each day may need to travel to meetings with colleagues occasionally. It may be that they prefer to meet regularly in order to maintain the team spirit.

In theory a telecentre which transfers its work electronically could be located anywhere with good telecommunications but the manager may still need to travel to meet clients. Consequently, access to transport is an important consideration. Unlike telecommunications, the availability and quality of air, road and rail services continues to be dependent on distance from the major population centres.

There are other operational issues which need to be considered when assessing the suitability of a location for teleworking. Remote areas are more likely to suffer from power supply interruptions which may cause real difficulties for some teleworkers. Also, the further the distance from the population centres, the more difficult and more costly it becomes to obtain maintenance for PC and other equipment.

It is therefore clear that distance is still a limiting factor but much less so than in the past, due to the availability of reliable communications. There are no hard and fast rules which define the critical distance beyond which it is not feasible to telework. This depends to a large extent on the specific application and the personal preferences of the individuals involved. In many cases the location will already be fixed, particularly if the home and family are settled in an area. In any case the prospective teleworker will have to weigh the difficulties that the location presents against the benefits of not travelling to work every day, balancing travel time, cost, productivity, quality of life and so on.

When planning teleworking, it helps to draw a map showing the locations of company offices, company teleworkers, managers, commuting routes (expressed in time terms), delivery routes, customers, clients and suppliers. Computer literate managers can transfer the map to a programme to maximise journey planning and for efficient maintenance of remote offices. Organisations with extensive teleworking will see their network maps growing, taking offices closer to outlying clients and customers.

3.4   CONSULTING THE FAMILY

At a recent conference in the USA, where seemingly every aspect of telecommuting was examined, a delegate asked whether any studies had been done on the impact on the family of someone going home to work . The answer was a surprised 'no' and as an afterthought, 'but that is a very interesting question'. (The question was in fact explored in *Effects of Clerical Teleworking on Family Life*, a paper commissioned by BT.)

3.4.1   The home as an institution—the institution as a container

Collins English Dictionary gives the following definitions: 'Institution: An organisation or establishment founded for a specific purpose such as a hospital, church or college. Container: An object used for or capable of holding. Home: The place or a place where one lives. A house or other dwelling. A family or other group living in a house or other place.'

The home is the original and first institution to which we all belong. At any given time it contains all the stresses and strains of family life, this containment enabling its members to leave its protective boundaries and to function in the outside world. The home is defended against all invaders, both physical and psychological. An Englishman's home is his castle; an American's a definition of freedom. Yet surprisingly little emphasis has been placed on the invasive effect teleworking will have on the home.

The home like any institution holds expectations, both conscious and unconscious. Unlike the office institution, however, the expectations are implicit. For example, the culture in an office might be that it is all right to arrive five minutes late but not twenty, that people can chat over the coffee machine and that personal phone calls are not acceptable. The variations are endless but, within days of joining an organisation, the 'rules' will become clear. In the home, however, it is not necessary to spell out the unspoken, often unconscious, rules, yet, if the transition from the office institution to the home institution is to be successful, there must be an acknowledgement of the impact that the change will have on the home and the family.

All change is stressful. Two researchers into the effects of stress on health, T. H. Holmes and R. H. Rahe, developed a 'Life Change Unit Scale' to measure stress (Table 3.4). Death of a spouse scored highest on the scale. Even pleasant changes in lifestyle, for example vacations, were felt as stressful. The scale, first published in 1970, does not include the impact of someone going home to work, but a number of the events are analogous to such a situation.

Holmes and Rahe began to see that persons with many life changes—those with high life crisis unit (LCU) scores—were more likely to suffer from ill health than those with lower LCU scores. Moreover, there seemed to be a definite additive aspect to the scale; the higher the LCU score the more likely the person was to come down with an abrupt and serious illness. Using

Table 3.4 Life Change Unit Scale.

Events	Scale of Impact	Events	Scale of Impact
Death of spouse	100	Divorce	73
Marital separation	65	Jail term	63
Death of close family member	63	Personal Injury or illness	53
Marriage	50	Fired at Work	47
Marital reconciliation	45	Retirement	45
Change in health of family member	44	Pregnancy	40
Sex difficulties	39	Gain of new family member	39
Business readjustment	39	Change of financial state	39
Death of a close friend	37	Change to a different line of work	36
Change of number of arguments with spouse	35	Mortgage over $10 000	31
Foreclosure of mortgage or loan	30	Change in responsibilities at work	29
Son or daughter leaving home	29	Trouble with in-laws	29
Outstanding personal achievement	28	Wife begins or stops work	26
Begin or end school	26	Change in living conditions	25
Revision of personal habits	24	Trouble with boss	23
Change in work hours or conditions	20	Change in residence	20
Change in schools	20	Change in recreation	19
Change in church activities	19	Change in social activities	18
Mortgage or loan less than $10 000	17	Change in sleeping habits	16
Change in number of family get-togethers	15	Change in eating habits	15
Vacation	13	Christmas	12
Minor violations of the law	11		

the table as a guide, it is easy to understand the disruption of the change of routine on the household, experienced in working from home.

It has been demonstrated that understanding and anticipating problems mitigates the stress of new situations. It would be an unwise and insensitive parent, for example, who didn't prepare his or her three-year-old for the first day at nursery school. Doctors, dentists and teachers know the value of preparing patients and students for what lies ahead. Preparation for child-birth has been an accepted part of parenthood for 20 years.

In the collective unconscious there is an archetypal fantasy of home and mother, i.e. that they have an infinite capacity to absorb the pressures of life, one reason perhaps why so little research has been brought to bear on the psychological impact of teleworking on the family.

3.4.2 Case studies

The following couples referred themselves for professional help after having struggled alone for months with their difficulties. In order to maintain confidentiality, clients' names have been changed and details which might identify the families altered.

3.4.2.1 Case One

Mr A. was married with two children: Tom, a boisterous seven-year-old was at school; Helen was four years old. Mrs A. was a busy woman with many friends and hobbies. Life was hectic but under control. School runs ran smoothly, stresses of child care were alleviated by neighbours in a friendly and supportive way. Mrs A. had adapted to the many changes in her 10 years of married life, from career woman to efficient home maker and mother. For seven years she had waved Mr A. off to work and had applied her consider-able skills to the business of running a home. At the end of the day, neither had given more than a cursory thought to how the other had negotiated their day.

Anticipating the move: conscious expectations Mr A. thought he would be able to see more of his family and that life would be a shared experi-ence. Mrs A. thought she might be part of her husband's exciting business life.

Unspoken expectations Mrs A. felt the burden of child care would be relieved; another person to share in the car pool, listen for the phone, let the cat out, take the dog for a walk and be a friend to have a cup of coffee with. In fact another capable, responsible adult in the house to talk to.

Mr A. hoped to work in a less competitive environment—less stressful—no more boss to drop in unannounced. A warm peaceful environment where the smell of supper being cooked would replace the stale tobacco odour of his office colleague—freedom to drift in and out of his room at will—freedom to find his own pace.

Helen and Tom expected that Dad would be available for most of the day to play football, read stories and do all the things that previously had to be fitted into the end of the day or at weekends.

In short the family, which to date had managed life's changes well, expected that it would take Mr A.'s new routine in its stride.

The impact Within a month, life had become almost intolerable. Mr A was convinced he would never be able to conceive another creative idea in his working life. He didn't know how to respond to the continuous demands on his time. His office had become a repository for toys and books. Neighbours, discovering the joy of having a photocopier and fax machine in the street, were constantly dropping in to use them. He was the back-up for almost any domestic hiccup: the school run; the washing machine repair man; baby sitting—the list was endless. His wife, who had always appeared to be the model of efficiency and calmness, now seemed to be a chaotic and frantic woman, needing his constant help. Home, far from being the peaceful haven he had anticipated, was a noisy, untidy and disorganised zoo.

Mrs A. felt alarmed that her conscientious, capable and creative husband now seemed to spend most of his working day scratching his head. Far from having a companion in the house she sensed an ogre in the spare room. She was increasingly aware of the number of times the phone rang, of the frequency with which Helen demanded attention in a shrill voice. Mrs A. no longer felt her home was her own. Her space had been invaded and her customary way of dealing with the inevitable crises of bringing up a young family, seemed under critical scrutiny.

Helen and Tom were confused. The house had become a tense and anxious place to be in. Dad was there, but not for them. Mum was not herself.

Analysing the situation Previously clearly defined roles and activities had become fudged. Boundaries between home life and work life had broken down. The established patterns of communication no longer worked, and neither knew what they could expect of the other. It was as if they had been placed in a foreign land without maps and told that because 'they had each other' they would be able to find their way.

Acknowledging that there was a problem was a great relief to the couple. They thought that if they couldn't cope there must be something wrong with their marriage. Gradually they were able to highlight the difficult areas and then the business of defining the situation as it was began to take shape.

Thinking things through They realised they needed to recreate the boundaries that had implicitly existed before Mr A. came home to work. This was difficult, because it meant each of them having to say 'no' to some of the demands made by the other. For instance, Mr A. felt he couldn't concentrate on his work if he had to leap to answer the private telephone when his wife was out. Mrs A. on the other hand, wasn't prepared to change her established ways of dealing with the children now that Mr A. was in the house—if she needed to shout, she needed to shout.

The very act of negotiation freed both of them to say how intruded upon they had felt, and how much at times they resented the invasion of their space. Redefining their boundaries paradoxically meant they could allow themselves more freedom. They could now enjoy a cup of coffee with each other, and a walk round the garden together during the course of the day—two of the many perks of working at home.

The children too had to accept that their father wasn't always available, and that he could say 'no' without it meaning he was being angry or rejecting.

Resolution Mr and Mrs A. did resolve the problem of territorial rights, but it took some time and the help of a counsellor to do so. The problem was exacerbated because they found it difficult to admit to themselves and to anyone else that they were having problems. Mr A. felt he would lose credibility with his employers if he expressed his feelings about not coping—after all he had volunteered for working at home partly because of pride in his good relationship with his wife. No corporate officer had expressed interest in how the family was coping. Mrs A. was also reluctant to discuss the strain of dealing with the situation for the same reason—they both felt that the home, as an institution, should be able to cope and contain their anxieties.

3.4.2.2 Case Two

Mrs B. was thrilled when she applied for and got a design job which offered flexible working from home . The family, which desperately needed another income, had sorely missed her contribution to the family budget since she stopped working after the birth of their son, two and a half years earlier.

Anticipating the move: conscious expectations The shared and expressed expectations of Mr and Mrs B. were that their son would not have to be sent to a nursery, that continuity of care would be achieved and that between them (Mr B.'s hours were reasonably flexible) they would be able to be loving parents and earn two incomes. Mrs B. was a designer, so she had the advantage of being able to work to her own routine. It seemed perfect.

Unspoken expectations The unconscious belief was that neither would get tired, that they would be able to synchronise their working lives and that their baby boy was as aware of the new situation as they were. Both Mr and Mrs B. came from families where mothers stayed at home and looked after their husbands and children. Enjoying a well-run home was a mutual childhood experience and therefore an unconscious expectation.

They realised they would need some help with the baby and it was decided to employ an au-pair.

The impact Mrs B. soon began to feel something was terribly wrong. She was completely exhausted and felt continually guilty that she wasn't doing anything well. Her little son couldn't understand why his mother didn't respond to his cries when she was so near and Mrs B. found it well-nigh impossible to not comfort him when she heard his distress. She felt always at someone's beck and call and quite unable to separate one aspect of her life from the other; after all, it was all taking place in her home. If she had a coffee break she would use the time to put the washing in or take it out, or to cuddle the baby, or to cheer up the au-pair.

Mr B. helped, but, although he could vary his hours a little, when he was at work he was out of the house. Soon Mrs B's design work got pushed into the evenings and she was often to be found at work in her office at 10pm when finally the home was quiet.

Analysing the situation Both wanted to live in an environment which was reminiscent of the homes they grew up in and, because Mrs B. was still in the home, it was all too easy for them to accept (albeit unconsciously) that she would continue to do the job of making a home. Mrs B. found it impossible to ignore the demands on her from the immediate environment. She was a conscientious, hard-working woman and so her professional work did not suffer. No-one quite realised that she was, in fact, doing two full-time jobs for the price of one.

Thinking things through   As with Mr and Mrs A. above, the first step out of the problem was to recognise that there was a problem and to look more realistically at what they were expecting of themselves. Trying to balance jobs and a home life is a recognised modern problem. The fantasy is that one way of reconciling this difficulty is to combine the two. But then the situation is reversed. It becomes a dilemma of how to separate work life from home life.

Resolution   Mr and Mrs B. are still working at the problem. Much of the pressure has been relieved by a more structured timetable being introduced. Now Mrs B. goes to her office in the house early in the morning while Mr B. dresses and gives breakfast to their son, before leaving the house in mid-morning. Mrs B. then allows herself to be at home for much of the day, working again in the early evening when Mr B. returns. The au-pair bridges the gap but doesn't have to hold the fort for too long. Both Mr and Mrs B. recognise that the situation isn't entirely satisfactory but they also know that it will improve as their son grows up. Recognising the difficult logistics and the need to think things through has given Mrs B. a sense of being taken seriously, which means she takes her own needs more seriously.

3.4.2.3   Case Three

The reasons for the success or failure of someone working at home are not always easy to see and may need more help to understand than either of the cases above. Another couple, Mr and Mrs C. who decided they needed professional help, had no conscious idea that their troubles began when they started to work at home.

Their situation seemed ideal. Their children were at school all day. The house was large with room for quite separate office facilities. The wife was a busy woman who accepted her husband's decision to work at home without much thought.

What came to be understood during the course of their counselling was that Mrs C.'s father, an architect, had worked at home when she was a child. He was a violent and demanding man and the household had revolved round the need to keep quiet because 'daddy is working'. When Mr C. started to work at home, her unconscious childhood anxieties and fears were aroused. Without realising she was connecting her husband with her father, Mrs C. resented his presence in the house. The bewildered Mr C. had found the atmosphere intolerable and had begun to express the anger that was reminiscent of Mrs C.'s father, thus confirming Mrs C.'s unconscious fears that having a man working at home was a worrying and stressful situation.

The way people work and the environment needed to facilitate that work are as different and varied as the jobs they are doing. One may need complete privacy and quiet in order to gather his thoughts but another can only work on the kitchen table surrounded by family life. A creative introvert might, even if living alone, be quite happy to contemplate working at home, whereas it could be anticipated that young single people are motivated above all by working in a busy office, with the chance to meet other young people.

Implicit in the notion of working at home is the idea that life will be more flexible and relaxed. From the case histories represented here, it is obvious that this is not necessarily the case. The family is as much an institution as the office and, as such, the same consideration should be paid to the impact upon it of change, as is paid to many of the other aspects of teleworking.

3.4.3 Recommendations

In order for the change to take place successfully, there has to be a recognition that working at home is not without its difficulties. If the employer acknowledges the potential difficulties and creates forums during which they can be explored, a container will be created which will release the employee to concentrate on the business of settling down to work, safe in the knowledge that any family problems encountered have been anticipated and will be dealt with.

If a number of people are going home to work, the company might consider running a group once a week for a few months for teleworkers and their families to discuss the experience. Not only will there be relief in realising that other people might be having difficulties, but they will also be able to draw support from other families.

It should be accepted that employees and their spouses might want to have one or two counselling sessions in order to think things through. This should not be seen as a sign of failure, but rather as an intelligent acceptance that change needs to be managed.

Included in the counselling sessions might be the following points for discussion:

- Boundaries
  —Territorial battles

  —Where is the office to be?

  —Is the office out of bounds?

  —Is the company equipment available to the family; if not, how is the ensuing disappointment to be dealt with?

  —Is the teleworker available for any chores?

- Extra costs
  —Who pays for extra tea, coffee and food consumed?

  —Can the teleworker expect help from the family?

  —What will the neighbours think?

  —How are business calls and visitors to be handled?

- Follow-up discussions

The above situations are common to all but, given some time to think about their own particular situations, each individual will begin to explore his or her preoccupations.

The employers would benefit, therefore, as would their employees, from a follow up session with the teleworker and spouse or partner if there is one, six months after she or he has started to work from home. This would enable all concerned to learn from the experience.

Included in these discussions might be the following questions:

- Are the family enjoying the new regime?
- What problems are they experiencing?
- Do they benefit from the teleworkers' increased leisure and family time?
- Do they welcome business visitors?
- Do others benefit from the teleworking equipment?
- Have household costs increased?
- Does the teleworker feel supported by the family?
- Do the teleworker and family feel supported by the employer?

It has long been acknowledged, in actuarial tables for insurance and pension companies, that men live shorter lives than women and that statistically men are likely to die a few years after retirement. We could speculate that the major change from a highly structured, institutionalised office environment, from which many people draw their identities and self-value, to a less structured home life, causes too much stress at the age of 65 or thereabouts.

By negotiating and dealing with the wider aspects of life at an earlier stage, through experiencing teleworking at home, men may become as resilient to change as women have had to be in the past—and perhaps therefore suffer less stress at such a vulnerable stage in their lives.

While thinking about the effects of working at home, more questions are raised than there is remit to explore here. Working from home might be open to abuse and exploitation, especially of women, which may be unacknowledged and unrecognised if the privacy of the home is used as an excuse not to study the impact teleworking has on the family.

3.4.4 Summary

It has been stressed that change is difficult and that, by acknowledging the major changes inherent in working from home, the transition from working in the office institution to the institution of the home will be facilitated.

Given the support and understanding recommended in this section, the transition into teleworking could prove to be a stimulating and exciting event. Indeed the family, given time, might discover new dimensions. Dimensions denied to all but a privileged minority during the past half-century, which has seen increasing divisions between home and work.

3.5   SUPPORT FOR TELEWORKERS

3.5.1   Training and promotion for the individual

In all organisations employees have an expectation of being 'in touch' and a need to be connected to the information network. These expectations are not often achieved, and the refrain, 'I never hear about new initiatives!' or 'You never told me!' is an indictment on any company. Both large and small organisations, with or without teleworkers, constantly have to review the best methods of keeping their people informed.

This is even more vital for the teleworker, who has a legitimate concern about being isolated from daily contact. Being uninformed hinders performance, commitment and morale. People need to be in touch with a range of ideas and issues to develop their skills, and be aware of promotion and career opportunities.

This section considers ways of implementing and maintaining an information package for the teleworker. Being employed as a teleworker means giving up spontaneous and daily contact with some colleagues, and the employer should offer an alternative system that will meet the need for information, news, and social interaction. These crucial issues for teleworkers will be considered under the following headings:

- Formal and informal information
- Support from managers and the core team
- Business imperatives for training and promotion
- Developing new skills

This section emphasises the need for regular contracted information channels that will not disadvantage the teleworker but will enhance his or her contact with the company and with colleagues.

3.5.2   Information systems

Information is a particularly essential tool for the teleworker. People need to keep in touch, not just for information, but to feel part of and feel included in the organisation. Managers of teleworking groups have to define and agree the frequency, type and content of information required. Teleworkers may not feel connected to performance imperatives and organisation demands if they are isolated from the mainstream of formal and informal information.

3.5.2.1   Formal information systems

There is a range of basic information that will support and encourage the individual. This is summarised in Table 3.5.

Table 3.5 Regular information for teleworkers.

Type of information	Content	Frequency
Performance	Team and individual	Monthly
Statistics and new requirements	Performance targets and specifications	Prior to implementation
Reports from HQ and colleagues	Statistics, ideas projects, improvements, career moves, news	Monthly
Central/HQ news	Business imperatives, trends, morale messages	Monthly

This information has to be distributed as good quality, paper copies, as poor documentation will not reinforce high standards. When people use electronic mail (e-mail), faxes and voice bank communications an acknowledgement system needs to be in place. Many people assume that sending information means that it has been read. Organisations which have no acknowledgement system have no record about the information being read, understood, activated, filed or discarded.

In restating the need for effective formal information systems, the baseline is that the teleworker should be made to feel that as an individual worker he or she is an essential part of the whole organisation. The benefits of excellent distribution systems, particularly for remote teleworking and for people who have infrequent office attendance, far outweigh the cost.

3.5.2.2   Informal information systems

In addition to formal information systems, there needs to be a focus on informal networks. One of the drawbacks of being away from an office for periods of time is losing spontaneous contacts with colleagues. Informal 'office corridor' meetings are invaluable for sharing and developing ideas, solving problems, or sparking off a new idea to improve a product or service. These contacts need to be seen as valid and valuable. In the case of a dispersed team, a replacement system should compensate for the 'office gossip' network. The time and financial costs of informal contacts, whether face to face or via teleconferences, are minimal in relation to the goodwill, morale and team-building that accrue to the organisation. If a manager has concerns about a specific employee abusing the informal network, there are a number of mechanisms to exercise control, e.g. call monitoring, performance or productivity targets, deadlines, or quality control.

A manager needs to build a close working relationship, despite remote office bases, so that any 'abuse' of freedom and trust can be tackled with the individual and not by tighter control of the complete team.

3.5.3   Support systems

Organisations which have installed and trained employees as teleworkers (with all their equipment, tasks, targets and information systems in place) need to develop a support structure to maintain the work and the worker. Maintenance is not simply monitoring performance and oiling the clockwork. Maintenance as described by Herzberg is an extra preventative 'hygiene' factor that will enhance commitment to the task and the organisation. The experience of a British charitable organisation working in a variety of community projects developed a strong effective management culture of delegation, trust and self authority. They worked using a model of dispersed Project Management and refined the most effective and cost-efficient support system as:

- Monthly visits for supervision at either the local site or at the national base
- Bimonthly HQ team meetings at the centre
- Irregular but planned visits between team members
- Joint project work between team members, at local sites
- Residential conferences and training workshops
- Annual general meetings with local presentations

3.5.4   Support from the manager for the individual

The individual teleworker and the dispersed team need to know in advance the level and frequency of support they will receive. From a human resource perspective regular individual supervision is a basic requirement. These meetings should be planned and booked and only changed in real emergencies. As a minimum these meetings should be monthly with enough dedicated time to cover the following agenda items:

- Targets
- Performance
- Objectives
- Problems
- New initiatives
- General issues
- Training needs
- Managing work/home issues
- Personal changes (i.e. any domestic or health changes that may affect the performance of the worker)

The meetings can take place at the central office or at the remote site; ideally alternating between the two.

3.5.5   Local visits

It is important for the manager to make a commitment to visit the home or remote site, though with prior agreement and respect for the teleworkers' privacy while working from their own home bases. These visits can give a new understanding of their specific environments and can demonstrate that distance is no barrier to effective teamwork. During the visit, the manager has a chance to pick up clues about the efficiency and suitability of the local office, and share the teleworkers' experience directly.

3.5.6   Central office visits

The main advantage of meetings at a central site is the reinforcement of the team and organisation connection, giving visibility to the distance worker, and maintaining a 'space' for them in the core team. For teleworkers who do not make regular office visits, these should take place every two or three months and be linked with team sessions, training, team reviews, briefing sessions, or annual audits and planning. These central office visits contribute to team identity and an opportunity to contribute to wider issues in the organisation.

3.5.7   *Ad hoc* support

In addition to regular supervision the manager needs to be available for occasional discussions or one-off decisions. These contacts become less frequent as the individual worker gathers confidence. Experience of regular supervision gives the worker a mandate and clear authority for their workload, and requests for intermittent advice diminish.

Teleworking managers should watch for signs of a lack of confidence or ineffective performance and be ready to increase their level of contact and support. Frequent requests for reports can be seen as performance monitoring, and may undermine confidence. Instead, the manager may check on the frequency of contact with other colleagues, set aside time for longer calls or visits, and invite the worker to additional training.

3.5.8   Training as a support

If teleworkers are not rigorously selected for their experience, they may need a variety of skill development sessions in addition to the work-based technology or functional knowledge of their normal job. As written reports are a vital link for teleworkers, an investment in a writing skills course is especially valuable as they may need to sharpen their writing skills, to provide concise, and effective communications.

Another area for skill development may be in the use of the telephone, which has a different focus when used as a main communication system. There are telephone techniques and manners that can improve working relationships, as a badly timed call can be unprofessional and obtrusive, and the teleworker needs to review and update their telephone techniques to include, for example:

- Making appointments for long calls
- Not assuming that a phone call has priority
- Checking if people have time to talk, and if not when?
- Introducing yourself and your work context
- Leaving clear messages
- Developing interpersonal and listening skills
- Preparing agendas for long phone calls
- Not keeping people on 'hold'
- Assertively telling callers if a different time is needed for a useful discussion

Time-management for the teleworker is very different than in an office culture, where people are guided by their colleagues' behaviour and the work ethos. This needs to be recreated and self managed in a home or remote office. It is not an easy change and any techniques that can formulate an efficient use of time should be on offer.

Apart from the direct value of skill development, there are other investments in training which show employees that they have worth in terms of time and cost to the organisation. They also have a chance to meet their colleagues, and to discuss any changes in their group, or in the culture of the organisation as a whole. These spin-offs indicate that training courses rarely have a single outcome and a manager of a dispersed team should consider training as an additional support system, as well as for its primary function of skill development.

3.5.9   Support from the core team

Irrespective of the numbers or status of the members of the core team, their main value is their consistent availability. They are the information hub of the team. They know where people are; they record and relay messages; they filter urgent from ordinary work, and they are often the initial customer-facing contact. At their best they can remind, encourage, take initiatives to pass on information, and make connections between people. The key to an effective support role for the teleworkers from the core team is to 'exploit' their availability as the matrix of the dispersed teams' information system.

3.5.10   Opportunities for training and career development

A major fear for teleworkers is missing training and career opportunities. This concern is fed by opportunists in the company who always seem to be in the right place at the right time, and may deter able workers from accepting a teleworking role. The onus is on the employing manager to allay these fears and to establish positive strategies for training and career development. The following suggestions could be part of a package that confirms to teleworkers that they have an ongoing value to the company.

Training   Teleworker training should aim to limit isolation, and extend the skill base. A training workshop should also provide social time for people to exchange news and views about their company. It is a time for people to measure themselves against the skills and knowledge of their peer group and to test their readiness to move to a more demanding job.

Mentor and non-managerial supervision   The inexperienced teleworker will benefit from meetings with a mentor. Typically a mentor is a higher-level manager, sometimes called a sponsor, who provides resources, ideas, information, introductions and personal contacts for someone less experienced in the organisation. Such meetings create links into new areas of the organisation, generating ideas about training and career opportunities.

Visits and shadowing   Keeping in regular contact with colleagues has already been highlighted, and shadowing a colleague can give the inexperienced teleworker a chance to observe 'live' working practice. The 'shadow' should observe and review, thus giving both people an opportunity to question the motives and principles behind each activity. The development opportunity for the shadow is to extend their skills, integrate new ways of working, and use the visit as a benchmark for their own abilities.

External conferences   Conferences also counter the potential isolation factor for the remote worker and introduce new ideas into an organisation. Internal and external conferences are hothouse opportunities for development and contacts. The teleworker benefits by meeting people from other organisations and will be able to import fresh energy back into their own organisation. Teleworkers who feel they are at the end of the line for ideas and information will find that attending a conference is a way of reversing the flow by importing new information. Being able to spearhead an initiative on their return gives an employee a showcase opportunity to demonstrate their knowledge to a wider forum. The teleworkers themselves should also be proactive about getting their development needs met. They will need to suggest projects and visits that will enhance their skills. This entails reading professional journals and taking responsibility for keeping in touch with new developments in their field of expertise. Their employer should encourage these opportunities not simply as morale-boosting, but as investments in the individual teleworker who may, one day, return to the core team, or another part of the organisation, in a more senior role.

New skills Some essential skills have been mentioned, e.g. computer literacy, time management, and report writing, as basic requirements. Inexperienced teleworkers also need to develop more than usually competent interpersonal skills. They need to make effective working relationships without face-to-face meetings. Their reports need to be clear, concise and pertinent, whether over the telephone, in videoconferences or in writing. They should learn to edit and select the optimum presentation media and develop a disciplined work style that plans and meets deadlines. They become more self-motivated and authoritative about their work, and develop clear boundaries to meet the energy demands between work, domestic, personal and professional demands and responsibilities.

Having an experienced and skilled teleworker is an asset to the company. However, they may also develop the confidence to consider a career change as they will have a wide range of transferable skills to offer to a new employer or self-employment. As the teleworker grows in professional stature with a greater ability to market his or her skills, the employing organisation needs to find ways to motivate loyalty . So training and developing an excellent teleworker also means guarding well one of the organisation's most valuable assets.

3.5.11   Returning to core team

Despite the careful planning, support and training of teleworkers, a proportion, perhaps a third, of those who try teleworking may need to return to the core team at some stage.

Whatever the reason, whether personal or professional, the transfer should not be labelled as a failure. Organisations need to consider the teleworking relationships with an open mind, and if it is unsuccessful changes must be made to limit unproductive work. The return should be planned (with a month's notice) to allow colleagues to readjust their work patterns, alter administration systems and pass on information about the change.

3.5.12   Summary

Authorising employees to work away from a central office base is a sophisticated balance of trust and control. The manager needs to inform, support and supervise work to make teleworking cost-effective. The teleworker needs to repay the trust by maintaining communications, remaining part of the team and working to agreed targets. In fact the healthy teleworking organisation is no different from any business, except it pays more attention to communications and contacts.

3.6   LANDLORDS, NEIGHBOURS AND CONFIDENTIAL BUSINESS

3.6.1   Household and office space

Teleworking makes huge areas of space available. In the next decade, if the teleworking prophets are right, New York and London will have an additional 180 million and 90 million sq ft respectively of empty offices, due to increased teleworking.

There are approximately 22 million and 91 million households in the UK and the USA respectively. The average space per person is 350 sq ft (32.5 sq m). The USA has *circa* 86 billion sq ft (7.98B sq m) and the UK 19 billion sq ft (1.76B sq m) of domestic space. In comparison work space is only a fraction of living space, being an average of 120 sq ft (11 sq m) per working person, or 14 billion sq ft (1.3B sq m) in the USA and 3 billion sq ft (0.27B sq m) in the UK (1988 statistics).

Telecommuting or teleworking at home (excluding traditional home pieceworking) is practised by *circa* 3% to 5% of the workforce, implying potential reuse of 98 million sq ft (9.1M sq m) in the USA and 437 million sq ft (40.59M sq m) in the UK of office space. A small percentage of home-based teleworkers (0.15% of the workforce) retain full office space both at home and at central office; thus 21 million sq ft (1.95M sq m) in the USA and 5 million sq ft (0.46M sq m) in the UK is duplicated space, used part-time but with rents and costs running full-time.

3.6.2   Future values of property

It is probable that teleworking is having an effect on property values and rents. It can be seen that there is no shortage of domestic space to use for both living and working and that, given the changing nature of work patterns, the distinction between commercial and domestic property will be blurred. This is already evident in London and New York where commercial and domestic rents are converging; it is particularly evident when 'reverse premiums', paid to entice tenants into commercial space, are deducted from the future rent-roll.

Well-planned telecommuting releases commercial space; the employer saves the rent and other costs and the property is re-let or stands empty. The basic economic mechanism is time-share or shift work. Offices are generally occupied for only 40 hours a week out of 168 hours. Home offices are available for living and working for the full week or for three work shifts, and taking up this option has a trickle-down effect on all other property. When teleworking reaches its predicted 15% of the workforce, some 2 billion sq ft (0.18 sq m) in the USA and 493 million sq ft (45.79M sq m) in Britain of office space will be released onto the market—sufficient space to easily house the homeless of both nations.

Figure 3.1 The 'Harpy': the teleworking home and office of Mr and Mrs Andrew Wadsworth

3.6.3 Building an office at home

Experienced teleworkers may find that sharing space with domestic activities restricts their freedom to choose their working hours and their control over their own environment. When the novelty wears off and the fear of isolation is replaced by irritation at being interrupted, most teleworkers will hanker after a little place of their own.

Financially, building or converting a space is affordable. All teleworkers save around £700 ($1000) a year which at 8% interest will support an additional mortgage of £8000 ($12 500). A fully finished, double skinned, insulated and electrically heated wood-built office giving 150 sq ft (14 sq m) will cost about that amount. Building in brick onto the house will double the cost, but increase the house value, and converting loft or garage space costs about the same as a wooden structure.

Beware, however, of ending up in an isolated and inaccessible roof space, where any visitors have to pass the bedrooms and bathrooms and children leave bear traps on the stairs in the form of wheeled toys and used diapers.

A separate entrance at ground level is ideal. Basements are all right if the lighting is thought about.

Planning permission—local zoning DO NOT apply for permission to build an office 'as refusal often offends'. Most authorities allow a percentage of existing domestic space to be added without a new permit, but if permission is required, simply add a study or garden room or some other domestic area. Teleworking rarely contravenes any business use conditions but applying for commercial use in a residential area will almost certainly fail and will delay building by months or years—despite the fact that millions of people are known to work at home, including the US President and the UK Prime Minister.

Landlords and mortgagors Similarly there may be covenants in any domestic mortgage, lease or rent agreement, prohibiting business use. Such covenants do not apply to an individual staying home to work. The landlords are protecting the area against deterioration, thus maintaining property values, and are protecting themselves against multiple tenancies, for example, a small firm or corporation acquiring tenant rights in a domestic property. Such multiple tenancies would create legal mayhem if the landlords needed to apply to the courts for repossession.

Applying for change of use to accommodate commercial use directly challenges both the local zoning and the landlord's restrictions. It is the formal change of use which alarms neighbours and officials, opening the floodgates, if successful, to all manner of traffic and noise in the neighbourhood.

Smart buildings When working space is added, remember the electronic revolution and incorporate as many power and telephone points as possible. Only the boldest feel they can predict precisely the equipment and wiring required over the coming years. Smart office buildings allow for floor and ceiling spaces to hide dozens of electrical and electronic connections; they are worth a study to help design your own home office (see Chapter 6.13).

Elbow room While 70 sq ft (6.5 sq m) is the immediate desk and sitting area required, if you are going to build—build big. Average office building space is 120 sq ft (11 sq m) when common areas are counted, and workshop/laboratory space (except at impoverished universities) is 300 sq ft (28 sq m). Make as much space as possible and try to allow for an assistant or colleague working with you from time to time. Allow for acres of shelves and cupboards; the paperless office remains an elusive dream.

Be individual One of the joys and efficiencies of teleworking is controlling your own working times and environment. Take design advice (Chapter 6.13) but be yourself and have the office the way it suits you—not how the Vice President would like it to be—whoever is paying for it. The Vice

President is not going to have to work and live in it. Natural light, artificial light and fresh air are fundamental to good workstation design.

National budgets for home offices Over the coming decade, if 10% of teleworkers build home offices they will spend $22 billion in the USA and £3.5 billion in the UK on building trades and materials. To equip teleworkers at home, whether or not they build offices, will create a market for desktop, user-friendly information technology of $82 billion in the USA and £12 billion in the UK.

3.6.4   House values

As teleworking increases and more people work at home, houses in remote areas will become accessible for permanent occupation, residents no longer needing to be close to railway stations and main roads. Houses which provide separate rooms for offices will be at a premium. Such properties are not necessarily rural. As the New York and London loft or warehouse conversions over the last 12 years have shown, many people want to live in the inner cities, provided that the areas can be made clean and safe. Teleworking does not spell the end of inner cities, or a sprawl of rural and suburban developments as some commentators predict. Teleworking enables people to live where they work and work where they live, without needing to be close to commuting routes or central offices.

People like cities, and have done so for thousands of years. It has been the 20th century growth of exclusive and prohibitively expensive office blocks which has dehumanised city centres and driven people out, making ghost towns of business areas at night. As commercial and domestic values converge, partly thanks to teleworking, city centres will come alive again.

3.6.5   Neighbours as a nuisance

Isolation is the great fear of new, full-time, teleworkers. Workshops for teleworkers held in Oxford as long ago as 1983 discovered that isolation is quickly replaced by friends, family and neighbours 'dropping in' for a brief chat, firstly from curiosity as to why 'you are not going to work any more' and secondly, the persistent ulterior motive, to use the teleworker's office and communications equipment.

Teleworkers are a godsend for local organisers, local events, local charities and children with homework. People will invade teleworkers' offices and quickly establish their rights to 'borrow' paper, envelopes, postage stamps, fax machines and, for the more sophisticated, e-mail and network connections. Their interruptions can be quickly controlled with a few firm commands and if they insist on using facilities, a stiff office bureau charge will dissuade even the most persistent.

Overlooking documents Such neighbourly and family interest dies away as time passes but even occasional visits will catch the teleworker unprepared, personal computer screen ablaze with corporate secrets, or confidential documents being compiled on the living room floor (see Chapter 5). This is the opposite side of the coin to the neighbourhood fearing the teleworker will degrade the area with commercial activity and is worth taking into account when planning where to place equipment. Ideally, it should be possible to leave the desk in the middle of confidential work, certain that it cannot be overlooked by casual visitors. If this is not possible then negotiations with regular callers will solve the problem. As a last resort, a memo from head office spelling out the confidential nature of all the documents and equipment should be produced and shown to intrusive callers.

3.6.6   Noise

Neighbours and family, particularly youngsters, can generate a deal of noise in suburban areas where they cannot reasonably be expected to move their activities away from the home office.

Noise in cities is at high levels and in busy offices can be as high as in manufacturing units. Noise affecting a home office is usually lower in decibel terms but can disproportionally disturb the teleworker for two reasons. First, in the quieter rural or suburban environment any persistent noise can intrude and irritate a teleworker. For example, one home-based worker became obsessed with a low frequency hum generated by grain-drying fans a half-mile away. In a particularly wet harvest season the fans ran for days and he tried (a hopeless cause) to have them stopped. Eventually moving home, to another rural area, was the only tolerable solution. The second problem is family noise, which has embarrassed teleworkers when it intruded into telephone calls or meetings. This is a common problem for new teleworkers who feel the local sounds reflect badly on themselves.

(Interestingly, some of the operators taking part in BT's Inverness, Scotland, experiment (see Chapter 6.0) found just the opposite. Local callers to the Directory Assistance service, who were aware of the experiment through articles in the local papers, identified the teleworkers by the *lack* of background noise.)

Both sets of noise intrusions could be solved by going to war against the perpetrators. It is, however, likely to be a long and bitter engagement and ultimately doomed to failure.

More intelligently, teleworkers have overcome the problem by comparing the noise levels at central office (and while commuting) to those at home, and by realising that they are not personally identified with noises outside their home offices—however closely related the source might be. One teleworker related the difficulty of concentrating in meetings when his child/children/dog was raising hell outside the room, until he recalled working for two years in a city office across a narrow street from a building site, the noise from which was probably over all known safety levels but did not stop his meetings or phone calls which were conducted by shouting. The difference, he realised, was that he felt no responsibility for the building noise but had felt responsible for the family sounds. Until he regarded family noises as natural hazards, he was in danger of making his own and his family's life miserable.

4

Economics

> '...teleworking can provide many benefits to industry
> with greater output of work, more flexible employment
> opportunities, cleaner air and fewer traffic jams.'

Steven Norris—Minister for Transport in London—1993

4.1 BASIC ECONOMIC FACTORS

Financially speaking, teleworking affects most aspects of business, personal
and national life. The basic economic factors include Commuting and
Travel, Office Space, Environment and Health, Taxation, Productive Time,
Leisure Time and Efficiency.

4.1.1 Roll them mountains

All the developed nations enjoy or suffer from morning and evening commuting on every working day. The cost of commuting, and the environmental damage caused by it, are directly related to the weight being transported.

The US commute weighs in at *circa* 146 million tonnes which represents
some 108 million vehicles carrying drivers and passengers to their work
places and then home again.

The UK equivalent weighs 33 million tonnes and the total European commute is in the region of 200 million tonnes. Europe and America together
move 379 million tonnes before 9am each morning and back again before
8pm every evening. The average commuting distance is 24 km (15 miles).
This is equivalent to lifting a third of Mount Everest, carting it 15 miles, and
repeating the exercise on five days of every week of every year. **If the commute didn't already exist, only the maddest of mad economists would
invent it.**

Telecommuting reduces this Herculean, energy consuming effort, at
present by around 3%, or some 11.4 million tonnes. The costs in money

terms can be estimated by applying standard AAA or AA rates. An average car with driver weighs 1.5 tonnes, a full train per commuter weighs 1 tonne. The Internal Revenue Service calculates and allows up to 30 cents a mile. The Euro–US commute costs therefore some $852 million, morning and evening. The amount saved by telecommuting is some $51 million a day or $12 750 million a year.

Added to this saving are 3% to 5% of the costs of maintaining the road network, traffic police, traffic accidents and the health costs caused by heavily polluted air.

4.1.3   Office space

Most employed people, in the developed world, enjoy two spaces: 330 sq ft (30 sq m) each in their homes for relaxing in and 120 sq ft (11 sq m) each in their offices or workshops for working in. The home tends to serve two eight-hour shifts a day and the office serves one shift.

Commuters pay for a house, the largest contract most of us sign in our lives, make it comfortable and matching to their personal tastes, then close it up each weekday morning and return, often after dark, to enjoy its benefits only at night. Meanwhile, the air-conditioned, modern office is closed down from 6pm to 8am. Virtually empty, it is cleaned and heated (and often lighted) for those 14 hours, to await the return of the commuters.

This duplication of space stems directly from the need to congregate around the information required for work. In offices, for the last 200 years, the filing cabinets were that focal point. Now that a standard $2000 desktop computer can access mainframe computers which can hold the equivalent of many thousands of filing cabinets, teleworkers are able to be as efficient at finding and applying information from a distance as they could be in the office. Most teleworkers claim to be more efficient. Dr Becker at Cornell University has found that 25% of floor space can be saved in most offices, due to the average number of unoccupied desks on any day (see Chapter 7.1), although the proportion of empty desks due to telework is not known.

Teleworking enables space to be saved, or used differently—perhaps for residential purposes, or simply made available to allow central office people (the core team) to spread out and be more comfortable and suffer less from 'sick building syndrome'. The current recession has highlighted an over-supply of commercial space in much of the developed world of at least 5% which has depressed some rental values. It remains, however, a major expense for a business to be centrally located in the heart of an inaccessible city in 'one-shift' office blocks. The pre-computer and pre-telephone rationale of bringing the entire staff together in a high density area with similar businesses close by, was the necessity for speed of vital communications. At 300 000 kilometres a second on a copper pair, the standard telephone line, the human office messenger can no longer compete.

The presently estimated 3–5% of teleworkers in Europe and the USA, or some nine and a half million people working at home or from vehicles, involves up to 1 billion sq ft (93 million sq m) of office space on the two continents. This could save their organisations the rent, property taxes and overheads of city offices to a total of $10B a year, plus the costs of providing support staff and contributing through taxes or directly to commuting infrastructure and travel costs.

4.1.3   Environment and health

Teleworkers tend to be healthier. A bank which has monitored its teleworkers for two years (LNC) and whose results are featured later in this book (Chapter 4.8) found that the average sick leave for those people halved from 6 days to 3 days per annum. This is a common and unsurprising finding, as commuters to city offices are exposed to air heavily polluted by traffic fumes, to every airborne germ, to water system-borne viruses, to bad weather, to sick building syndrome (ascribed to low frequency vibrations from machinery and to polluted air conditioned air), and to the stresses of commuting and of working in often noisy and crowded conditions.

Average UK sick leave was 18 days per man and 9 days per woman; in the USA it is half these figures, averaging 7 days per person. Assuming teleworkers are generally well motivated and healthy, they could, like the bank employees, average some 6 days a year prior to and 3 days a year following teleworking—a 50% improvement.

Taking the estimated Euro–US numbers of teleworkers above, the healthier teleworkers, at a conservative output of $35 per hour, each year contribute to the economies an extra $7.5B from lower sick leave.

The savings in direct health care are more difficult to estimate as taking sick leave may incur no more treatment than taking a couple of aspirins. If the cost of every sick leave day is assumed as 15 minutes of a doctor's time at $40 per hour, then $284m a year are currently saved by teleworking.

Air pollution from car, bus and train exhausts are also reduced by 3–5% equating to a reduction of noxious fumes of nearly 10 million million litres (2.5 million million US gallons) of exhaust gases a year. This may relieve some asthmatic and chest problems but the health implication is too intricate a calculation to make here.

4.1.5   Taxation

The extensive sections on taxation in this book (see Chapters 2.9 and 3.1) show that teleworkers should benefit from tax relief allowed on their home offices, bearing costs of some £750 or $1000 a year and gaining tax relief of *circa* $300 a year each. The Euro–US 9.48 million teleworkers should benefit by $2.8B a year. This is a small price for the Treasury to pay for the benefits to the economy the teleworkers bring.

Depending on the level of fuel tax, the Treasury will also lose tax revenues on some 5 billion litres (over 1.3 billion US gallons) of fuel, which at, say, 10% equals $22m per year.

4.1.5   Productive time

Most teleworkers produce more work and, ideally planned, do so at lower costs per unit due to the lower support and property costs involved. This has been calculated elsewhere (see Chapter 4.3.11), as a 45% improvement in efficiency. The improvement stems from teleworkers having more time in which to work, saved from the commute, being fresher for work than their commute-wearied colleagues, from having fewer interruptions and, as calculated above, from less sick leave. A 45% improvement for 9.48 million Euro–US teleworkers who contribute $35 per hour to output equals a $194B a year increase in output.

4.1.6   Leisure time and efficiency

'A happy worker is a productive worker' and one of the greatest personal benefits to home based teleworkers is the extra leisure hours they have available. If not dissipated and if carefully valued from the outset, all the saved commuting time can be well applied. Some telecommuters save two hours at the start and end of each day or 20 hours a week, amounting to 1000 hours a year. Working at home means they can finish at 6pm and be ready for leisure activities at 6.15pm. The value to the individual has been judged as the amount per hour they would earn if they took a second job and forwent their extra leisure. A manager works some 1800 hours for say $35 000 or $19 an hour. Saving 1000 commuting hours a year is theoretically valued by the individual at $19 000, though this is not available to them in cash.

This leisure benefit contributes to the finding that 68% of employed teleworkers do not want to return to central office working.

4.2   ENVIRONMENTAL FACTORS

The word 'environment' is used as a generic term covering major global issues such as depletion of the Earth's natural resources, the destruction of the ozone layer and the greenhouse effect; regionalised effects such as water and soil pollution, biodiversity and acid rain; and local concerns such as an individual's quality of life in material terms, the rural landscape and visual amenity. Any assessment of environmental impact must take account of all these factors but can be further complicated by the fact that the issues are not necessarily complementary. For example, concerns for the local environment, epitomised by the NIMBY (not-in-my-back-yard) syndrome, can often mask, or on occasion outweigh, wider, global considerations.

At a superficial level teleworking might seem to be all good news for the environment. It can lead to an improved quality of life (a 'better' place to live and a release from stressful commuting) and, on a national level, reduced demand on the country's transport infrastructure. A more detailed investigation, however, reveals that while these benefits can accrue there can

Figure 4.1   Big Ben hidden in a shroud of unhealthy chemical fog (photo Sunday Times)

also be environmental costs associated with teleworking, and that to maximise the benefits, while minimising the costs, will require both careful planning as well as a personal sense of responsibility by individual teleworkers.

While it has been estimated that, in the UK and USA alone, around 5 million people now telework, there have been very few published studies
describing actual changes in travel behaviour and even fewer publications
covering the wider environmental implications.

4.2.1 Travel

In many countries the car has quite rightly been identified as the culprit of
much atmospheric pollution. Although modern cars are undoubtedly
cleaner (especially since the widespread adoption of catalytic converters)
the ever-increasing numbers of cars on the roads means that improvements
to air quality resulting from cleaner engines are likely to be short lived. It
must also be remembered that catalytic converters do not reduce carbon
dioxide emissions (in fact they slightly increase them) and there seems little
indication of any move towards significantly more fuel-efficient cars. In the
UK, government figures predict a 19% increase in CO_2 emissions from the
transport sector over the next 10 years.

Signatories to the 1992 global Convention on Climate Change at the Earth
Summit in Rio de Janeiro accepted the precautionary principle with respect
to global warming and agreed to prepare programmes to limit their emissions of CO_2 and other global warming gases to earlier levels by the year
2000. Teleworking may have a contribution to make in achieving this target.

The average UK commuter travels 14.4 miles per day getting to and from
work. The majority of these journeys will be by car, with an average occu-
pancy unlikely to be much above one. Public transport is more frequently
used to travel into city centres, but in these cases the average journey length
is likely to be much higher, often counteracting the environmental benefits

Table 4.1 An estimate of annual atmospheric pollutants, in thousands of
tonnes, generated by 5 million commuters travelling 3456 miles per annum
using three different types of car.

Fuel type	Fuel consumed (million litres)	Carbon monoxide	Nitrogen oxides	Hydro-carbons	Carbon dioxide
Petrol	2600	158	24	28	6048
Petrol with 3 way catalyst	2900	61	2	9	6653
Diesel	1700	9	10	7	4527

Note: There are 4.5 litres in a UK gallon and 3.8 litres in a US gallon. 2600 million litres converts to 572
million UK gallons and 687 million US gallons.One gallon of petrol consumes 1800 gallons of oxygen
when burnt, creating, for these 5 million commuters, some 1.4 million million UK gallons of 'fumes' at
street level. Around 120 million US commuters produce 38.5 million million gallons of exhaust fumes
and 22 million UK commuters produce 6.0 million million gallons of fumes, each year.

arising from the switch to a more fuel-efficient mode of transport. As a guide, Table 4.1 shows the annual atmospheric pollution generated by 5 million people travelling to work alone in different types of car.

It has often been argued that while the widespread adoption of teleworking undoubtedly reduces the pollution generated by commuter travel, teleworkers will have more leisure time and could be inclined to make increased use of their cars for leisure purposes. Firm support for this hypothesis would need to come from scientific investigations into changes in people's travel patterns as a result of a move from a traditional commuting job to homeworking. For example, by logging the daily number of car trips made by each worker it would be possible first to demonstrate the saving of the two daily commuting trips, and then to monitor any additional leisure journeys. To date there have been very few such investigations but it is interesting to note that studies in California and the Netherlands not only showed the expected saving of two commuting trips per day, but even indicated a possible *reduction* in the number of journeys made for leisure purposes.

Data from the California State Employee Telecommute Pilot Project showed that, on average, telecommuters reduced their travel requirements by at least two trips per day. There was even some indication that family members of telecommuters may also have reduced their number of non-work-related trips. However, it was recognised by the investigators that this observation would need a more comprehensive study with a larger sample of people before it could be properly drawn as a conclusion of the work.

An analogous investigation in the Netherlands came to very similar conclusions. In this case, teleworking resulted in an overall 17% reduction in car trips per teleworker. Peak-hour travel by car reduced by an impressive 26%. An interesting, and unexpected, result of this work was that other members of the teleworker's household also appeared to travel less.

Teleworkers operating from telecentres are still likely to make use of their car to travel to work and, until the concentration of such centres approaches one per community, commuting distances of telecentre workers are unlikely to show any deviation from the norm. Even when the density of telecentres increases to a point where there is a measurable reduction in average commuting distance, it should always be remembered that vehicles are most polluting during the first 2 to 3 miles of a journey. Indeed catalytic converters will only work when they are hot and people making a significant number of short trips would be advised to select a diesel car in preference to petrol. In view of these transport effects the environmental benefits of telecentres are likely to be second order compared to the first order travel savings of the homeworker. Such second order savings, however, are not insignificant and are attributable to both home and telecentre workers.

Most large towns and cities now suffer from traffic congestion which gives rise to high concentrations of atmospheric pollutants and can be directly linked to the production of photochemical smogs. A number of solutions to this problem have been proposed, including car sharing, road pricing, car-free zones, car travel restrictions, electric cars and, of course, teleworking. Apart from improving air quality in large cities any reduction in rush hour traffic will lead to the additional benefits of fewer accidents (more likely in heavy traffic) and reduced pressure for improved travel infrastructure.

In the UK, Roarke Associates have proposed telecentres located at railway stations. This, they claim, would allow people to spend part of their working day in the telecentre and part in the city office. They project that a wide scale adoption of this working pattern would reduce peak loadings on the country's travel infrastructure and lead to significant financial and environmental savings.

Cities in most developed countries have efficient public transport systems. In the developing nations, however, capital investment in transport infrastructure is often low, and rail services poorly developed. This has meant that some of the world's worst photochemical smogs have occurred in places such as Mexico City. The early introduction of teleworking concepts in these countries would bring immediate, and significant, environmental improvements. Such a policy could also prevent some of the other undesirable social and environmental effects that result from large urban sprawls.

4.2.2 Offices and workshops

Traditional office accommodation takes up valuable land, uses significant quantities of materials in its construction and consumes large amounts of energy to run. Full-time working at home reduces the demand for new office accommodation (saving on extraction of raw materials, construction energy consumption, further expansion of urban sprawl, etc.) and, perhaps more significantly, provides for savings in running costs. In environmental terms the greatest saving is likely to be in office energy consumption. The average amount of energy required to heat, light, air-condition and service US and UK office accommodation has been estimated to be around 2000 kWh per worker per year.

For a worker moving from office to home there will, inevitably, be an increase in the domestic energy bill but, as shown below, this incremental increase is less than the savings made by eliminating traditional office accommodations. Unless a desk sharing programme is in operation, part-time teleworking will lead to an increase in heated and air conditioned empty office space and will only therefore provide environmental benefits from reduced travel demand.

Heating a house all day instead of just early mornings and evenings leads not to a doubling of the energy heating bill as might at first be expected, but to an average increase in energy consumption of just 14%. This is because a substantial fraction of the energy supplied to a home is used to heat the fabric of the building rather than the space, and that once heated, the building acts as a storage radiator. Since the working week usually consists of five days, a switch from office to homeworking will increase domestic energy consumption for heating purposes by around 10%. The average increase in domestic energy consumption due to the introduction of a full-time home teleworker will therefore be around 1000 kWh per year, offering savings over office accommodation of approximately 1000 kWh per person per year.

In most respects telecentres will have energy costs similar to those of other commercial buildings. In view of this there will be little difference in terms of heating and lighting energy consumption between the traditional office worker and a telecentre worker.

4.2.3 Equipment and materials

Home teleworkers will have a typical equipment portfolio of computer, telephone, fax machine and printer. In some cases there will be additional data transmission equipment such as an ISDN link or conventional modem. In many offices the fax and printer would be shared, so the home office can represent an increase in equipment resulting in associated environmental penalties in terms of use of raw materials, impact from manufacture and disposal costs. Such penalties are, however, minimal compared to the potential travel and infrastructure savings and may even be irrelevant as many homes now possess computers and, increasingly, fax machines.

Telecentres offer the opportunity to share equipment and will be environmentally neutral in comparison with traditional office working. Again, and unless desk sharing is in operation, part-time teleworking offers the worst of both worlds with duplication of office equipment.

Many large companies are now taking environmental considerations into account in their purchasing decisions. To equip a home office for a teleworker from a large organisation such arrangements are likely to continue. However, the provision of consumables such as paper, pens, print cartridges, etc., is not so straightforward. In this case the environmental benefits of central purchasing will need to be offset against the pollution generated by additional transportation and it may be better to provide individual teleworkers with lists of approved consumables, and then encourage local purchase, possibly against corporately agreed contracts with local suppliers.

4.2.4 Waste disposal

There are two main issues under this heading. The first concerns recycling of waste materials and the second involves the disposal of industrial and commercial wastes.

Large communities of people working in small areas such as an office block make the logistics and cost-effectiveness of recycling programmes for office wastes attractive. For home-based teleworkers, and for all but the largest of telecentres, recycling of waste paper and other consumables will rely on the availability of local collection programmes. The employer could arrange his own collection programmes but this would be prohibitively expensive and would lead to the environmentally unacceptable transportation of small quantities of waste over large distances.

Employers of teleworkers cannot, however, easily dismiss their responsibilities so far as waste disposal is concerned. Any waste generated as a result of their teleworkers' business activities belongs to the employer and should be dealt with as commercial waste. In the UK the Environmental Protection Act makes it technically illegal to place commercial waste in the domestic dustbin. While the odd piece of paper or paper clip is likely to go unnoticed, it would be wise for the company to ensure that it has an approved system of disposal for end-of-life electronic equipment, batteries (especially NiCd rechargeable batteries) and any other material that could be deemed hazardous or otherwise environmentally damaging.

4.2.5   Energy

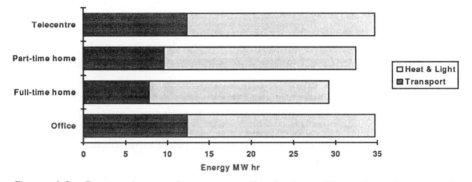

Figure 4.2   Personal annual energy profiles for four different modes of work

One of the largest, and probably the most easily quantifiable, of the environmental aspects of teleworking concerns energy consumption and associated CO_2 emissions. Based on a study by BT Laboratories, Figure 4.2 shows the energy consumption profiles for four different kinds of worker. In this figure transport energy refers to the average energy used per UK worker on private car journeys per year, including travel to and from work. The heat and lighting figure refers to the average energy used per UK worker to heat and light their place of work and home. The part-time home profile refers to someone working at home two days per week, with the other three days spent in a non-desk-sharing office. In addition to the energy consumptions shown in Figure 4.2, there may also be a small increase in the energy used to power the telecommunications network as a result of increased teleworking, but this is expected to be negligible at around 200 kWh per worker per year.

These figures show that, on an individual basis, total energy savings of around 16% can be achieved by moving from conventional office-based work to full time home-based teleworking. At a national level the effect of 5 million people working at home would save around 28 billion kWh of energy per annum. Based on the current mix of UK fuel sources, i.e. gas, oil, coal, nuclear and renewables, this would save about 8 million tonnes of CO_2 per annum, equivalent to 1.4% of UK total CO_2 emissions.

4.2.6   Conclusions

In energy terms, on average there is little difference between the traditional office worker and the telecentre worker. The environmental advantages accruing from telecentres are therefore second-order, i.e. reduced demand on travel infrastructure and improved quality of life.

In the case of home-based teleworkers, in addition to the second order effects, there could be noticeable improvements to local air quality in major cities and significant energy savings. Care should, however, be taken to ensure that proper arrangements are in place to supply materials to home-based workers and to cover disposal of their wastes.

4.3   BENEFITS AND COSTS TO THE ORGANISATION

4.3.1   The growth of telecommunications

Telecommunications corporations are currently one of the world's leading engines of growth. Most major organisations have an investment in or rely heavily upon the rapid financial and technological growth of this sector.

This growth is equipping the planet for worldwide television, telephones and computer networking at lower prices every year for the networks of cables, exchanges and transmitters and for the many peripherals for end users.

The USA claims the most advanced telecommunications network in the world. Over $10B (£7B) have been spent in the last 10 years to connect the homes and offices of the USA to optical fibre or wide band cable networks; the latter are generally financed by and for cable television but , with tens of thousands of times the carrying capacity of traditional copper-pair telephone wires, they are also capable of networking computers, videophones and videoconferences. To date, regulatory barriers prohibit TV cable companies from competing with telephone networks, and vice versa, but recent announcements that AT&T, BT and Bell are to offer video rental via telephone lines from early 1994, and compete with TV companies, may change the ground rules.

To a greater or lesser extent every developed nation is following suit. Japan may be in second place and Singapore is threatening to overtake both the front runners. Less developed countries are competing for funds to extend their telephone networks and are inviting Western telecommunication giants to build private, often cellular-based or radio, networks. In March 1993, President Clinton announced plans for America's Information Superhighway, cabling the entire nation at a cost variously estimated at $100B to $400B.

4.3.2   Be physically present or telecommunicate?

> **tele-**: from Greek. comb. form. 1. FAR (esp. in names of instruments
> producing or recording results at a distance.)

Telecommunications are not a recent development. From the times of mes-
sengers running with the news, relays of horse riders, drum beats, signal
fires, flags, semaphore and Morse code, the human race has conducted
important business via telecommunications. The 20th century electronic revolution may have improved the quality, quantity and speed but the methods date back to the beginning of civilisation.

In these days of instant voice communications to most places on earth, fax
transmissions, telex in emerging nations, high quality video and telephone
conferencing and extensive postal services, why do so many executives
travel long distances by land, sea and air to meetings? Arguments for and
against travelling to meetings implicitly examine the largest immediate
direct saving that telework brings.

There are compelling, perhaps more compelling, arguments for communicating at a distance than there are for travelling to meetings.

4.3.2.1   Face to face

If cables and electronics can transmit data at millions of units per second,
think how much data is being exchanged in a face-to-face meeting. Human
beings still value their instinct and intuition, informed by all five senses acting simultaneously and instantaneously, to gauge colleagues and competitors.

Travel broadens the mind and it will always remain true that experiencing
a thing directly will inform us more thoroughly than any amount of sym-
bolic representation. Even the spoken word is only an attempt to communicate an experience by selected symbols and will never be able to convey
more than a fraction of the total information available to the five senses. It
might be vitally important to hold first meetings in person, but subsequent
meetings will be subject to fewer distractions and, therefore, be more efficient, if focused via a telecommunication channel.

4.3.2.2   Language zones

Communicating across language barriers remains difficult; even if an accurate mechanical translation is provided, the room for misunderstandings
and errors is large. Britain and America are two nations divided by a common language, where one might order 'Gas' (the airy stuff) but get 'Petrol'
(the liquid smelly stuff). Being able to point and touch the products and
cross-examine a live translator remains important.

Computers are currently available with improving translation systems.

Having a printed text, which can be carefully considered before responding, loses the spontaneity of direct contact via a human translator, but will arguably be a more accurate communication. The need for a common world commercial language is addressed by AT&T's Language Line service, with on-demand interpreters for more than 140 languages or dialects via audio-conferencing.

4.3.2.3 Time zones

It isn't always easy to transact across time zones via telecommunications. Messages sent at midnight can be lost or scrambled or simply ignored, and communication may break down. Being on the spot can be just as frustrating, but a business traveller's commitment to getting results is increased in proportion to the time and costs invested in the journey.

A world standard of acknowledging messages is required to reduce the frustration of wondering whether contact has been made. However, important matters usually don't get ignored and it seems excessive to catapult a 160 pound human being 6000 miles through the air burning up 180 gallons of fuel, instead of transmitting a weightless message, or even a series of messages, at 186 000 miles per second, at the cost of a few dollars.

4.3.2.4 Human energy

The quantity of energy generated in a meeting tends to govern the quality, the concentration and commitment, applied. How much information passes in a large meeting or at a convention, generating a palpable and often vital 'mood' amongst the participants, is unmeasured and immeasurable. But most recognise that group psychology is very important in human affairs.

Experience of videoconferencing and audioconferencing confirms that group psychology and a common 'mood' is generated between the participants. A senior European manager of an American multinational company who used videoconferencing for the first time during the 1992 Gulf War found it 'just like being in the same room but without the jet-lag'. While much of the emotional flavour may be lost when using telecommunications, the counterbalance is that people prepare more, ramble less and have shorter, more effective meetings (see the Thorn EMI study, Chapter 4.4.1).

4.3.2.5 Adventure

Travelling and meeting people always has an element of risk and of potential which intrigues the human psyche. Who knows what turn our lives may take when we jet-off to distant lands armed with nothing but our wits and our international credit cards?

Telecommunications offers less excitement. The compensation is that it costs far less and is far less stressful. Downsized organisations, scratching for profits, may no longer afford to have managers spend days away from their desks, however much they enjoy the adventure.

4.3.2.6   Time out

Driving on a throughway or cruising at 30 000 feet at 700 miles an hour makes us feel busy and purposeful while being insulated from the pressures of work. As the study of a videoconferencing facility (Chapter 4.4.1) shows, people enjoy their days out travelling even when the journeys are tedious and dangerous.

Out of a standard 2080 hour working year, the average office worker uses up to 700 hours a year in non-productive activities, including time spent travelling between locations. For example, the UK Law Society calculates that its members, even working exceptionally long hours, can only bill 1100 hours a year, due to holidays, office politics, sickness, administration and non-chargeable travel time. If 'time-out' journeys are replaced with telecommunications, then it is reasonable to interpose some other stress- and tedium-relieving activity. Spare time could profitably be used for recreation, instead of being spent on motorways or in airports.

4.3.2.7   Status

Air travel and Big Shiny Cars remain major status symbols for the majority of us and for the advertisers who reflect our values. Enjoying exclusive rights in cars, hotels, restaurants, airports, planes and trains and visibly reinforcing one's status is heady stuff, may be as addictive as heroin, more expensive to indulge in, as dangerous to health and just as difficult to give up.

As travel has become commonplace and traffic slows to walking pace in most major cities, the new status symbols are not having to travel for business and not being responsible for parking a car. Having an office at home and having the option of working there is seen as a privilege for high status managers, who also benefit because regular teleworking is healthier than commuting (see the Lombard study, Chapter 4.8).

4.3.2.8   Inertia

Inertia is one of the most powerful physical forces; balanced by gravity, it keeps the Earth in its orbit, the planetary system functioning and many economic systems ticking over on automatic pilot. It is an equally powerful force in the affairs of individuals, enabling us to carry out repetitive tasks efficiently and without much conscious effort. Learning new methods and changing our habits slows us down, forcing trivial details on our attention; compare the pain of learning to ride a bicycle with the joy of an expert swooping down the Alps in the Tour de France. Much executive travel and commuting is due to habit and to the philosophy 'If it works don't fix it'.

Well-designed teleworking projects show the worth of challenging corporate inertia. They give an immediate 20% boost to productivity (see Chapter 4.8.2). 95% of teleworkers find that output goes up and that costs come down shortly after shifting to home offices or telecentres. The average teleworker is highly motivated to succeed, will usually produce more quality work per hour than core team colleagues and will generally put in more productive hours.

These eight arguments for and against travelling long distances to meetings can also be applied to commuting daily to central offices and to operating in very large groups. The economics of teleworking are financially and sociologically of sufficient value to have persuaded thousands of senior managers to change corporate habits and working methods to adopt teleworking.

4.3.3   Teleworking cost centres: effectiveness

The eight topics above provide a sound foundation for studying employers' costs and benefits of teleworking. Whereas the majority of individuals benefit in lifestyle terms, and most save cash every year, an organisation must constantly consider the balance between costs, savings and productivity or, as a US consultant has defined it, 'effectiveness'.

Effectiveness is a measure against a known baseline and can be defined as the short, medium and long term production of work, measured in units, multiplied by costs, and accounting for long term motivation. Better motivation brings lower hiring, firing and training costs. Effectiveness is thus the product of productivity, unit cost, and quality.

The baseline should be measured at the outset of teleworking or, if later, by measuring a control group in the core team against a similar group of teleworkers. Teleworkers and their managers quickly come to appreciate the value of 'measurables' or 'deliverables' or results, as compared to the 'present and correct' or turning-up criteria applied in some organisations.

Effectiveness of teleworkers may grow to be as much as 45% greater than the baseline or control core team. Such a level of improvement is not uncommon. It is the greatest benefit to employers and stems directly from reducing travel and increasing communications.

The next seven sections explain how greater effectiveness is achieved from teleworking.

4.3.4   Time is money

One of the first and key measurements applied is the value of the teleworkers' productive time. Professionals who charge their time to clients are very

5.15pm Tuesday evening

Figure 4.3   Time is money

aware of their productive hours, which are recorded hourly and tabulated and reported weekly. Lawyers, accountants, computer experts and consultants of all kinds usually charge by the hour or the day. A few quick calculations will show that most employees contribute to their organisations' Gross Revenues at rates very similar to those charged by professionals. Just as professional fees are the Gross Revenues of their organisations, so each employee in any organisation contributes at calculable hourly rates to the Gross Revenue.

Therefore, for all employees, work out the hourly rate contributed to Gross Revenue. The information needed for any organisation is almost certainly available in their published Annual Report. Follow this simple calculation, reproduced by kind permission of John Waddington and Company, who trade in the UK and the USA, to find the average hourly contribution:

John Waddington plc, security printers, printers, packagers, games manufacturers; year ended 31 March 1991.

Gross Revenue was £227 602 000 ($323 194 000) or £227.6 ($323) million. Dividing by the average number employed in the year (3806) gives £59 895 ($85 050) per head contribution to Gross Revenue.

The normal hours worked are 48 weeks × 40 hours, or 1920 hours per year. Deducting the average UK sick leave of 18 days × 8 hours (144 hours) and the average workplace slack time of 20% (384 hours) gives 1920 − 144 − 384 = 1392 productive hours.

Dividing this figure into the average Gross Revenue gives £43 ($60) per hour worked.

For any such analysis, ensure the figures are for a year. If not, annualise them by dividing by the number of months in the report and multiplying by 12 months. To calculate for different levels of pay, divide the Average Contribution to Gross Revenue (ACTGR) per hour by the average amount paid per employee and multiply by the amount actually paid to any individual, to arrive at the contribution they are (theoretically) making—or get a friendly cost accountant to do it. The products of these simple sums will usually be close to the rates charged by professionals.

Some calculations give surprising results. Nippon Telegraph & Telephone Corporation's 1991 results give an astonishing £150 or $213 per hour earned (ACTGR) by every individual in the business, including the office cleaners. Wall Street or City firms tend to not publish Gross Revenue but report their 'net earnings' which robs us of the opportunity for real comparisons. Merrill Lynch announced $894 (£629M) net earnings in 1992, after paying more than $4M to each of five executives. At salary rates of *circa* $2000 per hour, it would be interesting to know what the average contribution to Gross Revenue per hour was in the same period; the usual two to four times the salary paid puts it between $4000 and $8000 (£2800–£5600) an hour for those five executives.

Establish the ACTGR rates per hour for your teleworkers and core team control group. They should be the same in each group; but the *cost* of employment per hour will eventually vary between the two groups. Monitor the main *time* differences discussed in the next three sections.

4.3.5   Sick leave

Lombard North Central, a UK secondary bank, has found from monitoring their teleworkers for two years that sick leave halved (see Chapter 4.8). This occurred in a group of already well-motivated people who in any case, as members of the core team, took less than half the 1991 13 days national average sick leave. In 1993 the UK average was reported by the Trades Union Congress as having fallen to 8 days per working person, or some 1400 million hours nationally. The US average is 7 days per head per annum or 6700 million hours nationally. An average 500 person office suffers a loss of 32 000 hours through sickness a year. Using the industrial output figures from John Waddington, above, this level of central office sick leave costs $1.9M (£1.34M) a year in lost output per 500 people. The saving by teleworking all 500 employees would be half this figure or just under $1M (£0.7M) per annum.

4.3.6   Commuting time

Commuting time is also money and reducing time spent travelling increases employee effectiveness. In Chapter 4.9 the value of commuting time saved is calculated from the individual perspective, based on the amount a tele-worker might earn per hour if that time were devoted to overtime or a sec-ond job. The value to the employer may be conservatively set at cost of employment but realistically should be set at the output rate or ACTGR per hour.

Reduced commuting benefits in three direct ways. Firstly, most telework-ers start earlier and finish later, using some of their saved commuting time to boost their output. They also work those days when travel disruptions prevent core team employees from getting to the office.

Secondly, while travelling to work can be an exhausting process, tele-workers arrive at the desk as fresh as possible. They also save the energy that commuters spend getting home in the evenings, enabling teleworkers to be fitter for work the next day.

Thirdly, by not travelling and not engaging in office politics each morn-ing, teleworkers maintain greater concentration and continuity for the task in hand, generally producing better quality work than they did at central office. They tend to work at their personal peak times and can often be 'early birds' or 'night owls' to suit their own biorhythms.

The average commuter spends 20 minutes a day travelling. Commuters into major city centres, however, spend over two hours and there are many examples of people spending four hours every day commuting back and forth. Applying the 20 minute per day average and assuming the time were instead devoted to work, US telecommuters in 1993 saved an estimated 1.3 million hours, equivalent to an output of $78M (£55M) each working day or $18.7B (£13.1B) in the year. The UK saved approximately one quarter of this amount. A standard 500-person office converting entirely to teleworking would save $2.4M (£1.7M) per annum from the commuting factor alone.

It is valuable to record the commuting time spent in an office by all the personnel, categorised by salaries, and to calculate the increased output which might be achieved by cutting commuting.

4.3.7   Office corridor politics

A known component of lost time is the common incidence of chance meet-ings in corridors or by 'dropping in' on colleagues. The value of this very human and social activity in passing on useful information and in affirming corporate identity is explored in Chapter 3.5. The time cost has been calcu-lated as being up to 18% of the working week or a working day per week per person. Well-designed teleworking projects build in the opportunity for casual conversations between colleagues but, allowing for these, it remains true that teleworkers spend less than a fifth of the time that the central office teams consume on office politics.

Employed, as opposed to self-employed, US teleworkers in 1993 saved an estimated (Chapter 7.1) $2073M (£1459M) and the UK saved $518M (£365M) from this factor. A 500-person office, all converted to teleworking, would save over $1M (£0.7M) a year.

4.3.8   Health and vitality

Teleworkers avoid commuting crowds and office crowds. The reduced opportunity to enjoy mingling with massed humanity has the advantage of reducing the number of exposures to infection. Sick building syndrome, thought to be due to low frequency vibrations from machines and air fans, to polluted air-conditioning and office water systems and to the sometimes heavily polluted air outside offices, is a complex issue that is thought to reduce effectiveness in large buildings. In addition to the fewer days taken as sick leave, teleworkers tend to be healthier and more energetic at work, partly due to being able to choose and adjust their working environment, and partly due to their increased leisure time.

4.3.9   Employment costs are money

The basic economic factors (Chapter 4.1) looked at the national costs (transport, office space, environment and health, taxation, productive time, and leisure time and efficiency) of operating an organisation and meeting a payroll. However employers cut the cake, they ultimately absorb all the expenditure and efficiency problems of their employees. Some costs are direct or mandatory, such as salary, health insurance, office space, time off, unproductive time, assistants and back-up, training, recruitment, company pensions, redundancy packages, business travel and other expenses.

Other costs are indirect, perhaps met out of the employees' pocket, but it is the employer, in the majority of cases, who fills that pocket: employees' commuting costs, the family or company car, relocation costs, personal phone calls and other communications, hospital bills and, inevitably, taxation.

In times of high employment or when competing for scarce skills, organisations must design their employment packages to cover what the employee may reasonably need in salary, expenses and lifestyle to carry out the proposed job efficiently.

Teleworking will reduce employment costs and in turn reduce the cost per unit of work produced, however the unit is measured.

4.3.10   Transport

It remains true that over 40% of all journeys are commuting journeys. People can spend as much as £100 or $140 a week getting to and from their offices. These costs are not tax deductible in the USA or the UK, and must come from after-tax income, the gross amount of which is provided by the employer. Using the average cost of $15 (£10) a week or $720 (£507) a year and grossing up by 30% tax (remember payroll taxes), it costs $1028 (£724) a year gross pay. Five hundred average office workers spend over $500 000 (£352 000) a year on commuting and need wages to cover this cost.

Many UK employers supply cars to higher grade personnel and in the USA mileage payments are sometimes made. These costs increase as car costs rise, partly due to environmental taxes. 'London Loading' (or 'London Weighting'), additional salary to compensate having to live in or commute into central London, is another traditional way of paying for commuting. Some employers assist with train season tickets, acknowledging the need to transport staff to their city centre buildings

Employers should re-examine the costs of commuting to see if significant savings can be made. They are certainly possible. For example, an employer pays, say, 30 cents (21 pence) a mile including commuting mileage to 500 staff with average round trips of 50 miles a day. By teleworking 4 days a week the saving is $1.4M (£0.98M) a year. Whoever's pocket it saves in the short term, the employer will be able to reduce costs in the short or long term.

4.3.11   Annual net benefit

Summarising the above calculations, Table 4.2 gives the potential savings for an average 500-person office converted to teleworking in ideal conditions.

Table 4.2   Annual net benefit for 500-person office.

	Savings per annum (millions)	
Sick leave	$1.0	£0.7
Commuting time in output	$2.4	£1.7
Office corridor politics	$1.0	£0.7
Health and vitality	(see footnote)	
Transport—commuting	$0.5	£0.3
Total	$4.9	£3.4

Health and vitality are difficult to assess in financial terms but of real value to employers. Note: The above figures are calculated using lost output or ACTGR (Average Contribution to Gross Revenue) rather than cost per hour of employment.

Ideal conditions are not found in real life and organising 500 employees to telework so as to achieve the potential $4.9M (£3.4M) annual benefits is a major reconstruction for any organisation. A start can be made however, with a minimum of disruption and with a relatively small capital outlay, as Thorn EMI Electronics found, in the next section, when opting to save on journeys by introducing 'weightless travel' into one of their UK companies.

4.4   WEIGHTLESS TRAVEL: A CASE STUDY OF TELECONFERENCING

Longer business journeys are a cost which teleworking will reduce by video-conferencing meetings. The following case study is reproduced by kind permission of Thorn EMI Electronics.

4.4.1   Thorn EMI inter-company television

Thorn EMI Electronics, a high technology UK electronics company, serving the defence sector, have premises in Wells, Somerset (635 people) and in Crawley, West Sussex (1000 people), a round trip of 290 miles. The sites have been recently linked by a dedicated BT Megastream data and telephone line. Every week an average of 30 people travel between the sites to attend meetings. The management team took the initiative to install videoconferencing equipment, ready for use from 1 January 1993.

4.4.1.1   Cost justification

Table 4.3 gives calculations of the costs for 30 people journeys per week (290 miles). It is assumed that 50% require car hire (50% shared or pool cars) and 30% require overnight accommodation.

Table 4.3   Weekly costs of travel between sites.

5 hours/day per car × 30 days travel @ £12 per hour	£1800	$2556
15 car hires @ £50/day, incl. fuel	£750	$1065
9 hotel nights	£900	$1278
Total costs per week	£3450	$4899

Note that the travellers' time is evaluated at cost, £12 ($17) per hour, assuming an average salary of *circa* £15 000 ($21 000) p.a. More logically the ACTGR (Average Contribution to Gross Revenue) should be applied, as the company loses output, not just the cost of employment. Applying the UK national average of £35 ($49.7) ACTGR per person, the loss per week is £5250 ($7455) not £1800 (£2556) as assumed above. On this basis the total costs per week are £6900 ($9,798).

Comparing the weekly cost to the capital required (excluding interest, time and space) to buy the videoconferencing equipment for *circa* £107 000 ($149 000) shows a 16-week payback, or 31 weeks if cost of time is applied.

Apart from quantifiable costs, the journey, around the M25 London Orbital Motorway and west on the M4, is crowded and dangerous, taking its toll of the energy of the travellers.

Due to the relatively short payback time, the managers felt it unnecessary to look at details which include:

- Transmission charges
- Maintenance
- Power charges
- Studio space
- Consumables

- Lighting
- Furniture

A high value was placed, by all the personnel who travelled, on face-to-face meetings with colleagues. Designing and manufacturing high-technology components requires the facility to pore over technical drawings, consult computer simulations and data, see the manufacturing processes and handle the finished product. In addition, experts, managers and junior staff could meet their opposite numbers, meetings which facilitated good working relationships between the two groups, normally separated by up to 3 hours of driving.

4.4.1.2   The equipment

£107 000 ($149 000) plus an estimated £7000 ($9940) per annum maintenance bought a BT set consisting, in both locations, of two personnel cameras, each preset to focus on three delegates giving a range of six presettings, with zoom close-up on to each place. The presettings are coordinated with table and chairs placed in fixed positions. For crowd scenes, at least another six delegates can stand behind the six seated ones and Thorn EMI Electronics had managed up to 15 delegates, all clearly viewed by the two cameras. The main cabinet, some 6 feet long and 3 feet high, also houses three screens—a 'confidence' monitor which shows the picture being transmitted and two large screens which show the remote studio. In 'preview' mode, one of the large screens displays documents, personal computer screens and other displays (see Chapter 6.7).

'Preview ' mode displays the subjects of two further cameras fixed at one side of the tables, one focused on a whiteboard across the room and the other focused on an overhead projector immediately below it. For a further £7000 ($9940) the third screen can also be used to display computer screens, enabling delegates to bring their laptops into the meeting and display data and visuals. A memory stores the last document/picture transmitted or received, which can be recalled from memory.

The equipment is controlled by a remote device, held by the two chairmen (one in each location) of the meeting, who dictate who is on camera, and what is on display. Chairing meetings will never be the same again now the role is combined with that of a film director who can flatter and insult simply by switching people on or off screen. There will be a new industry training people how to succeed in videoconferenced meetings; e.g. Maynard Leigh, a major London training house for media appearances, already offer such courses.

4.4.1.3   Switching to videoconferencing

In January the first videoconferences were held and bookings were made ahead. Twelve o'clock to two o'clock was reserved for emergency use, only bookable the same day. Close attention was paid to users' comments and suggestions and by the end of the second month the managers related the following:

1. 10 to 12 hours had been utilised to allow large groups of 15 to 20 personnel to meet their opposite numbers. They took 15 minutes per group, sitting and standing, and were introduced to people they may have telephoned for years but had never seen. Appearing on television was most enjoyable for everybody and an invaluable team-building exercise.

2. Delegates had to be reminded to clear the memory before leaving the room as documents which had been on display were stored and would show on screen to the next group to use the facility.

3. The transmission was only as secure as a telephone call and therefore confidential information could not be displayed or discussed. The managers were considering an encryption device and were aware that optical fibre cables are extremely difficult to tap into. They felt the encryption device would be sufficient to protect any transmissions over public lines.

4. There was a pressing need to add a fax machine to the studio equipment and that was in hand. (Thorn EMI Electronics report that it is now installed.)

5. Having the delegates' name plates displayed on the tables would be useful.

6. Meetings had become more concise due to two factors. Firstly, people prepared more thoroughly, defined objectives more clearly and brought required information into the meeting. They also turned up on time. Secondly, the meeting times were booked and, as the facility was immediately popular and fully used, there was no time for meetings to run on.

7. Operating the equipment was simple and all delegates became comfortable with the medium within a few minutes. The majority could quickly forget the medium and the novelty of seeing themselves on screen and could behave normally.

8. It was felt that there was good training value in people seeing and hearing themselves on the monitor screen, which would improve presentation and communication skills.

9. Most delegates found the overhead lighting intrusive and tiring. The managers at Wells had reduced the recommended power and had angled the lights away from delegates with no perceptible loss of picture clarity, but at the Crawley end people were still exposed to the full glare. In both studios, delegates found they needed a break from the artificial lighting and from 'being on camera' after an hour. The managers recommend comfort breaks at least every hour in extended meetings.

10. Delegates missed their days out, particularly those who had been used to leaving suburban Crawley and driving to beautiful, rural Wells, with a good lunch and a quiet hotel to round out the day. The escape from routine and the space to think one's own thoughts while travelling may be important for refreshing memories or allowing new ideas to emerge. Such recreation may have to be structured into the working year in some other way.

The verdict was overwhelmingly in favour of the new technology and it seems likely that Thorn EMI Electronics will extend its use by plugging in to

ISDN (Integrated Services Digital Network, see Chapter 6.1) public lines, to enable them to videoconference with customers and with their USA corporations. Savings on air fares, hotel bills, executive time and individuals' stress will accelerate the repayment period considerably.

4.4.2 International videoconferencing: example

Inertia, or 'if it works don't fix it' thinking, keeps the old patterns of travelling to meetings in existence, even where videoconferencing would obviously save time, money and stress. On an international scale the savings can be substantial.

Table 4.4 gives possible costs by a US/UK international business, with main offices in New York and Brussels whose top 20 managers meet in New York twice a year, 15 of them travelling by air.

Table 4.4

Air fares	$ 10 500	£7 400
Hotel bills, 2 nights	$ 4 500	£3 150
Travelling time—15 hours round trip executives		
Output value—say $160 per hour	$36 000	£25 350
Costs per meeting	$ 51 000	£35 900
Costs per annum	$102 000	£71 800

The annual cost of $102 000 (£71 800) would pay a quarter of the costs of a system suitable to switch the two offices onto videoconferencing, and the transmission charges would be less than the costs of taxi fares for the traditional meetings.

4.4.3 Reducing costs of equipment

Mobile units are available which can be wheeled into any office where there is a suitable telephone line and plugged in to a standard wall socket. The price of such units is likely to fall and the amount of use to increase, giving an even better cost/benefit equation than for the Thorn EMI Electronics setup. For security transmissions and for ready access to the peripherals, however, dedicated studios may remain more convenient and necessary. The cost of studio equipment is also likely to reduce significantly and will put executives to the task of cost-justifying journeys to meetings instead of teleworking them.

4.5 OFFICE PROPERTY

Teleworking is most commonly practised by employers with large office staffs. The most obvious saving is 11 sq m (120 sq ft) of office space for each teleworker, which in city centres can cost from £100 to £650 per sq m or from $12 to $60 per sq ft per year, for rent and local property taxes; an average of $2880 (£2028) a year, which may be doubled by heating, lighting, maintenance, security and other property costs to cost over $5500 (£3870) per annum.

Less obvious is teleworking applied to high-tech research and manufacturing units, like those of Thorn EMI Electronics in the above example. With good quality videophones or videoconferencing, engineers and designers are able to discuss and show products and designs with clarity and can do so from home based laboratories or from customers' premises. Previously necessary workbench meetings can be reduced. Manufacturing industry property has been cheaper than offices but high-technology science and business park rents have narrowed the gap and this, with the larger average space per person of *circa* 30 sq m (300 sq ft) gives very similar costs per person.

Rationalising floor space, introducing shared desks and workbenches and combining these with teleworking will enable permanent reductions in area and costs. The savings are from the 25% to 40% of workspaces which are unused on any one day in the average commercial building (see Chapter 7.1).

Teleworking in a unit of 2000 personnel, with 500 working at home or out at customers on any one day, enables property costs of $2.75M (£1.94M) a year to be cut.

The costs include capital expenditure on telecommunications equipment, team training to accustom people to sharing central workspace, and home-office heating and lighting allowances. After costs, the property savings are in excess of $2M (£1.4M) a year.

4.6   SUMMARY OF EMPLOYERS' COSTS AND BENEFITS

The employers' costs and benefits can be calculated under the following headings:

EFFECTIVENESS

- Change in output or deliverables:
  —Quantity
  —Quality

- Change in employment costs:
  —Salary and expenses
  —Support staff
  —Office space and overheads
  —Tax deductible expenses
  —Training costs and staff gross revenue

- Change in motivation:
  —Hours worked

—Recruitment
—Retention
—Core team responses
—Health and energy

TRAVEL

- Commuting:
  —Company car expenses
  —Season tickets
  —Time lost by transport problems

- Local business journeys:
  —Travel costs
  —Communications costs
  —Meetings time
  —Productive time
  —Results or measurables

- Long distance business journeys:
  —Time travelling
  —Productive time
  —Air and hotel bills
  —Results or measurables
  —Communications costs

PROPERTY AND LOCATIONS

- Central office space per person cost

- Home/remote office cost

- Sick building syndrome, time lost

- Reuse of liberated space

- Need for large group work

- Effect on corporate culture

- Value of dispersed locations:
  —Customer contact
  —Colleague contact

- Team building and training by example

- Equipping central buildings or dispersed offices

ENVIRONMENTAL

- Clean Air Act, legal compliance:
  —National or federal laws
  —State, county or city laws

- Energy consumption per employee:
  —Travel
  —Office construction
  —Heat, light and power

- Organisation's environmental report:
  —Statutory report
  —Public image

4.6.1 Example of city savings

Table 4.5 shows calculations for an employer with 20 managers working virtually full time at home who previously commuted into central London. The costings reflect an ideal reuse of office space which was not achieved, due to the 1991–1993 collapse of office values and the large amount of surplus space.

Assuming reuse of office space the employer reduces costs by $30 676 (£21 303) per teleworker each year. Similar exercises on less expensive space in Manchester, UK, showed $11 360 (£8000) a year saved, and for a Birmingham, UK, factory office $8946 (£6300) per teleworker per annum.

Table 4.5 Corporate detailed costing of teleworking for 20 senior teleworkers.

Exceptional costs of change, divided by 5 years:

	£
New equipment, £3550 x 20	71 000
Manager's time, 70 hours @ £35/hour	2 450
Estimated loss of production @ £35 / hr	44 800
External course/consultants' fees	1 000
Less: retaining trained personnel	−(50 000)
Total over 5 years	**£−(69 250)**
Total per year	**£−(13 850)**

	Pre-Teleworking	Post-Teleworking	Difference
Annual office expenses:	£		£
Rent	86 400		86 400
Rates	21 600		21 600
Secretarial support / space electricity / air conditioning / heating	12 672	3 000	9 672
Building maintenance garage / parking spaces / fees	2 160		2 160
Buildings insurance security	10 800	4 000	6 080
Washroom / leisure facilities	2 496		2 496
Sick building syndrome	13 440		13 440
Clothing allowances	300		300

Continued overleaf

Table 4.5   (*continued*)

	Pre-Teleworking	Post-Teleworking	Difference
Annual commuting expenses:	£		£
Cars, capital per annum	no change	no change	no change
Car running costs	18 894	3 750	15 144
Train / bus fares / London loading adjustment	86 400	72 000	14 400
Time lost / disruption / sickness epidemic	11 200		11 200
Annual operating expenses:			
Teleworkers' salaries / fees / secretarial salaries / London loading	56 000	28 000	28 000
Managers' time	[3760 hrs]	[4888 hrs]	[−1128 hrs]
multiply by rate (£35/hour)			−(39 480)
Colleagues' time × rate,secretarial support time × wage, plus costs	164 500		164 500
Equipment (incl. secretarial), furniture, machines, Telecoms: rent / buy	see equipment line above		
Telecoms call charges	15 000	19 500	−(4 500)
Office contents insurance	—	—	—
Tea/coffee/food, etc.	—	—	—
Productivity up 11%:			
Productive hours x £35 per teleworker	[1410 hrs]	[1565 hrs]	£108 500
TOTAL			£439 912
Saving per teleworker per annum			£21 303

Achieving a saving of £21 303 ($30 250) per teleworker as shown in Table 4.5 may be possible in a central city office but provincial firms will find the numbers reduced in proportion to their distance from the city centre, just as rents and commuting costs are reduced.

4.7   AN AMERICAN CASE STUDY

A large US insurance company, with 1500 personnel in its Information Technology department, launched a telecommuting pilot project for 40 people in late 1990 and early 1991, termed a 'Home Access' programme.

The 40 teleworkers represent three types of work undertaken in the Systems Information Division:

● Production support—after-hours, emergency problem solving when the processors fail

- Overtime work—normal late after-hours working
- Pure teleworking—programmers requiring long hours of uninterrupted concentration

4.7.1 Background

The pilot project was approached with great care and long preparation, starting by analysing the problem in November 1989 and launching the first home offices in October 1990, followed by the others in the first quarter of 1991.

The Systems Information Division came under a particularly heavy workload early in 1989 when insurance products were redesigned. Personnel were required to put in regular overtime, often travelling home for a meal and then returning in the evening. Faults that developed and special supervision tasks had to be dealt with by specialists and managers, who were telephoned and brought from their homes during the evening or night. The mainframe computer may have had to stand idle until a specialist arrived and dealt with a problem.

With an increasing reliance on more sophisticated computers, the company needed to recruit higher-skilled, computer literate programmers, who were scarce in the surrounding area. Teleworking was considered as a means of helping this company attract these scarce workers, thus giving this company a competitive recruiting edge. It was also considered as a possible way to employ these skills from a distance, without the need for relocation.

4.7.2 Action

In July 1989 a task force was set up to study the costs and benefits of applying teleworking to the immediate difficulties being experienced. In November 1989 the task force called in a telework consultant to help plan the 'Home Access' programme. The plans were discussed with middle level managers and selection from a group of volunteers began in July 1990. Training the potential teleworkers took place in October 1990, though some of them had already commenced working at home in August and September. Technical and training problems delayed some of the home teleworkers from making the change. These were overcome by the end of the first quarter of 1991 when the 40 selected volunteers were established as homeworkers.

4.7.3 Operation

The care taken in planning did not result in stereotyped equipment or rigid timetables for the teleworkers. It did ensure that the work required was performed with all the confidentiality and security expected of insurance companies.

Teleworkers chose their own (IBM compatible) desktop and laptop computers. Most had a modem link to central office but a few simply carried diskettes to and from central office (see Chapter 5.9.10). Time at home and time at the office were agreed weekly in advance between teleworkers and managers, but both were prepared to change the schedule for urgent matters.

Evaluation meetings held in February 1991 found that only minor problems accompanied the start of the project, implying that the teleworkers, their managers and their core-team colleagues made it work efficiently. Further evaluation meetings were planned to include members of the teleworkers' households, to assess the effects of the 'Home Access' programme on all those involved.

The consultants to 'Home Access' believe the programme will be extended to involve more people from the same department and also to open up similar projects in three other departments.

4.7.4 Comments

Due to confidentiality undertakings, the contractual and financial details of this project remain under wraps, but in general terms some financial information can be extrapolated from the published reports.

The motivation for teleworking was not primarily to do with time wasted commuting, or the need to attract people to commute long distances (at high costs). While the latter was a planned outcome for the insurance company, i.e. the ability to hire experts at a distance as the local labour pool failed to produce enough high calibre specialists, it was not put into effect in the period of this study. Commuting for the Information Services Division team was relatively easy. The average time to drive to work was only 30 minutes, into a small city with relatively clear roads. On the traditional overtime system, operatives had enough time to drive home, eat and drive back again, without too much waste of time and energy.

The motivation was not to reduce the direct costs of office space, often the most visible financial benefit to employers. The office space was retained (though it might be argued that having 40 people provide their own floor space on any working shift releases about 5000 sq ft for other uses) and the teleworkers had effectively a desk at central office whenever they required one. It is likely that office space costs increased as the teleworkers' home expenses were reimbursed.

The main motivation for the company was to find a more efficient way of tackling a high-technology, team task, without disrupting the flow of work and without alienating any key personnel. It was a matter of using the human resources of the company in an intelligent manner, to produce the same output (keeping the system running smoothly and producing professional level documents), with less risk of failure and more time to do the job properly.

The extra resource released by the changes, to everybody's benefit, demonstrates again that the single highest value to an employer of teleworking is increased effectiveness (see Chapter 4.3) and a better motivated workforce. In this case 40 people working at home three days a week, having worked overtime with an extra round-trip commute each day, releases over 11 000 hours a year, normally spent fretting through traffic. As the company had planned from the outset, the computer programmers, thought to be 12 of the 40 teleworkers, would win their uninterrupted hours of concentration in which to produce a greater quantity and better quality of computer systems. On standard calculations, using a three-day teleworking schedule, they would avoid office politics and gossip to the tune of 2500 productive hours a year.

4.7.5 Financial benefits

On a professional ACTGR (Average Contribution to Gross Revenue) rate of $60 an hour (see Chapter 4.3.4) the total of 13 500 hours a year is worth $810 000 to the Department's budget and to the company's profits. Recovering only a part of that benefit, leaving the teleworkers and their families to personally benefit from the rest of the released time, explains the success of this quietly formulated, low key pilot project.

4.8 LOMBARD: TWO YEARS OF TELEWORKING

Lombard North Central (Lombard), Redhill, Surrey, is the largest finance house in the UK, employing some 3500 people, with a high proportion within 20 miles of London. The Deputy Director of Group Services (at the time of writing) kindly authorised the following report on Lombard's experience of teleworking.

> In 1991 Lombard launched a carefully planned and well-considered teleworking project for 10 professionals aged between 25 and 45, five men and five women, and monitored it for two years. One teleworker, a married man with a family, opted to return to the core team and was replaced, keeping the number up to 10.
>
> (Lombard/Rover Finance has 100 home-based sales representatives who are not regarded by Lombard as teleworkers.)

4.8.1 Contract and preliminaries

> Clear terms and conditions were agreed and were drafted as an addendum to the existing employment contract by Lombard's internal lawyers. The NatWest Staff Association and BIFU (the Banking, Insurance and Finance Union) were consulted and some of their concerns met by including the right of return to the core team at head office and the reassurance that all teleworkers would be volunteers.

The teleworkers spend, on average, nine days every two weeks at home and one day at head office. They must work at head office whenever required and the company has the option to recall any and all the teleworkers to work at head office as before, as the company sees fit.

Extra expenses were agreed to cover heat, light and power. Travel between home and head office is paid by the teleworkers.

Targets and means of measuring deliverables were set and a base for comparison was drawn up. The professional work was mostly Information Technology related and business research and analysis.

Further levels of security were acquired to control access to the mainframe computer and encryption and token exchange devices fitted to the teleworkers' business telephone lines, which the company installed in each home. Security of data transmission is now considered to be as effective as at any other company location.

Family consultations were held and managers visited each home to see the home environment and to advise on Health and Safety at Work issues and on physical security.

4.8.2   Lombard's teleworking in practice

Teleworkers were afraid of being sidelined and of becoming less visible in terms of consideration for promotions. This abated as three of them won promotion in the first two years.

All found the additional equipment simple to use and required no specific extra training.

Some managers in the core team were fearful of the 'how can you control staff if you can't see them' implications of the project but became committed to extending it.

Difficulties were experienced in monitoring results against the baseline but these were overcome.

Work output initially increased by 20% and after some months settled at 10% increase. The quality of work remains consistently higher. Traditional hours of work are not an issue and some teleworkers defer work and then make up their targets with an intensive period of activity.

Sick leave reduced to half the level for this group compared to the previous two years and remains at half the level at three days per annum. Loss of time due to commuting problems no longer occurs.

The high-tech head office space allows for reuse of the teleworkers' desks. Mobile locker units and shared desks are available for the teleworkers' time at head office. Lombard have numbers of peripatetic staff, making flexible desk sharing (hot-desking) practical.

Space used at home varies greatly, averaging 65 sq ft and, intriguingly, the managers report that some teleworkers wear business suits during work hours, which must help to differentiate between work-time and leisure-time.

A planned communication schedule is operated between head office and teleworkers which is reviewed from time to time.

Two of the teleworkers retain company cars and no mileage allowances are paid to any teleworkers.

The teleworkers saved the company in winter 1991 when a snowfall cut off the main computer installation and technical support staff could not get in to work. The teleworkers had no difficulties getting to work on-line and had sufficiently powerful equipment to enable them to keep the mainframe operating for the group. (A similar story comes from Inverness in Scotland in winter 1992, when snow stopped some of BT's operators getting to work, but the home-based, teleworking operators volunteered to work extra shifts to cover for their colleagues and keep the service running normally.)

All the teleworkers report an improved quality of life and would like to continue working at home.

4.8.3   Money matters

Lombard calculate they save £2500 ($3550) per teleworker per annum, enabling them to pay back the setup costs in 18 months. The teleworkers benefit by an average of £650 ($923) a year.

The heat, light and power and business telephone line charges, reimbursed to teleworkers or paid direct by the employer, are tax-relieved.

In the company's own words, 'huge costs' have been saved by retaining trained personnel who would have left Lombard if teleworking were not available. The training, knowledge build-up and continuity of professional staff are highly valued. Recruitment costs have also been saved.

4.8.4   Next steps

The current project is considered a success and will continue. There are plans to extend it to other staff when current downsizing has been completed.

A further plan to telework clerical staff is in hand at the head office, and a subsidiary company, Lombard Tricity Finance, is also launching a clerical teleworking pilot project of six people, drawing on the parent company's experience and helped by BT's teleworking experts.

4.8.5   Comments

The financial results seem to be conservatively and carefully calculated, as might be expected from a bank. If the ACTGR (Average Contribution to Gross Revenue) output formula is applied (see Chapter 4.3.4) then the 10% increase in productivity must contribute to the company some 1800 hours × 10% × £60 ($85) professional ACTGR, giving £10 800 ($15 336). The space at a modern high-tech office, which is re-used via desk-sharing and mobile lockers, is most probably 11 sq m (120 sq ft) per person, the national average space including common and circulation areas. The price of the space should include rent, local taxes, maintenance, energy and other building costs, which even in the current property crash may cost £5400 ($7668) a year per person.

Taking a long-term view, Lombard will ultimately benefit from the cash savings they have identified, the increased contribution to Gross Revenue and the saving of building related costs, to the extent shown in Table 4.6. Though not available yet to the employer, these benefits are possible and for 10 senior teleworkers will yield £187 000 ($265 000) per annum.

Table 4.6

Reduced employment costs	£2 500	$3 550
Increased ACTGR	£10 800	$15 300
Reduced property costs	£5 400	$7 650
Total per head	£18 700	$26 500

4.8.6   Environmental factors

As a subsidiary of the National Westminster Bank, one of a handful of UK companies to appoint an active Environmental Manager, Lombard might calculate the environmental effects. An average person commutes 15 miles per workday, in a car weighing 1.5 tonnes, which in its manufacture and disposal and propulsion (fuel) adds to pollution at approximately 25 pence per tonne mile. For the 10 professional teleworkers this calculates at £12 150 ($17 250) a year less pollution. The London public are spared 8.8 million litres (2.3 million US gallons) of noxious exhaust fumes each year, helping them to stay healthy. In office energy terms, if all the homes were previously occupied by day then there will ultimately be a net energy saving, reducing power station emissions (see Chapter 4.2 for details).

4.9   INDIVIDUAL BENEFITS AND COSTS

The costs and benefits to individuals are possibly one of the most important areas of advice to and of motivation for teleworkers. Whatever the environmental, national, and corporate or organisational budgets from teleworking, it is the impact on individuals which will hinder or enhance the growth of teleworking.

The information given here from both a UK and a USA perspective applies to most teleworkers in most countries. See the sections on taxation and costs and benefits to employers for more detail. However, the information and advice given, while based on experience and on case histories, is necessarily generalised and may not apply in particular cases. It is therefore not claimed to be complete or wholly accurate in any one case and individuals must consult their professional advisors or employers for accurate guidance for their teleworking budget and legal position.

Individuals should draw up a budget or forward plan of their proposed teleworking and consider the following from a financial point of view:

1. Commuting and travelling
2. Home office heating and power
3. Assistants wages
4. Child care
5. Office equipment, furniture and design
6. Stationery, postage and packing

7. Commuting
8. Insurance at home
9. Tax allowances and professional advice
10. Business and casual clothes
11. Food and beverages at home
12. Depreciation and upkeep of home office
13. Recreational time and costs
14. Sickness and keeping fit
15. Training and promotion at work
16. New skills gained and delegating
17. Cost of returning to core team
18. Cost of changing jobs
19. Contribution from employers
20. The value of time gained

An example of such a calculation is given in Table 4.7 for a homeworker living 30 miles from the office.

Table 4.7 Annual personal benefits and costs.

	Pre- Teleworking $	Post Teleworking $
Travel:		
Commuting @ 28 cents/mile	4 032	806[a]
Business: no change	—	—
Leisure @ 28 cents/mile (16% reduction)	4 000	3 360
Office:		
Light and power: increase 400%	200	800[a]
Heating: increase 250%	300	750[a]
Depreciation	100	500[a]
Furnishings and insurance	—	200[a]
Assistant	*Child care*	*Secretary*
	4 800	4 800[a]
Equipment and stationery:		
Capital: employer pays	—	—
Maintenance: employer pays	—	—
Personal use benefit say, $10 week	—	−(500)
Clothing:		
Business suits	300	100
Leisure outfits	200	300

Continued overleaf

Table 4.7 (*continued*)

	Pre- Teleworking $	Post Teleworking $
Meals:		
Office snacks, lunch etc.	1 200	240
Home snacks, lunch etc.	—	600
Beverages:		
Office coffee machine, 6/day	288	60
Home beverages, 4/day	—	100
Paid by employer:		
Travel costs: no change	—	—
Rent / electricity allowance	—	–(1 000)[a]
Uniform: not applicable	—	—
Taxation:		
Deductions allowed @ 30% tax	—	–(2 056)
Personal time used:[b]		
Commuting @ $15 per hour	10 800	2 160
Total net cost	26 220	11 220
Benefit to teleworker		**$15 000**

[a]These items are included in the tax relief.
[b]Personal time used calculated at assumed earning power for $27 000 per year working 1800 hours per year at $15 per hour.
The UK equivalent benefit would be approximately £16 500.

4.9.1 Employed teleworkers

Employed teleworkers will generally benefit as set out above. The main costs and benefits are identified in Table 4.7 which includes a $1000 or £700 contribution from the employer, which will probably be taxable unless offset by claims from the teleworker as depicted.

Budgeting Each case will differ and therefore each teleworker should anticipate the costs and benefits by setting out a budget. The tax allowances and charges will differ from country to country and from tax district to tax district within any one country. It is advisable for the teleworkers to persuade their employers to reach agreement with the Revenue Officers, although any agreement will still leave room for individual anomalies.

See Chapter 3.1 for detailed tax commentary.

Actual figures Teleworkers' budgets should be compared against actual costs and benefits, every six months, and discussed between them and their managers.

Valuing your own time Despite the sometimes bitter disputes over the past 100 years or more to win shorter working hours, the majority of employees do not address the question of how to value their own time. As something that would be fought for if any employer threatened to erode the rights to recreational time, it obviously has a high value to individuals. We price the marginal time at the beginning and end of working days (commuting time) at the amount an individual might earn per hour if they devoted that time to working.

Downside There are examples of unhappy home teleworkers. One-third of teleworkers may wish to return to the core team and it is advisable that the contract of employment should allow for this (see Chapter 2.6). Part of the motive for returning to central office may be hard cash; for people who live close to central office, perhaps walk or cycle to work, enjoy subsidised canteens, are issued with a uniform or overalls, switch off their home heating during the day and bask in the central office warmth, make some personal telephone calls, read their colleagues' newspapers and use office postage, stationery and other resources, the budget may well work against them.

A relatively small annual allowance to compensate for such costs will generally put the budget back in balance. It will not, however, compensate the trim, middle-aged woman who told her own story at a workshop on teleworking in 1990. She had enjoyed a few minutes' walk to work and relied on the subsidised office canteen for her main meals. When the local office closed, she was asked to telework rather than commute to the next town. She not only found it more expensive to work from home, heating her home all day, but, to add insult to injury, as she put it, she also put on weight.

4.9.2 Self-employed

The self-employed will in most countries benefit more than employed teleworkers from working at or from home.

Office costs Running a business, however small, from home inevitably incurs all the costs which renting commercial space would incur. Such costs, even if expended domestically prior to the business, are claimable against tax. An example is a domestic chair being pressed into service in the home-office and therefore becoming a claimable piece of office furniture. This inevitable blurring of domestic and business costs is generally beneficial to the teleworker, the downside being the invasion of privacy which occurs in having customers, suppliers and government officials calling.

Travelling One of the larger benefits is not only cutting out commuting time to and from a place of business, the costs of which are not tax deductible in most countries, but the fact that when the home is established as the office base, all business journeys start from the front door and the costs are fully tax deductible. Refer to Chapter 3.1 for more information.

4.9.3 Employed and self-employed

For both types of teleworker, the calculations are similar. In theory, but rarely found in practice, all expenses incurred in the course of business or employment can be claimed against tax. In practice, because governments promote entrepreneurs as putative employers (the 'small' or unquoted business sector employs up to 60% of the workforce) , self-employed people find it easier to win tax deductions than the employed. The largest benefit to both, however, is the reduction of commuting time and costs, not tax deductible by either sector. Commuting costs are considerable for the majority of the workforce and where the saved time is used for work, as is readily imagined in the case of the self-employed, the value of that time far outweighs any costs involved.

4.10 THE ECONOMICS OF TELECENTRES

Telecentres are being established in California, Hawaii, Jamaica, the UK, Paris, Japan and other parts of the world. The term includes telecottages, local centre working, satellite offices and other names (see Chapter 1.6.2). Telecentres contain workstations, typically between 10 and 20, equipped with office and communications technology. They cater for commuters who wish to reduce their mileage, and for nomadic workers who need occasional desk bases, and may be specific to one employer, shared by a number of employers or managed for public use.

4.10.1 Setting up a telecentre

Some telecottages are opened after very little cash expenditure, supported by educational institutions and government grants, with equipment donated by telephone and computer corporations. The costs, including donations, will however, follow the pattern below.

4.10.2 A 20-workstation telecentre

Including circulation areas (corridors, escalators, stairs), service areas (boiler room, switchboards) and common spaces (washrooms, general office, entrance hall), each person requires 120 sq ft (11 sq m). Allowing for three support staff, 2750 sq ft internal area and 3000 sq ft (280 sq m) external area is required—say a 75 ft (23 m) square 'footprint'. If a 'green field' site the land area will usually be double the footprint plus parking and access. For 23 cars, 10 000 sq ft (930 sq m) is needed.

4.10.3 Building structure

Telecentres are 'smart buildings' and as such require raised floors and concealed ceiling cavities to carry wiring and air conditioning to the workstations. A derelict building brought up to modern standards is perhaps 10% to 15% cheaper than building on a 'green field' site. This differential is smaller in the USA than in the UK as 'new' land and interest charges are substantially cheaper in America, where it can be cheaper to abandon derelict buildings and start anew. Interest charges in the 1980s added up to a third of all development costs to any building. The collapse of property prices and lower interest rates in the early 1990s helped to reduce finance costs.

4.10.4 Equipment

A telecentre aims to enable work at any level to be undertaken efficiently and to be transmitted to the tenants' central offices or clients. The equipment needs to be compatible with the tenants' IT skills and with modern central offices or networks. Plugs and junction boxes for tenants' portable computers and other peripherals are required.

To service 20 tenants, the general office requires two photocopiers, two fax machines and two laser or similar quality printers together with safes and fireproof cabinets. Stationery and stores capacity and security need to be greater than for the equivalent dedicated, traditional office. Advice is required on the most useful and robust telephone system and on the type and number of external lines or radio connections required.

A modern centre might include audio- and videoconference units.

Each workstation will typically occupy 60 sq ft (5.5 sq m) and be served with three or more telephone points and six power points. A tenant may require a desktop computer, a dedicated printer, facilities for a portable computer, a dedicated answerphone, a dedicated modem or ISDN (Integrated Services Digital Network) junction box and other facilities. A large desk, two chairs, and a lockable cabinet/filing drawer are basic requirements.

4.10.5 Capital costs

Table 4.8

	UK	USA
Land, 1/2 acre	£ 100 000	$ 80 000
Building costs	£ 150 000	$ 225 000
Air conditioning	£ 30 000	$ 40 000
Equipment and furniture	£ 120 000	$ 207 000
Design and project fees	£ 35 000	$ 35 000
Interest over 1 year	£ 18 000	$ 14,000
Car parking	£ 50 000	$ 70 000
Total development costs	£ 503 000	$ 671 000
Cost per workstation (20)	**£ 25 150**	**$ 33 550**

The costs of building and equipping a 20-workstation unit in an expensive commuter belt, 50 miles from a large city would be approximately as given in Table 4.8.

4.10.6   Running costs

A 20-unit telecentre requires the equivalent of one full-time manager to maintain services. The work is usually shared between two or three operatives.

Maintenance of the building is 2.5% of building costs per annum: approximately £7000 and $8500. Maintenance and updating of equipment costs *circa* 25% a year.

The approximate annual running costs are summarised in Table 4.9.

Table 4.9.

	UK	USA
Payroll	£ 20 000	$ 30 000
Building	£ 7 000	$ 8 500
Equipment	£ 30 000	$ 52 000
Overheads	£ 50 000	$ 60 000
Total running costs	£107 000	$ 150 000
Cost per workstation (20)	**£ 5 350**	**$ 7 500**

4.10.7   Alternative ownership and tenant policies

A telecentre could be operated profitably and commercially as an independent facility or by co-operative employers in a number of ways:

- Local government facility—non-profit making
- Consortium of employers—non-profit making
- Consortium of commuters—non-profit making
- Commercial facility—profit making
- Rented per workstation:
    —Long timeshare leases sold to employers
    —Annual timeshare leases sold to employers
    —Monthly licences let to individuals

4.10.8   Economics for employers

Assume workstations are occupied only for one eight-hour shift per day, for 5 days per week or 240 work days a year. Capital value remains constant. A 50-mile commute to the major city takes 1.5 to 2 hours per door-to-door journey, or up to 4 hours per day.

Costs are *circa* £1500 or $1200 per annum rent/interest per employee or workstation, and *circa* £5350 and $7500 per workstation per annum to maintain the unit.

Telecommuters are generally 45% more effective (productivity × quality × cost per unit) due to lower costs of employment, less tiring commuting, fewer hours lost through travel delays, fewer interruptions and fewer days' sick leave. Average Contribution to Gross Revenue (ACTGR) (see Chapter 4.3.4) is £43 ($78) which on an 1100 productive hour year gives £21 000 ($38 000) more contribution to Gross Revenues.

Assuming access to central office computers, telecentre tenants provide emergency back-up if transport disruptions prevent the core team from opening the main office on time (see Chapter 4.8).

Assuming central office space can be reused then the central office costs, rent, property taxes, maintenance, etc., can be saved.

Where an employee uses a telecentre for the majority of working days and is assisted with commuting costs (company car, mileage allowance, salary loading, season tickets etc.) then these costs may be renegotiated.

4.10.9   Economics for employees

On the same basis as in the previous section, the employee saves commuting costs for 50 miles of an average of £25 or $25 a day, i.e. annually £6000 or $6000.

An average of 2 hours a day or 480 hours a year (three full working months) of commuting time are saved.

Teleworkers report half the normal days' sick leave, thus saving medical fees and drug costs.

The employee may save on business clothes, depending on the culture at the telecentre and whether client meetings are attended. Four working days a week not wearing expensive suits for a year saves some £300 or $450.

Being home by six o'clock every evening gives more leisure and family time.

4.10.10   Economics for the environment

Heating and power will be little changed. Short-haul car commuting to a telecentre is equivalent to driving to a railway station, giving little change.

Travelling is a major polluter and saving 100-mile round trips for 20 people saves 720 000 tonne miles or 110 000 litres (29 000 US gallons) of fuel per year, which produces nearly 200 million litres (over 50 million US gallons) of exhaust gases—a net benefit for the environment.

4.10.11   Economics for the nation

Telecentres create more office and car parking space. They are usually one-shift offices, duplicating equipment and other resources.

Reduced travel reduces oil and car consumption (imports).

Telecentres are likely to create at least one permanent job local to the tele-centre, and building and maintenance work.

4.10.12 Siting a telecentre

Telecentres are ideally located near to railway stations in suburban areas where dormitory town commuters can reach them in a few minutes and where they will be convenient for telecommuters to journey to central office if required.

Existing unlet offices can be readily converted, creating local commercial activity without risking the blight of over-development.

Telecottages are often sited in rural areas of high unemployment where they provide training and recruit work.

Telecentres are ideal facilities for hotels, where meeting rooms and overnight accommodation already exist. They are also being planned for railway carriages, to enable long-distance rail travellers to be mobile tele-workers.

Libraries are regarded as ideal telecentre sites.

4.10.13 Tax allowances

The normal tax allowances on equipment, furniture and fittings are cur-rently available. There is an impact on fuel and carbon taxes and on com-pany car mileage related taxes.

Telecentres are also dealt with in Chapter 1.6.2.

4.11 PRICING YOUR COMMUTE

The verb 'to commute' has given birth to a useful noun. Thanks to the infi-nite flexibility of the Anglo-American language which has expanded its dic-tionary to be the largest and the most widespread of all languages, 'the commute' has been created. It is a noun which sums up all the hustle, bustle and hassle of transporting over 400 million commuters every working day.

The commute is an expensive, and relatively recent, practice for mankind and it is recognised as the single largest cause of street-level air pollution on the planet. People travel to work on horseback, on ox-carts, walk, ride buses, or cycle, in cars, trains, planes, and helicopters. The combined weight of vehicles and people on the move is immense (see Chapter 4.1.1) and corre-lates to the pollution caused and the costs of transporting them.

Commuting is a socially circular activity; the least and most powerful tend to have the shortest commutes while the middle classes live many miles from their workplaces. Millions of blue collar factory workers still live in the shadows of the smokestacks and walk or cycle very short distances to and from work. Some car factory workers increase their status by driving a

1.5 tonne car a very short distance to work. White collar workers move further out into the suburbs (away from the noise and smell of factories or barren high-rise offices) from where they commute. Managers and professionals move even further away from the monstrous factories and offices and commute many miles, in larger and newer cars, from and to exclusive settlements, in which commerce and industry are but distant, impolite memories. Highly successful entrepreneurs move to remote, inaccessible retreats and commute by aircraft over the huddled masses of canned humans below. The circle closes where many top politicians (Clinton at the White House, Major at Number Ten, The Queen at Buckingham Palace, Yeltsin at the Kremlin), top academics (cloistered in their ivy league towers) and business magnates (with penthouses above their offices), live as close to their workplaces as do the factory hands.

Celebrities and VIP's apart, the rule is that the higher up the earnings scale, the further the commute and the more time and money spent in the process.

Commuting has traditionally created traffic jams or, worse, gridlocks. Most commuters can relate personal experiences of being trapped for hours in immobilised public or private vehicles, on roads, rails or underground. Trapped commuters run engines to keep warm or cool, generating chemical smogs which they try to avoid breathing by running vehicle air conditioners, which create more chemical smog ... which they try to avoid breathing by upgrading the air conditioning ... which creates more air pollution ... and so on, into infinite regress.

Some economists believe that removing the motivation to travel, into ever more densely packed centres in ever larger, ever more airtight, ever more air-conditioned, ever slower vehicles, would collapse the world financial system. Some go further and see it as a vital public duty for all able-bodied citizens to join in commuting; to increase economic consumption. They reason that the majority cannot conceive of any better ways to burn off energy and time and create demand and that, therefore, commuting for at least 10 hours a week ought to be a mandatory responsibility for all world citizens.

4.11.1   What does commuting cost your business?

Over the past 15 years, some major employers have relocated their central offices, e.g. from New York City to Stamford, Connecticut (General Electric) or from London to Portsmouth (IBM-UK). Government departments have relocated to create jobs in depressed areas and new-age industries have sprung up outside existing major conglomerations, such as the famous electronics industry in Silicon Valley, California.

The very successes of these satellite developments, taking pressure off traditional major city centres, have attracted more industry and commerce, created more jobs in those places, more homes, more roads, more wealth and, inevitably, more commuting. The commuting is, however, vectored between suburban areas, while existing mass transit systems are still directed to major city centres; these 'cross-town' commutes can create serious traffic jams in previously quiet backwaters.

Businesses may have grown in or relocated to an area where commuting is still relatively hassle free, where personnel have short and sweet rural commutes which they enjoy. Half the workforce, however, still commutes to a few major cities, which are steadily increasing in both area and population. As the size of cities increases, the traditional status of living a fashionable distance away from work drives commuters to greater distances. The accumulated commuting and commercial journeys, in any densely populated area, increase costs to all businesses, irrespective of their own commuting patterns.

Traditional cost analysis methods, based on historical costs, may not produce an accurate picture of the real costs of transport. A shortcut for calculating the costs of commuting (or commercial journeys) is to calculate the weight moved and the miles travelled. The information can be collected by issuing a suitably worded questionnaire to each employee, set out as follows. (The weights shown are for 140-pound (63.5 kg) people travelling alone in a medium-sized car or on a full train or a full bus.)

Corporation .... Location ....

Daily commute:
1. Car Users No. ...... @ 3887 pounds × total miles .... = ... pound miles
2. Train Users No...... @ 2428 pounds × total miles .... = ... pound miles
3. Bus Users No........ @ 451 pounds × total miles .... = ... pound miles
4. Cyclists No .... @ 160 pounds × total miles .... = ... pound miles
5. Walkers .... @ 140 pounds × total miles .... = ... pound miles

GIVES Total pound miles = ... Pound miles per work-day

Average daily time Home–Office–Home ....hrs .... mins

Average daily cost $ .....cents ... £ .....pence ...

PLEASE LIST THE MILES YOU COMMUTE BY EACH OF THE ABOVE METHODS ON AN AVERAGE WORKING DAY. THE ROUND TRIP FIGURE FROM HOME TO OFFICE AND BACK TO HOME SHOULD BE USED.

The cost per person varies according to the degree of luxury as defined by the space, and therefore weight, that individuals need on the journey. For example, a large luxury car used by one person in the UK will cost between 40 pence and 50 pence per mile, including fuel, depreciation, insurance, road tax and all other costs. Motoring is less expensive in the USA due to fuel costing about one-third of the European price and vehicles being about one-quarter cheaper to buy and maintain. These 'local' variations mask the real 'world' cost of travel which can be measured in common units, such as weight, litres of fuel, life of rolling stock, etc., and which may ultimately be converted to an 'Energy Dollar' universal unit (see below).

However, for a single business, the direct costs are the most valid to use and accurate costs per mile are published by travel associations and by tax offices. The Internal Revenue Service in the USA allow a conservative 28 cents per mile, including all costs.

Common denominator To arrive at an across-the-board average cost per US ton (or tonne) mile for travel by any of the above five methods (car, train, bus, bike or foot), take the official costs per mile and divide by the weight of the car or vehicle. This figure will work, within tolerable limits, as a common multiple to price all forms of transport.

For example the 1992/93 IRS figure of 28 cents per mile relates to cars with one occupant weighing about 3750 lbs or 1.9 US tons. At 28 cents a mile the ton mile cost is 28 cents divided by 1.9 tons or 15 cents.

The UK equivalent works out to 22 pence a tonne mile.

Energy dollars The concept of reducing travel costs to the fuel, industrial and human energy consumed and expressing them in a common form such as 'energy dollars' is not yet, and might never be, a reality. Note that the costs per US ton mile used above include distortions such as taxation, customs duties and perhaps subsidies, reducing the commercial accuracy of the dollar (or sterling) costs. Currency-based calculations should, eventually, be able to provide a true measure. Scientists focus on the chemical reactions to provide a common measure, such as tonnes of carbon released into the atmosphere (see Chapter 4.2), but that oldest of all economic measures, money, might yet come to place a truer and more understandable value on the events. Money prices strive, through market and other forces, to value all the energy, including human energy, inherent in and added to raw materials such as crude oil. An 'energy dollar' value should therefore reflect all the energy, direct and indirect, which has gone into all the processes, both revenue and capital, reflecting all the energies consumed (basic crude oil, food for staff, pipeline laying, advertisers' staff, transport and distribution and all other costs).

4.11.2 Worked example

A real exercise (Table 4.10) will take the more complex route of collating all the questionnaires and accounting for people who use cars and trains and buses on the same day. This example assumes 500 straightforward personnel who use only one type of transport each.

It can be seen that this business pays $914 811 salary (plus employers' share of payroll taxes) to fund 3 days a week commuting which might be teleworked. The annual time spent commuting is equivalent to $9M of output. If the time saved by 3 days' telecommuting was worked, the output value would be $5.4M ACGTR for 500 people. This whole commuting time saved could not of course be recovered in productive time but 25% of it might be. This would give a $1.35M boost to the company's output at no extra costs.

Table 4.10 Calculation of commuting costs for 500 people.

Corporation *Global Faxnet Inc.*   Location *Philadelphia*

Daily commute:

Commuters	No	Weight (lb)	x Total miles	Pound miles
1. Car users	425	@ 3 887	12 750	49.5 M
2. Train users	40	@ 2 428	4 000	9.7M
3. Bus users	20	@ 451	300	0.1M
4. Cyclists	10	@ 160	100	0.01M
5. Walkers	5	@ 140	10	—
Total	500			59.3M

Divide 59.3M pound miles by 2000 to give 29 650 US ton miles (26 892 tonne miles) (43 269 tonne km)

Cost at 15 cents per US ton mile	= $4 447 a day

Say 3 days/week telecommuting = $640 368 a year
For a full 240 days a year = $1 067 280 a year

3 days/week, grossed up for 30% tax = $914 811 a year

Average daily round trip commute = 1 hour 15 mins
Average daily cost = $8.89 (£5.92)

Total annual commuting time (500 people x 240 days x 1 hour 15 mins) = 150 000 hours
Worktime value at ACTGR (150 000hours x $60) = $9M

Notes: All costs include depreciation. ACTGR means Average Contribution to Gross Revenue.

4.11.3 Comments

The rationale for regarding commuting costs ($914 811 in the above example) as an employers' responsibility is that the corporation, company, organisation or firm, consisting of all its personnel ('Company' means just that—a group of people accompanying each other in a commercial adventure; 'Corporation' borrows 'corps' from French—a body of people—and '...ation' signifies work being done; the often impersonalised 'multinational corporation' is in fact just a bunch of skilled people trying to make a living together) ultimately picks up the tab for all the normal and reasonable living expenses, including commuting costs, for all staff.

In recruiting staff, employers must offer a salary package sufficient to cover all reasonable living and travelling costs, net of tax, appropriate to the job specification. Viewed as a unit or team, employers and employees all eat out of the same dish and pay their bills out of the same treasure chest.

As teleworking becomes commonplace, new firms will spring up in the form of networks, not reliant on location (Chapter 1.6), enabling those firms to recruit personnel living less expensively in remote areas and without the costs of regular commuting. It may be that the budget currently allocated to commuting will still be paid by the employer but used by employees to make an efficient home-office, attend more group training and allow for extra leisure pursuits.

However the salary package eventually comes to be structured, the company (all its members) will have more time and more cash available as a result of teleworking.

The organisation should examine:

- Can commuting costs be cut to the benefit of employees, thus improving the employment package and increasing the quality of staffing?

- Can time spent commuting be put to better use, either for the employees exclusively or sharing the benefit with the employer?

Will teleworking address both these issues? The answer is 'Yes' as other costings in this book demonstrate (see Chapters 4.1 and 4.9). Teleworking cuts commuting time, costs and effort and gives individuals more leisure and family time, which in turn improves 'effectiveness'.

At a more detailed level, the costs of commuting should take into account time lost by travel delays (gridlock), days of sick leave and loss of concentration and output due to (excessive) office politics and sick building syndrome.

In a similar manner the entire transport costs of the organisation can be analysed including service vans, goods deliveries and business travel. Standard units need to be chosen for each sector which can then be reduced to ton miles or tonne km.

4.12 NATIONAL CONSIDERATIONS

4.12.1 Environmental legislation

The commercial impact of environmental improvements is a major consideration for all organisations and, in the USA, includes the pollution caused by their employees' travel.

Environmental laws have been drafted and are being introduced at every level of government throughout the developed world. All organisations will be obliged to produce an environmental policy statement and to establish an internal environmental audit team. Draft EC regulations already require this of UK organisations and the USA is further advanced with federal environmental laws incorporating air pollution control under which vehicle emissions have been controlled since 1965. Telecommuting is promoted by state authorities in California, New York and other US states, as contributing to the aim of zero vehicle emissions by 2010.

Banking on the environment Of immediate financial concern in the UK is a draft European Commission directive which *The Times* reported on 14

January 1992. The possible effect will be to make financiers responsible for their client companies eco-audits and for the eco-impact of assets pledged against loans. NatWest Bank, along with BT and others, have appointed an environmental manager to guide their policy and are selecting environmentally safer projects to finance.

Commuter polluters Moving people to and from work is expensive and consumes great amounts of energy. Most transport systems are not eco-friendly. In the USA some 120 million people commute daily to work, an average round trip of 20 miles. Fuel consumption is 1 US gallon per day per person or 29 billion US gallons a year. Increasing telecommuting from its present *circa* 4% to the predicted 15% would save 3 billion US gallons of fuel and could leave the nation self-sufficient in oil.

85% (556 billion passenger kilometres) of all UK travel is by car and 40% is commuting. This 40% computes to burning 34 billion litres of fuel a year or 136 million litres per work-day, adding gases to the street-level air we breathe at the rate of 245 billion litres of exhaust gas per day, which then ascend to increase the global greenhouse syndrome.

Over 50% of the greenhouse gases or global warming gases are produced by vehicles.

Family planning In Oxford in 1989 parents were advised not to have small (young) children in buggies or walking on the pavements at vehicle exhaust level, due to the health risk of diesel fumes from a surfeit of buses competing for passengers in the main shopping areas.

Hearth and home versus office power Modern offices are often better heated and air-conditioned than the office workers' homes. Setting aside the price discounts for bulk use of power, the environmental cost of heating/cooling offices must be compared to the extra energy consumed by a teleworker's home office.

On balance, previously unheated homes may consume slightly more energy than equivalent office space. Homes already occupied and heated all day, then used for teleworking, will reduce the national energy bill.

Teleworking occupies houses 24 hours a day and is therefore a more economic use of the building structure.

In three years of research, only one example of a home in the office has been found, but the 1990s slump in property prices is creating a convergence of commercial and residential rents, encouraging mixed use of office buildings in areas where traditionally no households have existed for decades.

Company cars In the UK, employers are still the major purchasers of cars, which they give to employees as part of their salary package. This is rare in the USA where vehicles and running costs are considerably less than in Europe. In theory, but not yet found in practice, teleworkers do not need a company car. They will typically use their cars 80% less than when commuting, creating a saving of £3000 ($4260) per annum, which translates into less industrial activity and therefore less energy consumption and pollution.

4.12.2 Health

Health is affected by the working environment and teleworking alters the balance and costs in the following areas:

- Commuting in crowded trains and buses spreads illness.

- Working in crowded offices spreads illness.

- The street-level air pollution caused by each unit (litre or gallon) of fuel burnt creates 1800 units of noxious gases, increasing respiratory disease and asthma.

- Sick building syndrome where the air, light and noise conditions can adversely affect health.

Teleworkers are reported to lose fewer days per year from illness than the national average of 8 days. Official sick leave has been found to halve (see Chapter 4.8), saving 20 million working days for 5 million US telecommuters, and some 4 million working days in the UK. This may be due to their ability to choose their own working conditions and to lower exposure to germs.

4.12.3 The main energy factors

Transport An increase to 15% teleworking (USA 18 million, UK 3.3 million) would reduce greenhouse and street-level exhaust gases and reduce traffic jams for all commuters.

Heat and light Increased teleworking encourages multirole use of buildings and reduces energy consumption, though a few teleworkers will consume more energy, not less.

Building costs Up to £8000 or $11 000 per teleworker could be saved, reducing consumption of tropical timber, still used extensively in new office blocks, and other resources.

Company cars At 15% teleworking in the UK up to 4 million cars would last five times as long, saving the energy for making and/or importing 1.6 million cars a year, a direct benefit to employers. Individual car owners in the USA would benefit from lower mileage and longer life cars, with an impact on imported vehicle costs.

4.12.4 Cleaning-up on profits

Commercial and financial consequences of teleworking will become inseparable from environmental considerations as the boundaries and responsibilities of organisations extend up and down the supply chain to include clean-up costs. Definitions of profits are having to incorporate eco-issues and the advent of a standard 'energy dollar' (Chapter 4.11.1) may be imminent.

Teleworking ranks as a practical and immediate 'green' benefactor to the community.

4.12.5   National calculations: effects of the recession

A *Time Magazine* report on information technology in the USA compared the predicted sales against the actual sales for 1990. It reflected the impact of the recession on electronics which correlates to a slowdown in the growth of teleworking. In the home, computers grew 15% against a predicted 50%; fibre optics grew 1% instead of 10%, and home banking recruited an additional 100 000 customers against 3 million predicted. Electronic mail (e-mail) missed target by half; videoconferencing missed by 70%—achieving $450 million.

Growth or decline   Since 1989 the number of UK employed teleworkers has remained almost static, while the number of pilot projects in major organisations has increased from 30% to 43% of those responding. The number of self-employed teleworkers has increased by some 18% of those newly unemployed who opt for self-employment.

4.12.6   National cost/benefit analyses

4.12.6.1   Commuting

'Only persons weighing less than 140 pounds will be considered' Assuming infrastructure maintenance and expansion costs to be equal for road and rail, in broad terms it costs 12 times as much to transport a lone commuter by car than on a (full) bus and 1.6 times more than by a (full) train. 85% of all journeys are by car; 40% of all journeys are commuter miles. The costs are proportional to the vehicle weight per person being moved; if costs rise substantially lean people may be rewarded with proportionately lower fares and employers will economise by hiring only lightweights.

Car or rail or bus?   The annual rail commuting cost from Norwich to London is £9000 per annum. From Princeton, New Jersey to New York costs $3000 a year. For 235 days' car journeys, for the same 230-mile round trip, a small Ford would use 1800 gallons of petrol, costing £3675 ($1800). Bus fares would be less than £3000 ($1500). From the commuter's viewpoint, who has invested in and maintains a car year-round for leisure, the incentive to use the car is strong.

L.A. Law   Cars are the most used and popular form of transport despite the increasing pollution from manufacturing them, running them and disposing of them, and despite the 50–60 days a year many car commuters waste in traffic jams. California's solution is to place a statutory obligation on car manufacturers to supply 1.7 million electric cars by the year 2000, and thereafter seven electric for every three petrol/diesel cars delivered by the year 2010.

Central London There are approximately 3 million people who work in Central London, 75% of whom commute by train, 20% on buses, 2.5% by car and 2.5% by foot/bicycle, giving 75 000 regular car commuters.

The rest of the UK In the London suburbs and the rest of the country, employing some 19 million people daily, 90% of commuters or 17.1 million people travel by car and less than 5% by train, 2% walk or cycle and 3% go by bus.

Potential UK savings Teleworking: would mean that 526 960 car-driving daily commuters would not travel in and around London and 11 250 would not enter Central London. Commuting-hours traffic jams would be substantially relieved on most trunk roads including the notorious M25.

Assuming an average 140 pound (63.5 kg) person to be teleworking instead of travelling, the commuting transport weight saved per UK commute, using the averages in Table 4.11, would be 4.9 million tonnes.

Table 4.11   Average vehicle weights per UK commuter.

Transport	Kilograms	Tonnes	Pounds
Ford Sierra (mid range UK), total 1700 kg			
assume 1 person	1 700	1.7	3 747
InterCity Train, total 592 000 kg:			
assume full			
—570 persons	1 038	1.04	2 288
Traditional London bus			
total 7 874 kg: assume			
full—56 persons	141	0.14	311

Petrol/diesel fuel to transport one tonne for one mile costs approximately 4 pence (would you push a one ton car a mile for 4 pence?) so the transport fuel saving for 3300 000 predicted UK teleworkers is £436 per year per teleworker.

4.12.6.2   Office rent, rates and local taxes

Inner London rent and rates per employee average £3600 per annum; Outer London and the Home Counties average some £2160 per person which applies in major cities in other parts of the country, and for the rest of the country an average of £1440 per person is reasonable.

4.12.6.3   Lost time and productivity

Telework researchers rely heavily on the UK Rank Xerox experience (up to 60% improvement in effectiveness was reported for USA Xerox's New York offices which, as possibly the first company in the world to do so, switched some staff into teleworking in the late 1970s). See the detailed section on effectiveness and productivity (Chapter 4.3.4).

Sick leave   In the UK, 432 million days were lost in 1989 through certified sick leave, an average of over 18 days per employee. Unrecorded lost time will increase this. One of the main factors in the reported 30% to 50% improvements in productivity of teleworkers is a reduction in days lost through illness.

Commuting accidents   17% of road casualties are due to commuter traffic. Telecommuting saves thousands of road injuries, and therefore health costs, and thousands of damaged vehicles per annum.

4.12.6.4   Skills and training

Accessing the productive workforce   Teleworking makes it easier to employ housebound people, including the disabled and carers, many of whom have valuable skills.

Retaining skilled people   Pacific Bell calculated that it costs $100 000 to recruit and train a systems analyst and that through teleworking they could have retained a third of analysts lost through relocation and other problems.

The Natwest Bank costs management training at an average of £10 000 per head and are currently seeking ways of retaining their skilled people. Another Central London multinational costs its manager training at £25 000 a year on top of salary costs and sees teleworking as a way of retaining women through child-rearing times and returning them to the central team months or years later, still *au fait* with the work.

Trained people who, without telework, would otherwise lose their skills are clearly a corporate and national cost to be counted.

4.12.7   Summary of national and corporate factors

Teleworking appears to be growing slowly and is likely to accelerate as the economy moves out of recession. Most HRM and senior personnel officers in major employers feel that it could work for their organisations, to a ceiling of 25% of the workforce, and 49% would themselves prefer to work at home. Many major companies operating pilot projects intend to expand the number of teleworkers.

Commuting and business travel Teleworking 15% of the workforce would save $864M in the USA and £1987M in the UK per annum in fuel costs at 1993 prices.

Office space and property 15% teleworking would empty 2.1 billion sq ft (0.19B sq m) in the USA and 396 million sq ft (36.80M sq m) in the UK of offices at annual rentals of $31B and £5544M respectively, but would create a US market for equipment of $62B and a UK market of £11.5B. Building conversion work for home-offices would be $20B in the USA and £3.3B in the UK.

Productivity, health, lost time These would improve by perhaps as much as 30%, which for 15% teleworking would add the equivalent of 1.75 billion days in the USA and 232 million days in the UK per annum to the nations' work, family and leisure time capacity. Damage to people and to cars would be cut. Increased numbers of skilled housebound people would be available. Lost training costs would be recouped.

Environmental factors These would be improved bringing substantial short, medium and long term benefits.

5

Security and Confidentiality

'Sometimes the best transportation policy means not moving people but moving their work. .... Millions have already found their productivity actually increases when they work nearer the people they're really working for—their families at home'

President George Bush—March 1990

5.1 DEFINITION OF SECURITY

(Quotes in this chapter are taken from Bill Landreth's book *Out of the Inner Circle*.)

It is important at the outset to define what is meant by security in the Information Technology processing environment. Understandably most people identify security in its physical form, that is, an image of a burly guard with an underfed German shepherd dog patrolling a barbed wire fence illuminated by high intensity lights. While these people provide a valuable function in protecting physical assets it is only one aspect of security.

In the context of information technology processing a security definition is 'the process of protecting the *Confidentiality*, *Integrity* and *Availability* of information'. This definition is used throughout this chapter.

These three elements are further expanded:

- *Confidentiality*—is the most common concept of security. It is protecting the secrecy of the information and making sure that it is only disclosed to those people who are authorised to have access to it (the *need to know* principle).

- *Integrity*—information is modified only by those users who have the right to do so. Only by maintaining a high level of integrity can the information be trusted by personnel and customers.

- *Availability*—information and other resources can be accessed by authorised users when needed. There is little point in having a fully up-to-date, accurate system containing information if it is unavailable for access when required.

5.2   IMPORTANCE OF SECURITY

The importance of security in all its aspects—physical, process, procedures, personnel and system—should not be underestimated. Security of information can be seen to provide a value-added service to a company or organisation's portfolio. Information is the lifeblood of companies and in many organisations protecting this information is paramount.

Customers will take confidence that their information entrusted in the custodianship of the organisation is secure if the organisation exhibits and operates a security culture.

Increasingly, industrial espionage is used to gain competitive advantage. The reduction of military objectives by Eastern European countries has led to an increase in commercial espionage.

Teleworking provides many social opportunities but also can provide opportunity to infiltrate an organisation or its information if security is not considered, implemented and maintained.

The originator of the information should identify the importance of the information to the organisation and develop procedures to handle, control , process, store and destroy that information. The responsibility for security lies with each individual who is part of the company or organisation.

Security does not always have to be expensive. Effective management of security features within computer systems or products can provide the requisite level of security.

5.2.1   Security awareness

Each company or organisation can improve its security by raising the awareness of its employees.

The commitment should come from the top and, akin to quality management, flow down and throughout the organisation.

A Corporate Statement of Security is essential if every employee is to understand the security culture in which they are expected to work. This statement will set the rules and processes to be applied and these will be appropriate in the teleworking, personal computer, office or mainframe environment.

Each individual system that supports the business processes should generate system-specific policies that will state the laws, rules and practices that regulate how assets and processes are managed, protected and distributed within a specific system.

In support and to implement effectively the policies, the organisation should develop a computer security improvement programme. The objective is to promote awareness, identify responsibilities and develop an education programme. The aim is to make people aware of their corporate responsibilities and provide the framework in which they are expected to work.

A programme of security compliance checks, reviews or audits is vital to ensure that security is effective, policies are followed, and improvements in the quality of security are implemented.

5.2.2   Is there a problem?

The convergence of information technology and telecommunications presents many legitimate opportunities to access vast stores of information to all sorts of people. However, it also presents challenges to many people who do not legitimately need access to this information.

Computer crime in its many forms is prevalent throughout the world. It varies from the intellectual challenge of gaining access to a system, deliberately installing a malicious computer virus, effecting fraud through misuse of telecomms links, to financing crime.

5.3   COMPUTING THREATS

All of the following are a threat to the security of the information or system. Regardless of whether that system is located in a secure environment or in a telecottage, teleworker's home or other designated location, the purpose of security is to minimise, prevent and limit the threat of a security failure.

These threats are dealt with in more detail later in this chapter.

5.3.1   Hacking

The most common vision of a hacker is portrayed in the film *War Games*. Hacking (in the UK this is defined as attempting or gaining unauthorised access to a system or network) has many facets:

- Novice
- Student
- Tourist
- Crasher
- Thief

The only two of these categories who are likely to inflict damage on computer systems are the Novice, who often causes damage unintentionally, quite simply because they don't quite know what they are doing, and the Crasher who is, to quote from Landreth, '... a troublemaker motivated by the same elusive goals as a vandal. If it weren't for computers he could just as easily be spray painting his name on the side of a building, or perhaps even setting the building on fire.'

According to Landreth, genuine hackers aspire to either student or tourist class. They hate crashers because they give hackers a bad name, they close accounts which hackers have spent time and effort to obtain, and they crash bulletin board systems on which hackers communicate.

5.3.2 Viruses

The important thing to remember is that computer viruses are *created* by people, and *spread* by people.

'A virus is a set of instructions, programmatic or otherwise, that propagate themselves through computer systems and/or networks deliberately set to do things unwanted by the legitimate owners of those systems. Key to this definition is that the introduction of a virus is a malicious act, not a technical malfunction. The potential for damage cannot be quantified, but it is unlimited in scope.'

5.4   MISUSE OF TELECOMMUNICATIONS LINKS

The more common report of this type of crime is the transfer of money from one account to an overseas account via electronic funds transfer or similar facility. This can only be effected if the security over access to the link, the controlling system and the account is weak or poorly administered.

Another example is the targeting of large telecommunications companies, particularly international traffic carriers, for types of crime that permit the criminal to resell network services for cash to finance other criminal activities such as drug trafficking.

5.5   COST OF SECURITY

No matter whether the system is going to be operated within one site or over many, designing security in at the start is more cost-effective than trying to 'bolt' it on afterwards. In 1991 some industry commentators calculated that designing security into a system from the outset relates to 9% of the system development cost whereas security 'attached' later is of the order of 20% of the system development cost. Those figures still hold good in 1993. However, to ensure that the security is cost-effective it is essential that a business impact review is carried out. The business impact review should ask and seek answers to the following questions:

● What is the confidentiality requirement of the information and system?
● What would happen if the confidentiality is breached?
● What is the impact on the company or organisation?
● Would customers go elsewhere; would the company lose revenue and market share?

- Would the company face legal or regulatory penalties?

Similar questions can be asked of the Integrity and Availability issues.

5.6   SECURITY RISKS ASSOCIATED WITH TELEWORKING

As a general principle there should be no more risk to security from tele-working than there is from working from a fixed location.

However, there are certain types of threat (theft of equipment, computer viruses) that are more likely because of the more flexible environment, but compensatory security mechanisms can be employed to counter these threats. It is the likelihood of these threats being realised that perhaps makes some organisations wary of adopting teleworking. In the case of theft of equipment it may also be that the information stored is of more value than the equipment. If the information was encrypted then its disclosure is less likely.

It is recognised that in practice the same physical and environmental security standards of an organisation's buildings or installations cannot be achieved for the teleworkers home or while telecommuting.

The distance of the teleworking facility from the organisation's main computing facility should not pose any greater risk, although the type of communications and the protective measures employed can influence this. The Public Switched Telephone Network is not the ideal medium for secure communications although it does have strength in its resilience. Determining the type and depth of security depends on what is being protected and this is discussed again below. The functional capability (speed, transfer rate, etc.) and operational requirement for access from the teleworker to the mainframe will also influence what type of security is required.

5.6.1   Types of attack

These can range from natural calamities (fire, flood, etc.), accidental damage (spillage of beverage over the keyboard), malicious act of violence to the hardware (wiping media with a magnet, attacking computer with an axe), deliberate or unintentional programming bug in an item of system software, to deliberate unauthorised access to the computer system or network component.

5.6.2   Types of threat

Ultimately any action or inaction, whether deliberate or unintentional, that for any reason causes a computer or computer system to fail, allow unauthorised access, modify data, or work in a manner that is not intended, must be considered a threat to the security of that system. The main areas of threat to computer systems are:

- Theft of data
- Theft of equipment
- Unauthorised access
- Loss of data integrity
- Loss of processing facilities

The security measures to be considered in countering such threats may be applied independently but more usually in combinations of:

- Physical and environmental security
- Identification and authentication
- Access control
- Software and data security
- Communications and data exchange security
- Security management
- Accountability and audit

All of these countermeasures can be applied in a teleworking environment although some are not as practical to introduce, such as physical security.

5.7   TELEWORKING IN PRACTICE

It is helpful in visualising how security can be employed in a typical tele-working environment to provide an actual working example. In BT (British Telecommunications plc), several members of the Internal Audit Department's computer audit team work from home. The nature of their jobs means that they are on site at any of BT's computer installations for weeks at a time. Their duties bring them into contact with sensitive information, weaknesses that may exist in systems and new projects and systems coming on stream. Therefore information security is essential. Those members of the audit team who work at home compiling their audit reports have personal computing, facsimile, telephony and storage facilities provided.

BT has developed a computer security policy and associated guidance which sets the baseline for security in systems and the operational environment. This is used as the template when providing facilities. In support of this policy is one standard which deals specifically with the security of information, its handling, marking, transmission, destruction, etc. Further policies have been developed providing rules for remote, secure access to mainframe computing from BT, and non-BT, premises.

Applying the policies and standards, it is easy to identify the threats to the information that the Audit team would process and to develop the appropriate level of security and countermeasures. For the computer audit team, the layers of security embrace access control to personal computing facilities, encryption of the hard disk, anti-virus software, transmission of facsimile (only when attended) and data, media and paper storage. The Computer Audit Manager ensures compliance with policy. This example demonstrates that the infrastructure (in the form of policies and standards, understanding the value and sensitivity of the information and providing security functions appropriate for the task, combined with managerial control) is essential for the teleworking environment. These principles hold good for any organisation adopting teleworking.

The first action is to identify the value and sensitivity of the information being processed and to anticipate threats to the computer system. If, for example, the US Internal Revenue Service or the UK Inland Revenue proceeded to instigate teleworking, an analysis of the type of work should be undertaken to establish the sensitivity and value of the information to be processed. 'Value' in this context includes asset value (data, equipment, software, communications links, etc.), its importance and potential corporate embarrassment, together with the cost of unauthorised information disclosure and any loss of critical services capability.

The requirement may be for staff to access a central database, download the information for local processing and upload at the end of the session. Such activity may require dial-back facilities (to authenticate the teleworker to the mainframe), communication software in the personal computer (PC) (thus making the PC incorporate some form of access control, i.e. password or token), local storage in the PC (perhaps encryption), registration of licensed software, and anti-virus software (to prevent upload and download of viruses). Security would be performed by the mainframe administrator and should ensure that access to the mainframe would be totally menu driven and therefore the teleworker would see only those parts of the systems that his or her security profile allowed.

5.7.1 Categories of teleworking

There are several variations of teleworker ranging from those who use stand-alone processing to those who support the administration of large mainframes. Relative to the teleworkers' function and the access privileges required to perform the job, the security functionality and requirement needs to be equally graded. There is greater risk of security failure on a large scale if, for example, the link to the remote system (central) administrator is breached than if a teleworker gains unauthorised access to a single electronic mailbox.

There can be no hard and fast rules about which organisations might confidently adopt teleworking, but security should not be a barrier to a decision. Security measures can always be implemented to provide compensatory controls over aspects that may appear, at first glance, difficult to secure.

5.7.2 Security responsibilities

Each employee of the organisation has a responsibility for the security of the systems they use and the information which they generate, process and transmit. Most organisations have specialist security personnel to formulate policy and standards, support, advise, monitor and provide technical support and detection capability. Security should, in the first instance, be the direct responsibility of personnel who administer specific systems.

There is, as yet, no formula that determines the ratio of security managers to numbers employed or to the complexity of systems within a company. Security has to be in the culture of the company. Companies which recognise the value of security should appoint a senior officer with overall responsibility for security, reporting to the Executive Board. In the teleworking environment security management should, ideally, be an extension of normal office procedures to the dispersed team and to their extended electronic network.

5.7.3   Security considerations

To determine security measures it is essential to value the sensitivity of the information and system. For example, if a system contains information of a National Security nature, that system is unlikely to be a candidate for teleworking access. On the other hand, a system in a commercial organisation holding information of value to a competitor may be opened to teleworker access, the security including encryption of all links and locally stored data. There are laws in force in most countries regulating how data are to be secured. Penalties exist should the laws be broken. Security planning needs to take account of the national legislation.

There is no universal formula that can be applied to determine the appropriate depth and strength of security required. Government, federal, national and similar organisations naturally require security far in excess of the commercial sector and their high standards may be too strict and expensive for most companies. Each part of each organisation must decide the appropriate amount of security in their case and must budget accordingly.

5.8   BUGS AND HACKERS

This is an area where it is prudent to retain trade secrets but to give sufficient information to raise readers' awareness. Until the 1970s, electronic security was largely restricted to military and government applications. It has spread to the commercial sector because the necessary equipment is readily available at affordable prices. As electronic equipment became available to businesses, so it did to the interested amateur or professional criminal.

Threats from 'bugs and hackers' fall broadly into two areas: (1) bugs and taps, and (2) TV-type receiving equipment.

5.8.1   Bugs and taps

It is important to define and describe the differences between the two.

Bugs are miniature radio transmitters which pick up the sound in a room

(room audio) through a very small microphone, and transmit radio signals on specific frequencies. Bugs can be battery powered, with a limited life, or line powered, i.e. drawing power from mains or telephone lines.

Taps differ from bugs in that they do not use a microphone to pick up the signal but intercept it directly from a line, such as (and most commonly at present) a telephone line. The resulting signal may then be either transmitted by radio or sent down the telephone line. A variation is the computer tap. This can be connected either to the computer network cable or to the computer itself. The resultant signal is not 'room audio' but a 'data' signal. Taps attached to computers are on circuit boards containing specially designed chips to transmit the intercepted data.

The bugs and taps described are freely available in the UK and the modified computer chip is freely available in the USA. Although in the UK it is not illegal to make, sell or own them it *is* illegal to use them.

5.8.2   TV reception

All electronic equipment, including computers, emits electronic magnetic radiation. Radio and TV waves are a form of electromagnetic radiation and electronic equipment emits varying amounts of radio (and TV) signals of varying power and on varying frequencies. The difference between 'emit' and 'transmit' is that transmitting intentionally sends out signals, whereas emitting unintentionally broadcasts signals. The video circuits of any monitor emit electromagnetic radiation that can be picked up and reformed into a picture by equipment such as a portable TV, with relatively minor modifications.

5.8.3   Electronic sweeping

This is the term given to checking a room or premises for suspected bugs, taps or electromagnetic radiation. This practice **must** be undertaken only by qualified and approved organisations. In the case of suspected taps and bugs on telephone lines the telephone company itself may undertake the sweep. There may be other implications which the telephone company would wish to consider in addition to the eavesdropping activity, such as intent to defraud the telephone company of revenue by misuse of the telephony service. Where the bugs or taps are located also influences the course of action required. The sensitivity of this type of operation cannot be overstated. There are few reputable companies and personnel able to undertake electronic sweeping.

5.8.4   EM radiation sweeping

As in electronic sweeping, the checking of terminals, personal computers and other equipment, by electromagnetic radiation sweeping is usually undertaken by a small specialist team. To overcome the electromagnetic radiation emissions, 'hardened' or 'Tempest' monitors are becoming available. Although primarily used by government and military authorities, their use within commercial organisations is increasing, despite the additional costs associated with these monitors.

5.8.5   Hackers

Hackers are unauthorised intruders into computer systems. Hacking is not restricted to personnel outside an organisation; it is just as much an occupation of employees, both while at work and from home, whether teleworking or at central office. There may be some telltale signs or alternatively the hacker may have covered his trail by the deletion of any security logs. A simple and effective check for unauthorised use is for the last log-in details (date and time) to be displayed when the system is next accessed. Thus the user should be able to verify if the date and time entries are correct or if some nefarious activity has been taking place.

Any discrepancies or variations in the log should be reported and investigations undertaken. But rather than rely on detection measures, it is better security practice to prevent the hacker getting in in the first place. Most hacking occurs via dial-in lines and therefore it is sensible to employ controls over these to restrict the opportunity. Teleworkers' access authorisations to central computers via telephone lines should be checked and use of modems or other devices restricted to the teleworkers.

Some practical advice is as follows:

- Monitor of the dial-up lines to the host system by the system administrator.

- Limit the number of attempts at getting the correct password (e.g. three) after which the line should be cut.

- Close down dial-up lines outside normal times of use (the host operating system may well have facilities to restrict or control day and time accesses—DEC VMS is an example).

- Implement dial-back procedures as part of the log-on procedures. This will enable the remote user to be verified by location and unique identification previously registered with the host system.

This list applies in general to those systems that are remotely accessed. Stand-alone personal computers (PCs) do not represent the same threat. A hacker would have to gain direct access to the PC and even then his actions would be limited to that PC alone. However, unauthorised access should not be discounted but can be prevented by applying the measures mentioned elsewhere.

Electronic security has been considered; just as important is the information generated on paper and its delivery and receipt.

5.8.6 Facsimile

The facsimile machine is a boon to any teleworker who wants to send or receive pre-generated paper-based information; there are some common-sense rules for their use:

- If there is a requirement for regular and consistent receipt and despatch of sensitive information then encrypted facsimile should be used.
- Confirm that there is someone at the remote end to receive the fax if encryption isn't used.
- Regularly confirm that stored short code dialling numbers are still current and to the location expected.
- If not using the facsimile machine for a period of time (holidays, etc.) then unplug from both mains and telephone line.
- If facsimile messages are to be retained for a period of time they need to be stored in a manner that prevents the paper from fading and discolouring. This often means photocopying the fax. Facsimile machines incorporating laser printers do not suffer from this problem.

5.8.7 Post or mail

5.8.7.1 Public service

Most countries operate a method of mail or post that enables the sender to record or register the item. Although this provides financial comfort to the sender, it does not prevent misdirection, or loss or theft during transit. The potential for a single item of mail to be intercepted is reduced by the great volume of items in transit at any one time, but perhaps the only sure method of secure delivery is direct by hand. It should be assumed that a motivated thief will use any means of interception, at any point in the delivery chain.

Just as determining protective and security measures in computer systems depends on the value and sensitivity of the information processed, the same criteria apply to paper-based information.

5.8.7.2 Couriers

Where couriers carry papers to and from teleworkers, care must be taken in the selection of the courier companies and, more importantly, in establishing a procedure for the authentication of the courier during the collection and delivery process. As an added precaution different courier companies could be employed and used on a random basis, preventing a regular pattern emerging that could be helpful to an industrial spy.

Where a magnetic medium (e.g. computer disk) is sent and received by mail, it should be checked for computer viruses by the recipient. The teleworker is not in a position to verify that what has been received is what was sent unless, under separate cover or by fax, is sent a listing of files, data, and file and data sizes to enable comparison. A further precaution is sealing magnetic media in bags with tamper-resistant seals. Delivering to untrusted mailboxes introduces a threat which is difficult to counter but one that could be lessened if particular types of mail, such as magnetic media, sensitive information, etc., were only despatched to a secure location known only to the sender and recipient.

Sensitive information that is to be sent direct to the teleworker's home may be double enveloped or wrapped in order to prevent accidental opening by other than the intended recipient. Clearly labelling the internal envelope with the recipient's name would aid the delivery process.

5.9   COMPUTER VIRUSES

The teleworking environment should not , if properly managed, increase the opportunity for infection by computer viruses. The following information is equally applicable to office-located PCs or those used at home. The Do's and Don'ts are commonsense rules learnt by many organisations the hard way.

Viruses are now, of necessity, being recognised as a significant problem to users of PCs. Numbers—of both strains and occurrences—are on the increase. They form part of a family of 'malicious code'. Some common terms used in association with virus are worm, Trojan Horse, logic bomb, dropper, trap door and back door, and these are explained in the following sections.

5.9.1   Virus

'A virus is a set of instructions, programmatic or otherwise, that propagate themselves through computer systems and/or networks deliberately set to do things unwanted by the legitimate owners of those systems. Key to this definition is that the introduction of a virus is a malicious act, not a technical malfunction ... The potential for damage cannot be quantified, but it is unlimited in scope.'

The definitive feature of a virus is that it replicates itself in some way. Replication can be confined to media devices such as floppy disk drives but, more often, can also involve an element of spread on the host's internal storage media such as a hard disk drive; this increases the chance of continued reactivation. The virus normally has some additional functionality, called a payload, that is triggered by an event (such as a particular date) which varies in functionality from a message on the screen to severe corruption or destruction of data on a disk.

5.9.2   Worm

'A worm is a program which copies and activates itself on other systems via an accepted communications channel.'

The most notorious example of a worm was the American internet worm unleashed by the son of a presidential security advisor. Although allegedly not intended to do any damage, due to a programming error damage was caused which was estimated at \$200M.

5.9.3   Trojan Horse

'A Trojan Horse is a program component that performs services beyond those stated in its specifications.'

It is executable software that does not perform the exact functionality that it claims to. The Trojan code is often 'joke' or damaging code but can also be 'back-door' or 'short cut' code. The writers of such code range from practical jokers, through disgruntled employees, to software developers wishing to leave their own personal mark in the program. The PC user is fooled into believing that the program is something that it is not and is tricked into running it on his computer.

Readers might like to consider whether they have run unsolicited software on their machines without any reliable information as to what to expect from it.

A classic example of a Trojan Horse is a little program which, if the DOS TYPE command is used to examine the contents of a file, redefines the PF keys, so that instead of PF3 repeating the last command, it deletes all the files on the disk. Another example, beloved by hackers, is a dummy log-on screen. It traps the user's password then passes the user to the real log-on screen. Most users will assume they got their password wrong and re-enter their User Id and password combination. In fact the log-on sequence was correct but was trapped by the hacker who could then masquerade as the user.

5.9.4   Logic bomb

A variant of the Trojan Horse is the logic bomb in which malicious code is inserted to be triggered later.

An example of this was when a disgruntled employee's name didn't appear on the payroll when the monthly run took place; he or she brought down the system so no-one got paid.

5.9.5   Dropper

This type of program is used to make the introduction of the Trojan or virus code more effective by making the process harder to detect by the user. A dropper program claims to perform one task but actually installs other malicious code instead. The code is often compressed or encrypted to disguise its real identity. In many respects dropper code can be considered to be a specific form of Trojan code.

5.9.6   Trap door/back door

'Trap doors are hidden software or hardware mechanisms that can be triggered to permit system protection mechanisms to be circumvented.'

It is amazing how many of these there are, often to help service engineers. It is also amazing how quickly they can become public knowledge.

5.9.7   Extent of problem

The concept of a replicating program has been recognised for many years and various experiments were performed to demonstrate this type of code across different computing platforms. Little serious attention was given to the idea by users of personal computers until 1986 when a PC virus was encountered that spread successfully around the PC community. Since then the number of types of viruses has grown with increasing pace.

Out of, perhaps, over 1000 PC viruses now reportedly in existence, there are less than 100 'family' types (of which 10 are prevalent) and the global occurrences are limited to a few tens of actual variants. The irritation, fascination and media sensation caused by early viruses seems to have been replaced by an ongoing intellectual challenge to originate new virus types and an even more dangerous form of hobby: the modification of existing viruses to 'improve' or debug them. Newer viruses are able to hide themselves from the user and to have disruptive payloads that make the virus an unpleasant presence on a PC.

The number of viruses is unlikely to continue growing at an ever increasing rate, however, because some growth-limiting effects also apply which may result in some viruses becoming extinct. For example:

- Increasing awareness of the problem in the user community and, especially, in support teams

- Increasing acceptance and use of anti-virus tools

- Improvements in detection techniques

- Reliance upon particular hardware features (e.g. particular disk drive sizes)

- Poor concealment techniques (e.g. presence/activity easily detected)
- Poor infection techniques (e.g. file/disk alteration effects easily detected)
- Obvious effects when payload is triggered (e.g. tunes, screen effects)
- Bugs leading to unexpected machine behaviour (e.g. system crashes)
- Design flaws (e.g. conflicts with other viruses)

5.9.8 Stragtegy for prevention

The strategy, viewed from the perspective of the virus problem, has four components:

- *Culture*—educating users as to the correct, ethical behaviour associated with the use of computers
- *Access control*—limiting the effects of the uneducated and the unethical
- *Anti-virus measures*—limiting the spread of virus outbreaks and detecting their incidence
- *Backup*—limiting the effects of educated users' mistakes and covering the cases where the other three components fail to prevent a disaster

The aims of an anti-virus strategy are:

- Containment of virus outbreaks to prevent further disruption
- Identification of the source of infection and support for any litigation process that is needed
- Removal of the infection and restoration of the normal computing environment
- Confidential documentation of the incident and calculation of the cost of any damage (real and consequential) to the business
- Dissemination of knowledge gained from the incident by revising policy and strategy

5.9.8.1 Do's and don'ts

DO:

- Only use software that comes directly from a reputable manufacturer, sealed in plastic. Where possible ensure that there is a contract clause which warrants that the software is virus-free.
- Keep master copies of software locked away.

- Use an access control package—including a password and floppy disk lock—to prevent unauthorised access to the PC.

- Ensure that data disks do not contain executable files. Currently viruses can only replicate themselves by attachment to executable files.

- Check all software prior to loading it on to the PC, by the use of a dedicated 'sheep dip', which is a dedicated PC especially designed and programmed to test all incoming and outgoing disks, or by the installation of anti-virus software already loaded on the PC.

DON'T:

- Borrow or lend software. As well as exposing a system to untrustworthy software, it may also be contravening the terms of the software licence.

- Swap disks or programs between computers within and outside the work environment without taking appropriate precautions.

- Load or play computer games on PCs issued for official use. Computer games are the perfect medium for computer viruses as they are swapped and borrowed so frequently.

- Download public domain software from bulletin boards or public computer agencies without appropriate precautions.

5.9.9 Likelihood of infection

Symantec, who market Norton Anti-Virus software, prophesied in 1992 that all PCs in the UK will have come into contact with a virus by the end of 1993. This is unlikely, but as there are over 1000 known strains and types of virus it is possible that without proper precautions the majority of organisations, throughout the world, have had some contact.

Most organisations have some software capability or procedure to check disks before loading them. It may be in the form of a 'sheep dip' machine (that stands alone and whose only purpose is to check disks for viruses), or it may be that each PC has resident anti virus software which is activated each time a floppy disk is loaded. Large manufacturers of PCs are bundling anti-virus software as part of the hardware build.

Teleworkers, if they permit their personal computer to be used by others and for purposes other than their official business, leave themselves open to attack and penetration by computer viruses. The simplest prevention strategy is to have an access control, such as a password and disk lock on the PC, with anti-virus software. This strategy could be extended to have a 'sheep dip' in the telecottage.

5.9.10 Computer disks

The threats identified above are those that can be anticipated should a third party be intent on stealing the equipment or media information or intent on intercepting mail. The unexpected threat may strike from within—destroying hours of work, effort, time and money. However, there are other perils that can be detrimental to the teleworkers' work or even their sanity.

Computer disks, although called 'floppy' disks, are now, certainly in their smaller variety, less floppy and more rigid. They contain a vast amount of information and should be treated with respect. The following points affect the security, i.e. the abuse, of the data held on a disk:

- Do not bend a floppy disk
- Do not touch the disk itself
- Do not allow anything else to touch the disk
- Keep magnets away from the disk
- When not in use, keep the disks in their jackets
- Keep the disks within the temperature range 10°–52° C and out of direct sunlight
- Do not throw disks about like Frisbees, or handle them roughly
- Do not write on labels already attached to disks, especially with sharp-pointed pens

Any of the above can cause the disk to physically crash, with consequent loss of data. Most of these points require little extra explanation, but it is worth a closer examination of where magnets can be found in the everyday teleworkers' environment.

While preparing this on an office PC, the work is surrounded by electrical equipment, capable of generating extraneous magnetic influences:

- PC monitor
- PC processor
- Printer
- Telephone
- Answering machine
- Electronic diary
- Facsimile machine
- Photocopier

Add to this list typical equipment that could be found in the home in close proximity to the teleworker's work area:

- Vacuum cleaner
- Video recorder
- Television
- Microwave oven
- Hi-fi equipment
- Electronic toys and games

The list is not exhaustive and is intended only to draw the reader's attention to the likely sources.

> A colleague who frequently completed his security survey reports at home, on his notebook PC, came in to the office one day asking for a copy of software that could recover lost data. Mysteriously his floppy disk had 'lost' its data. The occurrence passed but was repeated some weeks later. On enquiring of the layout and environment where he worked at home, nothing untoward was revealed until it was admitted that, to keep prying young fingers from interfering when he left the workplace, he hid his floppy disk under the answering machine. On his return he would activate the answering machine to replay any messages. Thus the culprit for 'losing' his data was identified. Needless to say he now stores his floppy disk in an appropriate container and locks it away in his desk drawer.
>
> Another teleworking colleague was pleased to return and find his home office sparkling and cleaned by a zealous assistant. By coincidence all data on his PC was lost. Several months later the same sequence occurred, again losing all PC data. Under intense interrogation the assistant admitted cleaning the dusty old PC with the household vacuum cleaner—inadvertently wiping out all data with the magnets in the vacuum motor.

There are many anecdotes of similar occurrences where humble domestic electrical equipment has played havoc with a floppy disk, simply because the storing of them in close proximity to electrical equipment was not considered an issue. So the question has to be asked, 'where do you keep the disks both when they are being used and when they are to be stored?'.

Ideally the disk storage containers that can be purchased quite reasonably from computer equipment suppliers offer an adequate level of protection and can be used for both situations. If located on the desktop or in a convenient drawer then disks can be safely stored temporarily or long term.

Portable or notebook-type equipment is most attractive to thieves and is particularly vulnerable when being transported in a motor vehicle. The widely reported case during the Gulf War of a military officer who, while looking at showroom cars, had his own car stolen with his war plans laptop PC, typifies the vulnerability of this type of equipment. While the hardware can be insured for its replacement value, the information contained cannot be and it may be invaluable. The recommendation for PCs carrying vital information is to store only the applications and operating software on the hard disk and all data files on floppy disks, which are carried on the person. This will not prevent the car from being stolen—only automobile theft deterrents will do that—but locating the data separately increases the chances of the information remaining confidential.

5.10   DOCUMENTS

The feeling of satisfaction of having completed an important task on time and in an attractive and well laid out format can soon evaporate if an external influence decimates the work. The potential perpetrators of such acts are the inquisitive child, the over-friendly domestic pet, the helpful office cleaner and even friends and neighbours.

While computer systems offer sophisticated facilities to clear screens, re-enter passwords, etc., in order to protect access, the same cannot be said for the completed paper output or report. Once the output has been produced it demands its own form of security: namely to keep it out of harm's way. The teleworker, working at home, may not be able to instil in the family sufficient loyalty and respect for the work. Therefore self-discipline and good office-keeping practices are sensible.What may seem important to the teleworker may seem of lesser importance to those nearby. It is not always possible to impose particular security or housekeeping controls on others; so 'Lock it or Lose it' should be every teleworkers' motto.

In the UK at BT, a 'clear desk' policy is mandated and checked by periodic out-of-hours audits to confirm compliance. The NatWest Bank avoided the embarrassment and costs of having thousands of pages of confidential documents scattered across London, in April 1993, when the landmark NatWest Tower had every window blown out by a terrorist bomb—due, the NatWest claimed, to their strict clear desk policy. A similar policy of clearing and locking desktop items, when leaving the desk unattended, is both suitable and practical for home teleworking and telecentre environments.

If papers have to be left in vehicles, common sense dictates they should be stored out of sight in a suitable container.

5.11   POTENTIAL HAZARDS

The typical teleworker may face several additional hazards:

- Car is stolen or broken into

- The contents of the car are stolen (work and equipment)

- His desk has been 'tidied' and papers 'filed' in the rubbish bin

- Final reports have been 'decorated' by his children/dog/cat [delete which one is not applicable]

- Computer is now fighting off space invaders with the help of child(ren) and friend(s)

- Disks are all being fed into the hi-fi Compact Disc player 'because they fit, daddy/mummy'

- Computer 'dies' during the up-load of the final report—the socket has been taken for the vacuum cleaner

- Floppy disks are boomerang shaped and battered around the edges 'but they fly, daddy'

A teleworker can survive all of these and more by recognising that they **can** happen and planning to prevent them from happening in the first place.

5.12   SECURITY EQUIPMENT FOR TELEWORKERS

The equipment provided to a teleworker for the purposes of executing his duties will be varied. Security mechanisms to protect that equipment must be equally varied. The type, depth and cost of security will be determined by what is being protected and against what threats. For teleworkers with access to a database (e.g. containing customer marketing information) and with local printing or storage of that information, encryption of the telecommunication links as well as the terminal or PC hard disk may be needed. Secure furniture should be provided for the storage of the printout.

Neither employers nor individuals want to develop a Fort Knox environment for the home that remains in force even when the teleworker has 'clocked off'. Therefore a compromise has to be struck, consistent with the value and sensitivity of the equipment and information. If the teleworker is provided with the capability of locally storing information in magnetic or paper form then, inevitably, some form of physically secure storage or protection is required, if only to prevent inquisitiveness by household members or co-occupants of telecentres.

Rules apply which are equally appropriate in the teleworker's home or in a telecentre.

5.12.1   Physical and environmental security

Personal computing equipment, facsimile machines, modems, videos, copiers, etc., are all attractive items liable to theft. Therefore restricting access to the equipment and its resources is the prime consideration. Achieving an access-controlled regime may be more difficult at home than in a telecentre, where the volume of equipment makes physical security (alarms, CCTV, etc.) more cost-effective.

Premises may require alarming either directly to neighbourhood police stations, to central alarm centres or even to the employers' central office. Burglar or intruder detection alarms use either the local telephone access network or radio to transmit to their chosen destination. Premises housing high-value equipment may be recommended by insurance companies to install an alarm. The organisation supporting the teleworker must decide whether the value of equipment and information is sufficient to install alarms. Layers of security can be employed to minimise security failures, ranging from physically securing the premises to individually securing equipment.

5.12.1.1   Theft

The threat of theft applies to media as well as equipment. The following provides guidance for protecting equipment:

- Equipment should not be located adjacent to or visible from a ground floor window

- Equipment should be located in a room that is lockable when not in use
- Equipment should be clearly and indelibly marked (either the user's post or zip code or the company name)
- Equipment should be provided with physical locks to the components. This may take the form of a lock preventing access to the internals of the component. In a telecentre, where there will be several people sharing facilities, securely attaching the equipment (especially the processor unit) to the desk may be appropriate
- Portable equipment should be stored out of sight during transit
- Media (disks, headed company paper, etc.) should be stored in a separate location when not in use

The motto 'Lock it or Lose it' applies equally well to teleworking equipment as it does to motor vehicle security.

5.12.1.2 Environmental security

Security is achievable to the desired standard at a cost. The cost has to be balanced against the threats and the likelihood of realisation of those threats. Conditions to be considered include the neighbouring accommodation.

In the teleworker's home it may not be appropriate to dictate the environment under which the equipment should be used but simple, commonsense rules should be applied:

- Equipment should not be located adjacent to an environment likely to generate smoke or fire such as kitchens. Inexpensive smoke detectors will provide an early warning but may not prevent the equipment being damaged in the event of an emergency.
- Equipment should not be located where there may be a risk of water leakage such as beneath bathrooms or in cellar rooms, near to central heating boilers and associated pipework.

5.12.1.3 Power supply

Equipment should be provided with an electrical power supply smoothing device capable of controlling surges or spikes. Most equipment will withstand *minor* variations in electrical power but additional precautions are sensible.

5.12.1.4 Physical security

Equipment that cannot be physically isolated and secured should incorporate compensatory security devices as an integral part of the equipment.

Hardware locks Equipment should have hardware locks, such as power supply, keyboard and disk drive locks to prevent unauthorised use of the equipment.

Security tokens To provide a greater depth of security, equipment could utilise a security token and reader. It could not be easily operated without the token.

Media Both magnetic media and paper should be stored in lockable furniture in a location away from the equipment.

Teleworkers generate output similar to that generated by their counterparts in central office and require the same facilities for storage, transmission and destruction of information as the core team.

If sensitive information is going to be processed by a teleworker, then the security will need to be incremented accordingly. Encryption of links, strong authentication of the teleworker to the host system and secure storage, capable of withstanding lengthy attacks (safes), combined with alarmed premises are all essential.

5.12.2   Typical security equipment for the homeworker

The room in which the equipment is to be used ideally should be lockable and locked when not in use. If this is not practical then the equipment itself will require some form of access control to prevent it being used by unauthorised users. This access control facility could reasonably be expected to be provided as part of the supply of the equipment and be consistent with the parent organisation's security procedures. (An example of a specially designed security desk is shown in Chapter 6.0.2 on the BT Inverness project.)

Media, both paper and magnetic, should be stored in lockable and removable containers that can be located in a different room when not required. The typical magnetic disk boxes advertised on sale in computer supply catalogues are adequate if they are supplemented by storing them out of sight and at a separate location.

Disposal of media may be by shredding or crushing. Although domestic shredders are available, they are generally noisy and generate a lot of dust. It may be more appropriate for media to be transported back to the parent organisation for disposal.

The building itself may need to be alarmed if there is a requirement by the insurance company, if the neighbourhood has a high crime rate and if the equipment and information value justify it.

5.12.3   Access summary

To summarise; security will need to prevent access to the equipment, prevent access to use of the equipment, prevent access to information processed or derived from the system, and detect any attempt to access the premises.

For those teleworkers whose job content involves more sensitive information than average, the above security will apply but they may need more stringent security arrangements.

A point to note is that people who routinely take paper documents home may be even more vulnerable to theft and loss during transit than the teleworker receiving information over a public telephone network.

End user products, requiring varying degrees of computer experience, are available to strengthen the security systems of any organisation, including those with teleworking networks.

Personal computers can be safeguarded by the LEKTOR range of devices to encrypt and safely store data. For example the LEKTOR 3600 is for use on IBM PC XT and AT compatibles. Its plug-in board and custom chip redefines the PC in terms of access and inward and outward transmission.

Designed and marketed by BT, New York and London, the LEKTOR range comprises four types and over eight models which are tailored for individual machines or, with personal access keys, for individual users.

BTACS access control systems are also readily available to authenticate incoming and outgoing messages for and from individuals.

When fitted and maintained by experts, such systems defeat most unauthorised users, and all casual interceptions are rendered harmless.

5.13   PROTECTING INFORMATION IN THE HOME OR LOCAL OFFICE

The transformation from working in a team environment within an office or large organisation with access to all modern conveniences to a singleton environment working at home with limited conveniences introduces some unusual security concerns. The central office environment offers employees the opportunity to discuss professional matters, business news and social matters within a group where corporate secrets are likely to be respected.

It is essential that anyone in the teleworking environment understands the parameters in which they are expected to work, including the disclosure of information. It may seem that a single teleworker may not have sufficient information of value or sensitivity to attract industrial espionage, but, if aggregated with information from other teleworkers from the same organisation, an individual's knowledge may develop into valuable information. Large organisations have developed policies on the disclosure of information that are mandated and are compliant with the laws of the land. Each employee should be aware of their responsibilities and have procedures on the disclosure of information. Before a teleworker is empowered to work from a remote location, the teleworker should be clear about the rules applying to the security of information and assets (equipment, network, software, media, procedures, etc.) including the disclosure and disposal/destruction of that information.

Where the occupation of a teleworker is known to a customer, supplier or competitor, their apparent isolation may make them a target. In the main office team environment such targeting is less likely. Communication is the means by which teleworkers are able to perform their work, albeit using electronic means as opposed to word of mouth. The need to talk face to face, and the social freedom that teleworking allows, may encourage the individual to talk about confidential work on visiting establishments, such as the local bar or pub at lunchtime, which they would only visit with team colleagues during central office attendance.

Of interest to hackers is the fact that the teleworker may be connected to a mainframe and the potential for accessing it. This could be more serious than lunch-time gossip, as it is likely that the mainframe has further connections to other systems thereby providing the would-be hacker with a web of networks for them to eavesdrop on confidential exchanges. Telecentres also present opportunities for the disclosure of information as they may be used by employees of more than one organisation. Teleworkers should not be put in a position of not knowing what the procedure or penalty is for the disclosure of sensitive information.

Once a teleworker has undertaken their allotted tasks, inevitably somewhere in the process their efforts will be recorded on paper or computer media. If these are no longer required they should not be discarded in the normal household or domestic waste. Sensitive information can be stored until of sufficient volume to be collected by appointed, secure waste disposal companies. The most secure method of disposal is by incineration but a shredder capable of shredding to strips of 3 mm or less may be adequate. There have been news reports of banking information and customer details found on public rubbish dumps. The embarrassment and subsequent loss of custom to the banks was also reported.

Information on computer disks can still be retrieved and read, by off-the-shelf software, after it has been erased **six** times. The British Army are reported to dispose of floppy computer disks, during field manoeuvres, in chemical lavatories to ensure destruction. This may be a bit extreme in the commercial or domestic world, but nevertheless indicates the seriousness of the problem. The only sure way of destroying a disk containing sensitive information is by crushing or cutting it. Commercial secure destruction companies offer destruction by crushing, grinding or pulping the magnetic media. Another method is degaussing (a strong magnetic field destroying the data but leaving the recording medium in place). If the teleworker cannot return papers and magnetic media to the central office, for secure disposal or destruction, then the incinerating of these by the local Council or Corporation or domestically burning them may provide an alternative but less secure arrangement.

5.13.1   Securing information from fire and explosions

This section is primarily concerned with the requirement for fireproof safes in the teleworking or telecentre environment with relevant background information.

Most large organisations have contingency procedures to enable their business to resume in the event of disruption from an emergency or disaster. This is especially true for companies that utilise large computers. What is sometimes overlooked is the equally important requirement to plan for business resumption in the support or office environment not connected to the mainframe. Whole office blocks that perhaps are the headquarters of the company can also be disrupted in the event of disaster. The terrorist bomb explosions in the Baltic Exchange building, London (1992), in the World Trade Center, New York (1993), and again in the City of London (April 1993), are clear examples.

Basic requirements are for securing valuable files. Any information processed on any computer system has its own value to the process of that business and should be safeguarded accordingly. The majority of information is administrative, supporting the operation of the company, and could be reproduced without too much difficulty and without affecting the ability of the company to trade. Some information is absolutely critical to the operation and the success of the company and is considered 'enterprise threatening' and therefore it is essential that it is kept secure.

In the teleworking environment it is likely that the information entrusted will not be enterprise threatening but may still have some major repercussions on the company if destroyed. Less important, but nevertheless a factor to take into account, is the time (cost) taken to produce and process the information and the time needed to recreate it.

When the question of fireproof safes is raised the usual consideration is for the ability of the safe to withstand the heat and temperatures associated with a large fire. Frequently overlooked is the ability of the safe to withstand smoke and the fire dousing agents such as water, CO_2 and foam. Computer magnetic media are particularly vulnerable to heat, smoke, dust and water from the fireman's hose. Equipping teleworkers with the same type of fireproof safes as are used in large organisations is prohibitive. Access, location, weight and insurance all have to be considered. However, it is reasonable to provide the teleworker with a transportable and lockable media safe (for storing transportable magnetic media) that can be located near to the equipment when in use and transported to a different location for secure storage. This will also permit removal of the media if an emergency arises and time allows.

Fundamental decisions on the type of media to be stored, the types of disaster the safe is trying to protect against (theft, fire, smoke, etc.), the location, access arrangements, key/combination holders, etc., have to be taken. It is sensible for the teleworker to have an approved product, particularly one that has undergone testing within their own country or standards organisation. Companies such as Chubb offer a whole range of suitable cabinets and safes. Prices vary and, as they say, 'You pays your money and you takes your choice!'.

Contingency planning in the form of secure retention of important information is an element of security that is often only paid lip service. There are several worldwide examples of companies which, in the event of a disaster, were unable to recover vital information. This was either through denial of access to the site (and failure to secure off-site copies) or through finding that when they could recover their information it was unusable due to poor storage facilities and was damaged by the recovery procedures. Organisations that have chosen their fireproof safes carefully and have had the misfortune to suffer a fire have found that the safe and the media stored within have been recoverable.

The teleworker will need to determine what should be stored within the fireproof safe, the domestic fire prevention arrangements (smoke detection, remote alarming, etc.) and the location and weight implications before deciding on the make and model. The insurance company may also be able to provide advice on types of fireproof safes that are recommended and for which they are prepared to insure the contents. They will usually rely on the safe manufacturers' contents valuation figures (derived from the length of time required to breach a safe). Although insurance will provide a financial recompense in the event of lost time due to a disaster, it is no substitute for adequately securing the information in the first place.

All teleworkers should be issued with desk and equipment stickers with the security industry slogan—'Lock it don't lose it'.

(Note: also see Chapters 6.1.14 and 6.5.1.2.)

6

Technology

'*John Sculley, president of Apple Computer, has estimated that an integrated network could help create a $3,500 billion market where new technology will fuse telecommunications, computers, consumer electronics, publishing and information into a sprawling interactive information industry*'

President Clinton's announcement of America's
$100–$400 billion Information Superhighway, April 1993

Figure 6.1 Videoconferencing: 'just like being in the same room, but without the jet lag'.

6.0   THE INVERNESS TECHNOLOGY

During the summers of 1992 and 1993 there was considerable publicity in Britain about an experiment in teleworking being conducted by BT in the Inverness area, Scotland. Although this was a limited-scale experiment, rather than the full-scale introduction of teleworking for a large group of people, it is worth a mention at this point, as the experiment was at the fore-front of the use of technology to support teleworking.

6.0.1   Aims of experiment

Before discussing the details of the experiment, it needs to be put in context by considering the aims of the experiment. The 'Teleworking Systems' Group at BT Laboratories, Martlesham Heath, near Ipswich, were looking at ways that telecommunications and Information Technology (IT) could be used to support teleworking, and help overcome some of the known problems. Experiments allow the exploration of particular working situations in detail, and enable the team to try out ideas for providing support using tomorrow's technology. A series of experiments is planned, each with a different type of job. For the first experiment, BT aimed not at the professional working at home—of which there are a number of well-known examples—but at the 'mass market': the vast bulk of people doing structured, clerical or administrative jobs.

BT chose, as the subjects for the first experiment, Directory Assistance operators. The work of a Directory Assistance operator involves receiving and answering enquiry calls from customers and interacting with a remote central database. This is a type of job that has been labelled 'Telephone Enquiry Agents'. There are many types of work which are similar to this basic form of interaction (e.g. booking agents, credit card clearance, telephone ordering). The experiment ran from June 1992 to June 1993, and involved 11 operators working at home. The results of the Directory Assistance experiment will be useful in providing teleworking solutions for other 'Telephone Enquiry Agent' type jobs.

The main aims of the experiment were:

- to demonstrate that 'Telephone Enquiry Agents' can successfully work at home;

- to explore how the facilities and support provided for office based workers can be extended to homeworkers;

- to investigate how the technical and non-technical problems of tele-working can be overcome;

- to assess the potential benefits of teleworking for all concerned; and

- to gain knowledge and experience in setting up teleworking systems.

The experimental system has been designed so that the job of the teleworking operators remains essentially the same as that of the centre-based operators. In designing the experiment, many of the issues discussed previously—selection, training, safety, isolation, supervision, and so on—have been tackled. In addition to the core team, setting up the experiment involved experts from numerous BT departments—Security, Personnel, Human Factors, Training, Industrial Design, Selection Methods, and so on—and involved the relevant Trade Unions from the start.

6.0.2   Facilities

'IT' facilities have been provided to support the homeworkers while they are working, and when they are off-duty. These support facilities include:

- Videophone—for dealings with the supervisor, and for socialising with colleagues when off-duty
- Emergency alert—for notifying the supervisor of a domestic emergency
- News flash—to broadcast urgent information to the homeworkers
- Electronic forms—to replace paper forms used in the Directory Assistance Centre
- Electronic mail—for messages (official and social) to and from the homeworkers
- Electronic notice boards—for work notices and for social notices
- Comfort break—to allow the homeworkers short, unscheduled, breaks
- Performance feedback—to give the homeworkers the same information as other operators

Not all of the technology employed is electronic, however. The solution to requirements of security, safety and compactness of the home terminal equipment resulted in a specially commissioned 'desk'. The desk is designed so that an operator has all the working space needed to work in an ergonomic position. When work is over, all the equipment packs away inside the desk, with a motorised lifting platform for the relatively heavy PC monitor. The desk can then be closed up to occupy the minimum space in the operator's home for the non-work time. A lock on the desk prevents unauthorised fingers getting at the equipment. A picture of one of the operators working at her workstation is shown in Figure 6.2.

Figure 6.2   Inverness teleworker

6.0.3   How it was done

The support facilities were provided largely by a central computer running the application programs, terminals in the teleworkers' homes with windows for each application and BT's ISDN2 (the Integrated Services Digital Network, described in Chapter 6.1) connecting the whole together.

Figures 6.3 to 6.5 show how the work is extended to people's homes and the how the support facilities are included.

Figure 6.3 shows the normal configuration of equipment in the Inverness Directory Assistance Centre. Incoming calls from the customers are distributed to the operators by the Automatic Call Distribution switch (ACD) which gives an even loading amongst the operators and equalises the call waiting time. The operator answers the call from a console (sometimes called a 'turret'), which consists of a desk-top unit and headset. The operator uses a special terminal to interrogate the Directory Database and find the

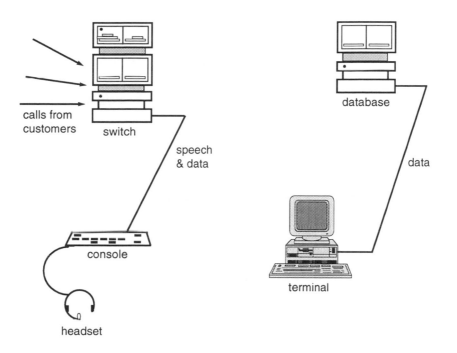

calls from
customers   switch

speech
& data

database

data

console

terminal

headset

Figure 6.3   Inverness technology: normal

telephone number required by the customer. All of the components shown in the diagram, apart from the Directory Database, are located in the Directory Assistance Centre. Operators' terminals are connected to data concentrators (not shown) which have high-speed data links to the remote database.

These essential elements, which allow the operators to do their work, can be extended into their homes using ISDN as shown in Figure 6.4.

However, when the additional support facilities are added, the situation becomes more complicated. Figure 6.5 illustrates the configuration of equipment which was used to support the teleworking operators. Multiplexers combine the data and voice channels for transmission across one of the 'B' (64kbit/s) ISDN channels. The ISDN videophone uses the second 'B' channel. Each teleworking operator has a 486-based personal computer which emulates the 'Centre' terminal (as shown in Figure 6.3). A specially designed keyboard was developed for this with the additional function keys necessary to interrogate the directory database. The operators' personal computers run a UNIX operating system with an X Windows Motif user interface. As this is a multi-tasking operating system and a windowing environment, the teleworkers can use all the support facilities simultaneously if desired.

There is a supervisor's terminal, located in the Centre, from where the supervisor can manage and interact with the teleworkers. A second supervisory terminal (not shown in Figure 6.5) is provided for the use of the

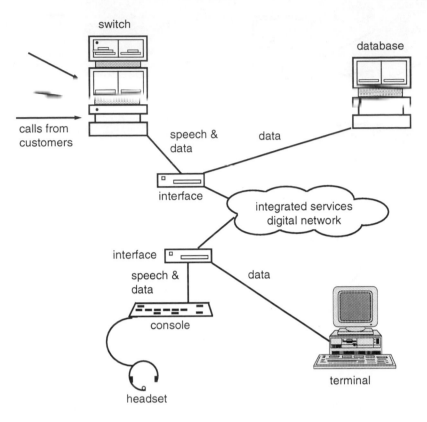

Figure 6.4   Inverness technology: extended using ISDN

Senior Operator responsible for the administrative functions of running the Centre, such as arranging duty rotas, holiday periods, overtime payments, and other matters.

There is also a terminal, with limited functionality, provided in the room at central office where the Centre operators usually take coffee breaks—to allow socialising between the homeworkers and centre operators (see Chapter 6.7.3). The Inverness experiment is further discussed throughout this chapter, in particular Chapter 6.14.1.

6.1   ISDN AND OTHER NETWORKS

6.1.1   History

The earliest form of telecommunications system was optical. Beacon fires to warn of anticipated dangers were followed in 1792 by the semaphore system which used large shutters or moveable arms mounted on hilltops for good visibility.

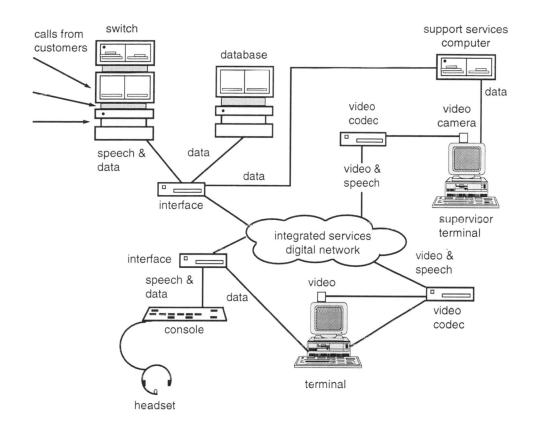

Figure 6.5 Inverness technology: support for teleworkers

In 1837, the first practical electrical telegraph appeared. In Europe, Cooke and Wheatstone produced a five-wire telegraph and Samuel Morse invented his system, although it took another seven years before it was put into service.

The telegraph which ultimately provided the telegram service dominated telecommunications for the next 40 years.

The work of Bell, Gray and Edison led the way to the development of the telephone service as we know it now. The expansion of the telephone network was so great that in the early 1900s the public telegraph ceased to be a dominant form of telecommunications. However, the need for a written record and the development of the page teleprinter in 1928 did lead to the development of the telex service. By the 1950s, most countries had three networks; a declining telegraph network, the telephone network and a telex network.

The telephone network was by far the largest and most popular owing to its ease of use. Based on a nominal 4 kHz bandwidth the network used analogue techniques throughout. In the local network, or loop, the transmission principles over copper pairs had not changed since 1880, and the signalling principles were the same as those used in 1910.

In the trunk network telephone signals were carried using Frequency Division Multiplexing over copper wires. Switching was electromechanical, either a developed form of Strowger's 1898 step-by-step technology or crossbar switches. The latter, developed in 1938, was a more refined form of electromechanical switch.

In the 1950s, two new technologies emerged, the computer and the transistor. An early benefit of the transistor was the development of the modem, a technique enabling data to be sent over the telephone network, initially in the 1960s at 100 baud but now operating at speeds up to 19.2 kbit/s.

In the 1970s the arrival of integrated circuits, together with optical fibre transmission technology, changed both the transmission and switching systems to become digital.

This digitisation has enormous implications. It creates an infrastructure of universal extent which can carry not only telephony, but also data at 64 kbit/s. As data and telephony can now be integrated on the one network it is now known as the Integrated Digital Network or IDN.

Analogue-to-digital converters located at the exchange's interface with the access network are used to convert voice signals into 64 kbit/s digitised speech. Digital transmission did not extend to include the local access loop to the telephone. These remained an analogue two-wire link. This remaining link, allowing 64 kbit/s access to customers, has now been completed (see below) and completes the last piece of the jigsaw of the Integrated Services Digital Network, or ISDN.

6.1.2   Overview of ISDN

CCITT defined the ISDN as: 'A network evolved from the telephony IDN that provides end-to-end digital connectivity to support a wide range of services, including voice and non-voice services, to which users have access by a limited set of standard multipurpose customer interfaces.'

6.1.2.1   Network user interfaces

ISDN is currently presented to the customer in one of two formats. They both offer the same facilities and services to customers.

Basic Rate Interface (BRI) This service offers a customer interface with two 64 kbit/s channels known as B-channels and one 16kbit/s signalling channel known as the D-channel. Collectively this can be known as the 2B+D service. There appears to be little logic to the choice of letters: B follows A which stands for analogue and D derives from the Greek letter Delta which means a small increment, in mathematical circles. Each B-channel can independently carry a speech or data call. The signalling channel is used to set up and clear calls on both B-channels. It is also used as a data link to convey small amounts of packet data in parallel with the B-channels. The service is connected to the exchange via a single copper pair and is presented to the customer in the form of a 'box on the wall' known as an NT1.

The NT1 is powered from the network which is in turn powered from the electricity mains. Networks continue to operate under mains failure because each exchange is isolated from the mains by battery back-up and/or diesel generators. TE1 equipment is normally expected to be powered locally from the mains; however, a small amount of current is available from the NT1 to allow a single 'designated' terminal to operate during power failure.

Primary Rate Interface (PRI)   Primary Rate ISDN provides the customer with 30 B-channels and one 64 kbit/s D-channel (30B+D). This service is usually used by business customers to connect large Private Branch eXchanges (PBXs) to the network. The service will be of great benefit to data bureaus which require fast data access and are currently restricted by slow analogue data modems. This service should not be thought of as a 2 Mbit/s service; it provides 30 separate B-channels. The user network interface is a standard transmission interface using coaxial cable.

In the USA this is provided as a 23B+D service delivered over twisted-pair wires.

6.1.2.2   ISDN services

Supplementary services   Both basic and primary rate services are identical. BRI customers will have the ability to make two calls simultaneously on the two B channels using speech or up to 64kbit/s data; PRI customers can do this for 30 calls. In addition to simple calls, a range of standardised enhanced facilities are provided by ISDN and these are known as Supplementary Services. There is a large number of such services either currently supported or being introduced shortly. Those most relevant to teleworking are listed next.

Supplementary Service	Description
Call Forwarding	Allows a customer to divert all calls, calls when line is busy or calls with a specific basic service
Call Hold	The customer can place a call on hold to make or receive another call. Calls on hold are still metered to the calling customer.
Calling Line Identification (Presentation)	Allows a customer to have his/her number presented to the called party prior to their answering. This allows the called party to confirm the identity of the calling party

Supplementary Service	Description
Call Transfer	Calls can be transferred to third party. Transfer may be initiated remotely or from the customers' premises as required
Call Waiting	Notifies the customer of an incoming call which can then be put on hold, ignored or answered
Conference Call	Allows up to 10 customers to hold one simultaneous call. Callers may be added to, or drop out from, the conference at any time during the call
Connected Line Identification (Presentation)	Displays the actual number a customer is connected to. This allows the customer to have knowledge of diverted calls
Connected Line Identification (Restriction)	Allows the called party to hide any call diversions. This is useful when the call has been diverted to an ex-directory number
Line Hunting	Allows calls to be evenly distributed over a number of line in a group. This is particularly useful for telesales environments to ensure all lines are used efficiently.
Multiple Subscriber Number (MSN)	The incoming line has 10 directory numbers mapped to it, each of which may be used to separately identify a terminal.

Network providers will package bundles of these supplementary services for specific customer applications. A 'solution' may well include CPE to interact with network services, thus providing a tailor-made network service package for the customer.

Packet access Future planned enhancements to the BRI service are:

- D-Channel Packet Access
- B-Channel Packet Access

D-Channel Packet Access has been identified as one of the major advances for the sale of BRI. This is access via the D-channel to the packet data network. An example of an application which would use this service is

Electronic Funds Transfer Point-of-Sale. Typically this type of application involves transmitting small packets of information and expecting a reply within a short time. Such transactions can take place independently of B-channel calls.

Conversely the higher data rate B-Channel Packet Access will be available shortly. B-Channel Packet Access uses a switched circuit call path to connect to the packet network and uses the B-channel to convey standard packets.

6.1.3   ISDN market

In the UK a PRI service based upon proprietary signalling was launched in 1988, and is largely used by PBXs. The BRI service was launched in February 1991 and conforms to international standards. A major factor in the recent past has been the availability of approved Customer Premises Equipment and much effort has lately been put into this issue. The main problem being experienced by manufacturers is the subtle differences between the implementation of ISDN in various countries. This results in CPE which requires modification in each country and hence increases costs.

Since the IDN is now largely in place in the UK, both PRI and BRI are available anywhere in the UK. Those exchanges which are not digital can be served by remote ISDN multiplexer units connected by megastream links, although this is not very economic and is usually reserved for customers making large purchases of ISDN lines. This picture is also true in the rest of Europe.

In the USA, most of the Regional Bell Operating Companies have some form of ISDN BRI service offering. Currently these are grouped into 'islands' of service with the longer distance routes only now being developed and installed. A recent initiative involving both network providers and equipment suppliers has attempted to coordinate the industry towards a common ISDN1 goal. The primary rate digital service offered mostly today is based upon 'bit-robbed' signalling which serves voice applications. Only recently have offerings of 23B+D become available.

The technology in the USA is now available to support a nationally available ISDN service. The next two to three years will determine how fast the deployment takes place. Strong customer demand will ensure its success.

6.1.4   ISDN products

Currently available equipment falls into six general categories.

6.1.4.1   High quality speech

In addition to normal speech quality over 64 kbit/s, available products can increase speech quality. Equipment is available which can deliver 7 kHz

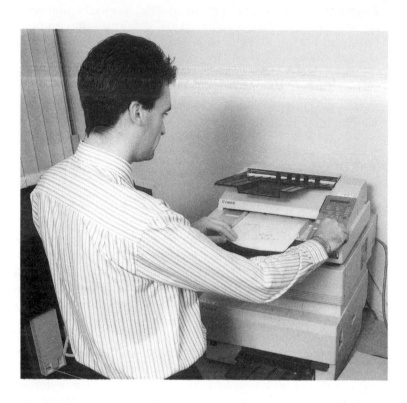

Figure 6.6   Group 4 facsimile

speech over a single 64 kbit/s channel using speech compression techniques. With the use of six 64 kbit/s channels to provide a higher bandwidth bit rate, it is also possible to deliver CD music quality (20 kHz bandwidth) stereo signals over the ISDN.

6.1.4.2   Facsimile

An analogue Group 3 fax machine can send a page of text every 30 seconds. An ISDN Group 4 machine is capable of conveying a letter quality image which can be delivered on plain paper using laser printing techniques every 10–15 seconds. Larger documents become particularly easy to convey on this equipment.

6.1.4.3   Photographic Videotex

The availability of technologies such as optical storage and graphic display controllers has made it possible to contemplate the storage and transmission of photographic pictures over ISDN.

An ISO signal processing and data compression standard known as Discrete Cosine Transform is illustrated in Figure 6.7 for differing compres-

Figure 6.7 Pictures produced using DCT (Discrete Cosine Transfer) compression. Top: at 0.08 bit/pixel. Bottom: at 2.25 bit/pixel

sion ratios (bits/pixel). An ISDN picture capable of transmission once every five seconds can be achieved with a compression of 0.5–1 bit/pixel. This is thought to be a good rate for browsing of databases.

6.1.4.4 Audiovisual

Again modern signal processing and data compression techniques allow a combination of video and voice signals to be compressed down to 64 kbit/s. Although at these rates the pictures are noticeably jerky and require a fixed

Figure 6.8   Telesurveillance

camera position to avoid excessive movements, remote surveillance
applications needs are satisfied.

In Figure 6.8, the operator has a menu of telephone numbers in front of
her, each of which has a slow scan surveillance camera connected. She can
view each camera at will on the associated television screen. The system
shown may access up to four cameras and display each on a quarter of the
screen. This has obvious applications for security (Chapter 5) and traffic
control.

Using the same technique, it is possible to both see and hear the person
over the ISDN using a videophone. Figure 6.9 shows a stand-alone videophone. Service can be provided over a single B-channel using 48 kbit/s for
video and 16 kbit/s for speech, or with greater quality over two B-channels
using 64 + 64 or 112 + 16 kbit/s for video and speech. As an alternative the
videophone function may be incorporated into a personal computer. In this
case, it is customary to have the videophone picture as a PC window which
may be moved and zoomed like any other window.

The intelligence of the PC may also be used to control a multipoint videoconferencing environment (Figure 6.10) integrated with other facilities
allowing the exchange of numerical and graphical information between the

Figure 6.9   ISDN videophone

participants. This leads on to the concept of a multimedia terminal. In the future, for example, during a videotelephone call, the user may wish to send a low data rate text on a facsimile picture, and having displayed the text or picture the sender may wish to control an electronic pointer to highlight a particular area of the destination display.

If greater picture quality is required, such as for videoconferencing, 384 kbit/s data rates are required.

6.1.4.5 Data equipment

Terminal Adapter units allow existing terminals to be connected to the ISDN. They are stand-alone units which provide a traditional interface, such as V24 or X21. Alternatively, personal computers may be connected directly to the ISDN by plug-in cards.

A wide range of LAN–LAN equipment is also available, ranging from simple multiplexers which emulate a private circuit up to complex intelligent servers which set up circuits via the ISDN based on the routing and traffic needs of the LAN. Larger versions may use primary rate interfaces rather than basic rate.

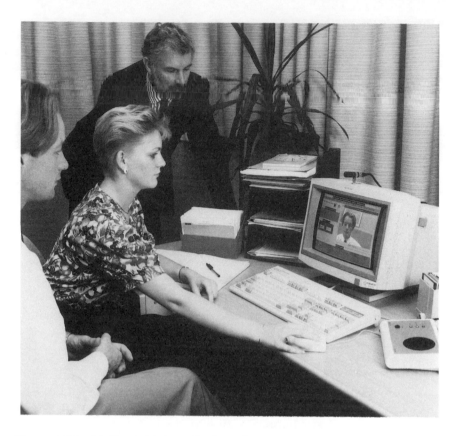

Figure 6.10   Multipoint integrated conference

6.1.4.6   N×64 kbit/s aggregators

There is now a range of products available which is able to provide a higher bit rate to the user than 64 kbit/s. This equipment does this by establishing N independent 64 kbit/s calls across the ISDN. Through a process of negotiation in the B-channel, the propagation delays of each call path are measured. These delay variations can then be padded out and the higher rate bit stream carried from user to user.

6.1.5   Impact of ISDN on teleworking

The teleworking population can be divided into three categories:

- Professional
- Clerical
- Nomadic

Two sub-categories also exist, real-time and off-line teleworking.

6.1.5.1 Professional teleworker

A customer would typically have a range of equipment at home, e.g. fax, PC, telephone. Multiple Subscriber Numbering would be required to allow incoming calls to be directed to the correct terminal. Being in close contact with colleagues and customers is important and would require frequent audio- and videophone calls. Such a worker would want a reliable service which is adequately served, and facilities such as Calling Line Identification (CLI) would be useful with dialback features. Call Waiting is also important.

Real-time professionals, typified by stockbrokers, would make small frequent transactions to the stock exchange or similar information operations. They will require either D- or B-channel access to the packet network and, in order to avoid long connection times, will require short dial up times giving the impression of a demand access.

Off-line professionals, on the other hand, are expected to rely on bulk data transfers, e.g. CAD/CAM, fairly often. At least 64 kbit/s will be needed to serve this need. Two or more channels may be better using aggregators.

6.1.5.2 Clerical teleworker

The off-line clerical teleworker can be characterised using a real ISDN-teleworking example. Crossaig, a company in Scotland, developed a teleworking application using ISDN2 to update one of the largest on-line databases in the medical sector called 'EMBASE'. This database is supplemented with entries from 3500 journals a month, a task which previously meant there was a 50-day delay between an entry being published and its being included in the database. To reduce this time to just seven days the Crossaig application software automatically sends the journal entries to a team of teleworkers who scan the journals and update the database entries. Each teleworker receives his/her next journal entry in a queue which is automatically controlled by the Crossaig system.

Using standard scanning resolutions of 300 dots per inch, a scanned page of A4 will produce 1 Mbyte of uncompressed information. This could be transferred to the teleworker in around two minutes using a single 64kbit/s channel. With data compression, the transmission time could be reduced to around 30 seconds. Having been processed, the return information will comprise those parts of the document containing images, which will be required to be returned unaltered, and text information, which would be converted to an ASCII format. This text conversion and editing will dramatically reduce the time required to send the return information. Since the processing time will be very much greater than the network transfer time, a single 64 kbit/s channel will be sufficient. This channel can be used either for sending or receiving work packages from the central system or for conversing with colleagues during timed social breaks. Data transfer could be limited to off-peak times to reduce transmission costs at the expense of additional storage in the teleworker's terminal to hold the day's workload.

Conversely the clerical real-time teleworker, such as a telesales or directory enquiries employee, requires relatively frequent, small amounts of data traffic and a dial-in voice channel. Calls would need to be distributed evenly over the number of teleworkers covering a particular shift. Following an incoming voice call the teleworker would initiate a database enquiry. This enquiry may result in the incoming voice call being transferred to a computer system for further processing, as with the simulated voice systems used to speed directory enquiries. In the event of an enquiry requiring interaction with the supervisor or another colleague, the voice channel will need to be held in the network so that an outgoing voice call may be made without needing to open a second channel. Having spoken with the appropriate party the original call could then be taken off hold and continued.

6.1.5.3   Nomadic worker

The nomadic teleworker's requirements can best be embodied in the phrase 'Roaming in the Fixed Network'. While being on the move, the nomadic teleworker will need to appear to be stationary for all those wishing to contact him. Each time the nomadic teleworker registers himself in a new location, voice calls would need to be diverted to that location until he moved on. Until it is more common to find an ISDN line on business premises than it is to find a PSTN line, nomadic teleworkers requirements will be mostly based on voice calls with enhanced signalling services. Digital information, such as fax and data transmissions, will need to be processed at the teleworker's normal office or sent to a bureau for holding, since these cannot practically be forwarded unless the teleworker can guarantee to divert to only ISDN lines.

In the long term, digital mobile radio terminals would allow slightly slower fax and database access to teleworkers.

6.1.6   ISDN conclusions

The ISDN is intended to provide a 64 kbit/s data and speech service over the fixed switched network. It offers fast call setup and clear times and provides a range of supplementary services.

It is clear that the ISDN is an ideal network medium for teleworking. It not only offers the bandwidth, services and supplementary services required by the teleworker, but also many products are available which are well suited to teleworking.

BRI has ideal facilities for the remote teleworker, offering two channels: two for work or one for work and one for domestic use. PRI is ideal for a central bureau, connected into either a PBX or a computer system.

6.1.7 Modems and multiplexers

Open up any periodical on communications or networking and you will be faced with a plethora of equipment and services, all promising to provide a trouble-free existence with your communications network. The choice is endless and, therefore, so is the possibility of error. The following is a limited discussion into the limitless world of communications. The communication channel between the home and the office can be provided in a number of different ways, largely depending on what services are required. Channels can be broken down into two main categories: 'switched' channels, which need to be dialled, have the ability to create a link to any other similar channel; while 'leased lines' or 'private wires' are run over dedicated, fixed lines. A switched circuit will be charged for as you use it whereas the leased line has a fixed charge regardless of its usage. Switched lines have the advantage of flexibility. If a group of teleworkers used switched lines then, in theory, any teleworker could create a connection to any other teleworker. These circuits, however, have the disadvantage that a connection has to be set up before information can be transferred. This problem is solved if leased lines are used as the connection is permanently established. If the connection is to be kept up for a majority of the day, then a leased line will be cheaper to run.

6.1.8 Data over the telephone

A telephone line is the most basic form of switched circuit. It provides a straightforward interface which is well understood and for which there is a wide range of equipment available. Furthermore, it is the least expensive option both to have installed and to run. With the right equipment, it is capable of transferring both speech and data, at the same time if required. It is, however, limited in the amount of data that can be transferred in a given time. It would typically take about half a minute to transfer a 10-page document across a telephone line although the actual cost of the transfer is likely to be the lowest.

6.1.9 Modems

If a telephone is to be used to transfer data then a modem will be required at each end of the link. These now come in many shapes and sizes depending on what data rate is required and how clever the modem is in transferring the data. The basic function of modems is to convert data into a series of sounds which can be transferred over a normal speech link and to convert these sounds back into data at the other end. In this way a block of data is transferred from one end to the other. Some modems offer to verify that the data has not become corrupted during transmission, and others will attempt to compress the block of data to enable it to be transferred more quickly. The modem at the other end then has to decompress it into its original form.

6.1.10   Private wires

If a telephone line can transfer sufficient amounts of data quickly enough but is used for more than a few hours a day, then a private wire may be better. It is likely have a higher rental charge than a normal telephone line, depending on how far apart the ends are, but there is no charge for usage. Furthermore, with no connection to set up, a private wire for homeworking provides a far simpler configuration. There are, however, limitations when it comes to connecting to other teleworkers or another office. As with the telephone line, data transfer will require a modem.

6.1.11   Digital private wire

If the amount of data which is to be transferred is high, or if greater quality is required, then switching to a digital line will be a better option. In the UK, the BT product is called 'Kilostream' (see Chapter 4.4) and can be supplied in a variety of data rates. A digital private wire does not need a separate modem, which will reduce the per operator equipment cost. Of course, if speech is to be transferred in addition to data, then additional equipment would be required. As with normal private wires, a fixed rental is charged depending on how far apart the ends are. The data link into a digital private wire will be in a format dependent on what data rate is being used. For low data rates the V.24 standard is normally used, which is compatible with standard PC serial ports. If, however, a higher data rate is required then the X.21 standard is normally used. It would take less than five seconds to transfer a 10-page document using a 64 kbit/s Kilostream link.

If you require the quality of transmission provided by a digital private wire but have a number of sites to connect, or the teleworkers need to communicate between themselves, then an ISDN2 line may be best—as described above. It has the high data rate and quality of a Kilostream without the limitations of a fixed link. It does, however, have the disadvantage of having to set up the call before a connection is established. Unlike Kilostream, an ISDN2 line comes with the same amount of equipment as a telephone, i.e. just the box on the wall. It is necessary to purchase either an ISDN telephone or, for data, a terminal adapter. Using both data channels the 10-page document would be transferred in less than three seconds.

6.1.12   Terminal adapter

The terminal adapter (TA), for most ISDN2 applications, is the standard access point. It will be via the TA that a call is set up and, where possible, call progression information obtained. TAs come in a number of different guises, depending on what form the data is in. In this way a TA is very similar to a Kilostream box in that, for low data rates, V.24 is used, and for high rates X.21.

6.1.13 Multiplexers

Down a single telephone line or a single Kilostream line you can, largely, only transmit a single type of information at a time, be it speech, a database file or a piece of electronic mail. However, using a separate channel for each data type would mean higher communication costs, under-utilised connections and generally an untidy solution. A multiplexer, on the other hand, combines a number of different channels of information, including speech, and transmits them over a single, composite, high data rate channel. Another multiplexer is required at the other end of the link to separate out the various channels.

Multiplexers come in a bewilderingly wide range of prices and facilities. Basically, two multiplexers, when placed at opposite ends of an established link, will attempt to synchronise with one another and agree how information from the various channels will be transferred between themselves. A simple multiplexer will have a number of configurable channels from which it will accept data. Using the protocol agreed with the other multiplexer it will pass that information over the composite link.

A multiplexer can transfer data in two basic ways, Time Division Multiplexed (TDM) or Statistical. In a TDM multiplexer a space is allocated on the link for each channel whether there is current data to be transferred or not. In a statistical multiplexer, space on the link is apportioned according to the amount of data there is to transmit on any given channel. Each type of multiplexer has its particular uses. For instance, if there were four data channels all of which were 90% busy then there would be little use in having a statistical multiplexer. However, for four high data rate channels all of which would be unoccupied for most of the time, a statistical multiplexer would be ideal, as it would allocate the entire link capacity to a single channel if it was the only channel active. However, it would attempt to share the link out fairly when more than one channel had data to send.

6.1.14 Security

The decision as to what form of communication and what communications equipment to use should include consideration of the security aspects of such a link. In general, the higher the data rate, and the more complicated the protocol used for the link, the harder it will be for a breach of security to occur. A high speed ISDN line transmitting speech encoded using a speech and data multiplexer is more difficult to intercept than a standard telephone line. Data that is similarly encoded will also present a problem.

The security aspects of a home to office link can be broken down into two basic types. First, there is the security problem of people eavesdropping on the link, and extracting the information. Second, there is the unauthorised use of the computer systems. The eavesdropper who can intercept what you are doing will only be able to access the data that you have accessed yourself. However, someone who can gain access to your database can gather all the information required.

Security from the eavesdropper can be improved using high speed links and equipment such as a multiplexor, which will mix up all the data channels together into one single, seemingly unintelligible channel. However, this may not be all that effective against the intruder who also has the same type of multiplexer, as part of the functionality of a multiplexer is to attempt to synchronise with another multiplexer. The task of deciphering the 'code' will be dutifully done by the multiplexers themselves! On the other hand, the use of a password system and other security mechanisms like dial-back, where the central office holds a list of permitted telephone numbers, and will dial you back before letting you into the system, will not be very effective against the eavesdropper, as you yourself will provide the access.

(Also see Chapter 5.)

6.2   COMPETITION IN TELECOMMUNICATIONS PROVISION

Until recently, choice for telecommunications buyers was simple. All types of network services were supplied by monopoly providers, in most cases a government department or state-owned industry. Even in the United States, with a private telecommunications industry, local telephony services were offered by local monopoly suppliers (of which the largest were the AT&T companies), and interstate, intercarrier and international traffic by AT&T Long Lines. Some countries (e.g. Japan) had two carriers, a monopoly national and a monopoly international carrier, but in most cases choice of carrier for the consumer, where available at all, was limited to a choice of where to live.

In addition, in very many countries, some or all customer equipment (telephones, private switches, ancillary equipment) was available only from the monopoly supplier of network services.

Over the last 15 years, however, competitive developments in telecommunications have snowballed, starting with the opening up of the customer equipment market, which will not be covered here.

Of far more consequence, however, has been the opening up of the network market, which has been facilitated by four trends, each affecting the others:

● The introduction of new types of service and carrier mechanism

● A belief amongst national governments and regulating bodies that competition stimulates effective and cheap services for the consumer, and that monopoly, or near monopoly, conditions tend to the opposite

● A requirement to look for non-governmental investment in telecommunications infrastructure

● The market pressure to introduce resale, either the selling of added value services over existing networks, or the resale of leveraged capacity on existing networks (simple resale)

Services in North America, in the UK and in Japan are currently the most changed through liberalisation and the introduction of competition, but the trend is virtually universal, and the arguments are now about when, rather than if, specific national markets will be fully open to competition, and, where they have been opened, how fast real competition will develop.

6.2.1   New types of service and carrier mechanism

In competition with the traditional fixed network/low access bandwidth telephony supplier three new types of supplier have recently emerged:

- Mobile and radio access networks
- Cable TV networks
- Competitive Access Providers (CAPS)/Metropolitan Area Networks (MANs)/Alternative Local Transport (ALT)

6.2.1.1   Mobile and radio access

The evolution of cellular radio systems to support mobile telephony, allowing far more customers to be served by a given radio spectrum, created a new market for telecommunications access, and offered governments and regulatory agencies the opportunity of inviting new companies to tender for licences. Indeed, in many countries, the introduction of cellular systems was the first opportunity taken to allow competitive networking, although, in the main, existing suppliers were either allocated one (of several) licences or allowed to compete, in partnership, for these licences. Cellular companies might be required, or might choose, to utilise fixed network links supplied by fixed carriers.

Similar opportunities are also now being taken in the allocation of licences to support radio Personal Communications Networks (PCN) and Personal Communications Services (PCS) and licences for Telepoint (CT2) public cordless telephone systems.

Licences have been awarded either for national services (e.g. in the UK) or for the local or regional services (e.g. in the USA) although certain companies (for instance McGraw in the cellular field in the USA) have put together portfolios of regional licences to create something analogous to national coverage.

6.2.1.2   Cable TV networks

A second set of opportunities for alternative carriers sits around the provision of cable TV services, where cable providers have been offered the opportunity of offering two-way telephony services as well as broadcast and interactive entertainment services.

The opportunities in modern cable installations, using coaxial access to the customer served by a fibre network, to offer high bandwidth as well as standard communications services may be very attractive, though it must be remembered that delivery of analogue television signals to the customer is not immediately compatible, over a single fibre system, with digital communications.

Those cable TV communications opportunities are already being exploited in the UK by a number of cable companies, many of them owned by US local telephony carriers. In the US itself many cable companies (singly or in consortia) have taken the opportunity to apply for licences to offer PCS, which may include radio access, but are unlikely, in most instances, to make use of existing installed cable network to deliver services, as much of that installed in previous decades is technically unsuitable.

6.2.1.3   Competitive Access Providers (CAPs)/Metropolitan Area Networks (MANs)/Alternative Local Transport (ALT)

Particularly (though not exclusively) a US phenomenon, CAPs (MANs, ALT) are high bandwidth networks which serve specific (often geographically very small) communities and customer groups, who have communications needs in terms of both bandwidth and functionality. CAPs offer facility bypass, diverting traffic from local carriers for point-to-point (unswitched) services. These services mimic more effectively, for a group of customers, fully private point-to-point networks traditionally leased by many companies individually, linking their sites for instance directly to inter-exchange carriers. Services are most commonly delivered on fibre and/or microwave. Some regulators consider that CAPs may also be useful in offering competitive switched services, although this may not be uniformly treated as an attractive proposition by all CAPs. US IXCs are now terminating directly on CAPs, bypassing local exchange carriers. Some people indeed see the CAPs as **'carriers'** carriers'.

6.2.2   Competition introduced in fixed networks

The two major models for this have been the USA, where AT&T's end-to-end (local and toll) services were broken up and competitive carriers allowed in the toll and international arenas (but where local monopoly provision remains the norm); and the UK, where a full service competitor (Mercury Communications Limited (MCL), now owned by Cable and Wireless) was allowed to compete with the previously nationally owned carrier BT, providing telex, voice and data services, a trunk network, international services and local access. A third carrier (Ionica) has been awarded a licence, and by the time of publication more are expected to have been awarded. In the UK, connection to a competitive carrier can be made either directly, through installed cables, or indirectly, via another carrier, using appropriate access codes.

It is now increasingly possible to choose a local carrier or carriers and toll and international carrier or carriers, as well as alternative providers of Private Circuits. Large companies frequently choose to have alternative carriers (dual source) to meet security and resilience requirements, and software allows calls made by these companies to be routed via the least cost carrier for the particular destination chosen.

In the UK, customers can be connected to a network by one carrier but choose to route certain types of call (normally toll or international) via a second carrier. In the USA customers must choose which toll and international carrier routes their traffic once it is handed over from their local carrier.

Competition to stimulate investment A driver of both the privatisation of state monopoly carriers, and the introduction of licences for new carriers, is to move the costs of investment in infrastructure from the public purse to that of private enterprise, and, for developing countries and those in the former Eastern Bloc, to stimulate foreign investment, of both capital and expertise. The 'payback' for the state is a modernised communications infrastructure which is seen as vital for all other types of economic growth. In the developed world similar beliefs encourage the creation of the 'electronic highway' linking individuals and homes, as well as businesses, into the high-tech infrastructure data and multimedia communications, a movement with particular relevance to teleworking.

Added value and simple resale competition A final type of competition which has emerged is that which utilises either the functionality, or the capacity, of networks owned by others either to offer services with added value (i.e. more than simple bit carriage) by adding service or management elements to simple networks, or to offer services more cheaply by partitioning bandwidth and selling it on.

The key to all these services (and to services provided by wireless and cable carriers) is interconnection. In order to ensure that historically dominant carriers 'share' their customer base with new competitors, regulators require that 'public network' calls which originate from any customer of any carrier must be able to be received by any customer of any other carrier. This means that a call may start on one local network, pass through one or more intermediate networks and terminate on yet another local network. Regulation ensures that the dominant carrier must be prepared to allow its network to be used by other carriers to route traffic through intermediate points, where they do not have a network, to ensure calls are delivered.

6.2.3 Role of regulation

The regulators (State Public Utilities Commissions (PUCs) or equivalents and the Federal Communications Commission (FCC) in the USA, the Office of Telecommunications (Oftel) in the UK, the Ministry of Posts and Telecommunications (MPT) in Japan and so on) must ensure that carriers provide adequate access at acceptable charges to each other, within the locally agreed competitive framework.

Regulators need to balance the benefits of effective competition against the dominant carriers (often the previous monopoly supplier), which lead to new services, greater customer choice, greater efficiency, and lower charges in areas of competition, against the continued requirement to provide telephony access to customers who are commercially unattractive to the new competitors, by virtue either of low comparative usage, or of relative geographical isolation. In the short term regulators also need to ensure a smooth transition to rebalance charges to reflect costs between different classes. Regulators may also wish to ensure an even-handed or balanced approach to investment in infrastructure which reflects long term public policy as well as short term commercial requirements and reflects the political imperatives of the governments (state and national) which they serve, and may change emphasis as these imperatives change. In some cases it can be argued that, at least in the short term, customers, as well as carriers, are restricted by the regulator from a 'free' choice of what to do, and this has led to restrictions from using a single carrier, for instance, to provide all types of communications services, where this might be desired by the customer.

6.2.4   Billing

Customers are billed either by the carrier they chose to use (even when their calls had to pass over an access network, e.g. to connect with their chosen toll carrier) or, in some instances, via a chosen third-party credit or charge card, where those facilities exist. In those instances the carrier bills the finance company.

Much effort is exercised by carriers and regulators to ensure that the billing carrier reimburses other intermediate or access carriers for use of their networks, although much heat is also generated about what a fair reimbursement actually means. Regulators wish to ensure that dominant carriers do not benefit from that dominance in their dealings with other carriers, and to that end may decide to come closer to satisfying the commercial aspirations of the smaller carriers. In some cases the stated aim of regulators is to act such that the dominant carrier is disadvantaged through regulation in a manner similar to that of being fully connected with all aspects of service, before nascent competitors can actually offer that competition.

International call billing   Past practice has led to a billing regime where carriers agree with foreign counterparts, on a bilateral basis, an 'accounting rate' for calls passed between them (each carrier 'owning' half of each international circuit linking them). They then pay (or receive) a fixed percentage of that accounting rate for each call passed between them, irrespective of what they actually bill their customers. This discourages a carrier unilaterally reducing prices to customers, since their billed revenues will fall, but their payments to the distant-end carrier remain the same. It is certainly anomalous that short distance calls crossing international boundaries almost always cost substantially more to the customer than much longer distance calls within one country. It is equally noticeable that calls may be charged at very different amounts depending on the direction they are travelling—internationally both the USA and the UK are comparatively cheap to call from, compared with many other countries.

Many commentators believe that the era of accounting rate regimes is (and should be) coming to an end, and that increasingly prices will more closely reflect costs (cost-based tariffs). Competitive local and international carriers, and carriers using liberalisation to gain presence in a number of different countries, will encourage this trend.

6.3 ELECTRONIC MAIL

The potential for electronic mail began as soon as it was possible to store computer data on removable media. Whether this consisted of data represented as holes punched in a card or magnetic fluctuations on a floppy disk, the opportunity existed to send the data by post to the intended recipient. Of course, the main use for these facilities was to make backup copies of valuable programs and data. Probably the thought of writing a message on a computer, copying it to a floppy disk and then sending it to someone in the post, would have caused fits of laughter and a suggestion to use that revolutionary technology known as pen and paper! It is worth considering what is meant by electronic mail. There are two elements that constitute electronic mail: the data, and the addressing information that defines who the data is intended for. This is a broad view, but as will be shown later, this is a broad subject, and a narrow definition would not do justice to electronic mail.

Electronic mail systems can be split into two broad groups: centralised and dispersed systems. A centralised system, such as Dialcom or Telecom Gold, has a large central computer system, which users access to read their electronic mail. Each user has their own personal mailbox, which can be considered as a pigeon hole, where all their mail is held until they can read it. This means that the storage and access are provided and maintained by the service provider. Often, centralised systems allow connection ('gateways') to other systems, for example to the latest stocks and shares information.

The other broad group are dispersed systems. Probably the best known dispersed system is Usenet, of which Internet is a part. The major difference is that the user's mailbox is local to their computer system and their electronic mail may pass through a number of computer systems to reach its recipient. The most obvious difference between the two systems occurs when the users are on line. For a centralised system, the user is on line to read and create mail. This is usually achieved by using a simple text-based interface. For a dispersed system, the computer is only on line to pass the electronic mail. The user uses a local machine to read and create mail. Generally the interface will be more sophisticated, possibly using a graphical user interface (GUI).

A typical electronic mail message will contain: who the mail is addressed to, who received a copy, the subject of the message, the date it was sent, and of course the message. One advantage of electronic mail is that more than one person can be specified as a recipient, and the copying and distribution will be taken care of by the mail system. Common features of electronic mail systems include distribution lists. These allow mail to be sent to all recipients named in a list. Another advantage is the opportunity to use the computer to search through old messages using keywords to find some particular information.

The nature of teleworking means that teleworkers may be distributed over a wide geographical area. Therefore it will be necessary for each teleworker to have some form of telecommunications link to communicate with one another. For many teleworkers the only communications tool they will have access to is a phone. For this link to be used by an electronic mail system, it must be able to transfer computer data from one teleworker's system to another. To use an ordinary phone link in this way requires a modem. A modem provides a link over the public telephone network that supports the transfer of data from one computer to another. For a centralised system the data link will be used to allow the user to log-on to the central system to read and manage their mail, whereas the dispersed system will use the link to transfer the electronic mail. This makes electronic mail accessible from almost anywhere; anywhere, that is, where a phone is available. The speed of the link, the protocols used and whether the link is error corrected, will depend on the capabilities of the modems connected and how they are configured.

An alternative way of establishing a data link is by using a network dedicated to transferring data, such as a packet switch network. These typically provide reliable, error free, high speed data links. They are generally only cost-effective for high volume data users, so tend to link commercial systems with high traffic. However, users can benefit from packet switch networks by using local access points. These can be accessed using a modem over the public telephone network, which will typically involve only a local call and provide a more reliable link.

Deciding what equipment to buy depends on a lot of factors, from the speed of the data link required, to the value of the data being passed. Fortunately the problem is not compounded by having to decide whether equipment from one manufacturer is compatible with another's, because the equipment is more than likely to conform to one or more standards. The problem can then be simplified to ensuring that the selected products conform to the appropriate standards. There are many standards bodies such as the ISO (International Organization for Standardization), the CCITT (Consultative Committee for International Telephony and Telegraphy) and the IEEE (Institute of Electrical and Electronics Engineers). A few common CCITT modem standards are shown in Table 6.1.

Many standards originate from one organisation and are adopted by another. One such standard is the OSI (Open Systems Interconnection) model. The OSI model was defined by the ISO, but was adopted by the CCITT to produce the X.200 recommendation. The OSI model is important, not only because it has been widely adopted, but because it provides a framework for network communications. This framework divides network communications into seven distinct layers. These layers range from the

Table 6.1 Typical modem standards.

CCITT Recommendation	Description
V.21	This is for a 300 baud link. Using this standard, data is passed between two modems at a speed of 300 bits per second
V.22	This is a faster standard, and allows data to be passed at a rate of 1200 bits per second
V.32	This allows data rates up to 9600 bits per second
V42	This is an error correction standard. It is a packet-based error detection and re-transmission technique

physical layer to the applications layer. Of most interest to teleworking are the higher layers. The presentation layer, for example, includes data compression and encryption, but of greatest interest is the application layer. The application layer provides a number of recommendations, but the two of most interest are X.400 and X.500. X.400 is a recommendation for electronic mail. The recommendation provides for more than simple text-based electronic mail. It provides for a variety of different message types, including text, facsimile and digitised voice. The X.500 recommendation is for directory services. These are analogous to the Phone Book, but map names of people and services to their corresponding attributes (electronic addresses).

The recommendations are ambitious and complex, which has led to implementations which only meet part of the recommendations. Even so, the recommendations provide the bases for an integrated international electronic mail system, which provides for multimedia messages and for electronic mail systems to talk to facsimile machines.

While standards offer a common way of doing something, they do not preclude doing something any other way. Indeed there are many existing commercial computer systems, such as NeXT and Wang, which offer electronic mail systems with which users can send spreadsheets, databases and voice, all in addition to simple text. However, users can only exploit these facilities with other users who have compatible systems. It is possible to put together a crude multimedia mail system with just a file transfer package and a modem. Whether using a drawing package, or a sound digitiser, it is likely the work can be stored as a file. This provides the opportunity to transfer that file to a recipient. Clearly this is very crude; the appropriate standards are used to obtain the data link, and proprietary systems are used to obtain the desired functionality. It is this lack of compatibility between different applications that has contributed to simple text being predominately used as the message in electronic mail, because the vast majority of willions and word processors can display it. It also has the benefit that it doesn't require much data to convey a message, compared with data-hungry applications like voice mail.

The predominance of text-based electronic mail has also suited the data communications equipment available for use over the public telephone network. However, the emergence of technologies like ISDN is changing that. In the USA the coverage is growing, but in the UK the coverage already exceeds 90%. For the UK, ISDN2 provides two independent data channels, which can be installed almost anywhere. Each data channel provides a 64kbits (56kbits in the USA) data link, which is more than three times the speed of data links possible with modems. In addition, call charges for each channel are the same as normal telephone calls would cost. This makes a cost effective way to exploit electronic mail. Applications which require large amounts of data to be passed, such as digitised voice and graphics, are more viable.

So far electronic mail has been considered purely as a messaging system, delivering messages from one user to another. However, this is only the tip of the iceberg. At a lower level, electronic mail systems provide a mechanism for moving data from one user to another, and from one location to another. Providing more advanced applications to process that data opens a whole new era in electronic mail. To gain an idea of the future of electronic mail, it is worth looking at a group of users whose primary communications link is not the public network but the LAN. The LAN or Local Area Network is a mechanism for connecting computers in a local area, such as an office, together. The computers are linked using ethernet cables, and data rates of over 10 Mbit/s are typical.

Use of LAN-based electronic mail is expected to grow dramatically over the next few years, and the high data rates possible have encouraged software vendors to develop more advanced applications based on electronic mail. These applications offer new ways of working. One new area is scheduling, which allows users to arrange meetings, check other users' diaries, etc. The scheduling applications use the electronic mail system as a 'transport system' passing messages between one application and another.

Probably the most exciting new area is work flow management. Like the scheduling applications, the electronic mail is used as a 'transport system', but in this case to replicate office procedures. A typical example is a travel expense claim. A user wishing to claim expenses uses an electronic form to enter the claim. The form can then be validated for basic input errors by the computer and then sent to the user's supervisor for authorisation. Exactly who the form is sent to, and under what criteria, will be determined by pre-programmed rules, defined by the office procedure. These systems offer companies the potential for improved efficiency over paper-based systems, and even greater opportunities for teleworkers.

Currently, the facilities offered by these systems will be limited to users attached directly to the LAN, although these systems often offer standard gateways to allow connection to other electronic mail systems, such as X.400, PROFS and SMTP. In the short term, teleworkers can gain full access to the facilities offered by these systems by using products known as 'ISDN LAN bridges'. These bridges exploit the data rates provided by the ISDN to link the office LAN to the teleworker's home. The advantages of these products are that they make the teleworkers appear as though they were directly attached to the LAN. This allows an easy migration path for teleworkers, allowing them access to office procedures as easily as office-based workers but from the comfort of their homes.

The full potential for electronic mail still has not been reached. The common perception of electronic mail revolves around simple text based systems. But the real potential for electronic mail is as a 'data transport system', the potential for which can just be seen in LAN-based electronic mail systems. As standards mature and interoperability increases, applications that today are only just starting to exploit LANs will be available on a worldwide basis. Companies with distributed teleworkers on an international scale could be informed and coordinated using electronic mail. Electronic mail is more than a messaging service; the potential applications based on it are enormous, and its benefits are only just starting to be explored, which makes it an essential tool for any teleworker.

6.4 FACSIMILE

6.4.1 Introduction

This section outlines the development of facsimile, showing how the earliest ideas have evolved into today's fax machines. Facsimile has emerged as the most widely used telecommunications service apart from the basic telephone service. It is perhaps remarkable that fax machines now cost so little, given their complexity, and no other computer product is as user friendly. Fax is an essential business tool and it is estimated that there are about 80 million fax users worldwide. Fax machines are sold in High Street stores as a consumer item and this is extending the use of fax to residential and small business applications.

Fax is not generally regarded as being a 'high-tech' information technology product. Its popularity is primarily due to its ease of use and the fact that it is universally accessible via the telephone network. People also like it because of its immediacy and versatility. However, the full potential of fax has not yet been realised and this section outlines some of the new applications that are expected to appear in the near future.

These applications are resulting from the integration of fax and computer applications. Fax boards for PCs are becoming cheaper; it is estimated that more fax boards are now sold than stand-alone fax units. It is not difficult to imagine the provision of a fax board as a standard facility on every PC. In the past some commentators have suggested that fax has hindered the paperless office; in fact the reverse may occur.

6.4.2 History

The invention of the fax machine is attributed to the Scottish physicist Alexander Bain who in 1843 published an English patent for a telegraph recording machine that used electrolytic paper. A second design was demonstrated by the English physicist Frederick Bakewell in 1851 but this was not taken beyond the demonstration stage. The first attempt at a commercial fax service was set up by Giovanni Casselli in France but the system only operated for about five years. Bain's invention established the basic principles of facsimile transmission, that is, it consists of scanning and printing devices which operate synchronously and are connected by a transmission line. Achieving acceptable results was difficult and many refinements were tried over the years. A major improvement was due to Dr Author Korn of Germany who, at the beginning of this century, introduced optical scanning and photographic recording techniques, together with the use of tuning forks to control synchronous motors.

By the 1920s, fax was being used regularly to transmit photographs for the newspaper industry and later began to be used by meteorological offices. However, machines were very specialised, usually incompatible with one another, and had to be used on private networks as the public telephone networks caused distortions in the facsimile signals. Some companies introduced office fax machines but fax was almost totally unknown in the business world.

Many fax machines of this period were based on the rotating drum principle. The document is placed in a drum which rotates at a constant speed and is traversed from top to bottom by an optical sensor attached to a screw device. At the receiver, the printing medium is placed in a similar rotating drum and traversed by the printing device. The scanning and printing devices must rotate synchronously to obtain good results. The electronics used in these machines were simple but mechanically they were very complicated.

In the 1980s, fax machines began to use CCDs (charge coupled devices) as the optical sensing mechanism and stepper motors were used to allow automatic sheet feeding. Synchronous operation was no longer needed and this made machines quieter, easier to use and more reliable, since their operation was now dependent upon electronic rather than mechanical devices. In the late 1980s laser printing was introduced, and more recently ink-jet printing is being used to provide high quality reproduction at low cost.

One of the key reasons for the success of fax has been the acceptance of international standards. By the 1960s, the potential use of fax for office applications became more widely recognised, together with the need to remove incompatibility between different machines. This led to the publication of

CCITT Recommendation T.2 in 1968 which defined an international standard for Group 1 facsimile machines operating on the general telephone network. This standard allowed A4 or North American letter sized pages to be transmitted in 6 minutes using an analogue transmission method.

However, Group 1 did not become a well-established standard and manufacturers began to try out new encoding methods that shortened the transmission time. This led to the definition of a new CCITT Group 2 facsimile standard which was published in 1976 (Recommendation T.3). This standard defines a simple analogue encoding method which reduces the transmission time of an A4 page to 3 minutes without perceptible loss of quality. This standard was widely adopted and for the first time documents could be transmitted reliably between machines of different manufacture.

6.4.3   Group 3 facsimile

Despite the success of Group 2, the big breakthrough in the popularity of facsimile came with the adoption of the Group 3 facsimile standards which were published by CCITT in 1980. Almost all fax machines in use today comply with these standards. They operate significantly faster than Group 2 machines as they use digital data compression and transmission techniques.

Group 3 operates by scanning and dividing each line of a document into 1728 picture elements (equivalent to about 200 pels per inch). The standard vertical scanning rate is 3.85 lines/mm (about 100 lines per inch) which is adequate for text. An optional fine mode (7.7 lines/mm) is provided for better quality. Using a CCITT V.27ter 4.8 kbit/s modem, a document scanned at the standard resolution can be transmitted in an average time of about 1 minute. This varies between about 20 seconds and 2 minutes depending upon the document content.

Over the last few years, significant increases in transmission speeds have been achieved by the adoption of faster modems. V.27ter modems have now been generally replaced by V.29 modems which operate at 9.6 kbit/s. Recently the CCITT V.17 modem standard has been adopted and this supports a speed of 14.4 kbit/s. In the next two years we should see the adoption of even higher transmission speeds—initially 19.2 kbit/s and later 28.8 kbit/s.

Group 3 machines transmit documents by using a run length encoding method. This regards each scan line as being made up of 'runs' of white and black picture elements (pels) which are represented during transmission by different digital codewords. By carefully matching the codewords used to the frequency of the run lengths, using a technique known as Huffman encoding, a high data compression ratio across a wide range of documents is obtained. This encoding method is defined in CCITT Recommendation T.4.

Another feature of Group 3 is that an 'electronic handshake' is used to set up the call between two fax machines, agree on the various features that are to be used and control the document transmission. This procedure is defined in CCITT Recommendation T.30.

Digital encoding is more sensitive to transmission line noise than analogue transmission methods and so the Group 3 encoding method provides
some protection against errors by preventing them from propagating
throughout a document. However, telephone networks have improved considerably due to the introduction of digital transmission techniques and it is
now unusual to find fax documents that are seriously damaged by transmission noise.

Despite this, an error correcting mode (ECM) has also been added to
Group 3 and this guarantees that documents will be received completely
free of errors. In brief, this works by dividing the encoded fax message into
numbered frames which can be re-transmitted if requested by the receiver.

In 1992, CCITT extended the Group 3 standards to allow machines to
transmit simple 'mixed-mode' documents, i.e. documents containing both
facsimile coded and character coded information. Also the standards have
been modified so that they can be used as a simple file transfer mechanism
that will support the transfer of any type of digital information. This can be
used, for example, to transfer word processor, spreadsheet and EDI files
between different machines, for either processing or printing. These facilities are, however, not yet commercially available.

6.4.4   Facsimile on digital networks

In 1984, CCITT defined a set of standards for a new class of fax machine, i.e.
Group 4, which is intended to operate over high speed digital networks such
as the ISDN (Integrated Services Digital Network) and in a computer-to-
computer environment. These machines use an enhanced coding method
and a communication protocol based on the OSI (Open Systems
Interconnection) model, which provides automatic and error-free transmission.

Today Group 4 is not regarded as being very successful and there are perhaps less than 10 000 machines in use worldwide. This is due to various factors, including the slow introduction of digital networks and the very high
growth in the use of Group 3 on the PSTN. A Group 4 machine should transmit a page in about 3 seconds but this is generally not achieved due to the
complexity in setting up the protocol stack. Also, most machines are very
expensive because they are more complex and have a high specification,
including the use of plain paper and higher scanning and printing resolutions.

Recently, CCITT has extended the Group 3 standard to allow these
machines to operate over the ISDN at 64 kbit/s. Some countries consider
that such machines will be cheaper than Group 4, but this view is highly
controversial since other countries want to promote the use of OSI applications on the ISDN. At present it remains to be seen which high speed fax
standard will become the most popular.

6.4.5   The fax market

From about 1985 onward the fax market escalated at a phenomenal pace; in some countries the growth rate was over 100% per annum. This is perhaps due to the introduction of new technology which led to greater ease of use, substantial price reductions and increased reliability. Conservative estimates indicate that currently there are about 30 million machines in use world-wide, including 5 million in the USA and 1 million in the UK. These figures are complicated by the recent high growth in the use of computer fax units which will be described further below.

Up to recently, the fax market has mainly consisted of the sale of stand-alone fax units to the corporate sector. The most significant new market for fax today is the sale of fax modems, particularly in portable computers. We can also expect to see an increase in the installation of fax servers on LANs (local area networks) which allows fax to be integrated with existing office tools and provides enhanced features such as automatic document distribution. In addition, very cheap machines are being sold on the High Street as consumer items and this makes the machines readily available for the residential and small business user.

6.4.6   Enhanced fax applications

The introduction of fax boards (or fax modems) for personal computers (PCs) has created the stimulus for many new fax applications. In its simplest form, a fax board turns a PC into a fax machine and a programmable interface allows computer programs to control the sending and receiving of fax documents. This can allow any information created on a PC to be converted to the appropriate fax format and sent automatically to one or more recipients. Also faxes can be sent at predetermined times and retries can be automatically carried out if the recipients are busy. The advantages are savings in time and costs and improved document management. The reception of fax documents on PCs is often less useful because the documents will be in bit-map format. To process the documents, they will need to be converted to text by means of OCR (optical character recognition) techniques. However, as mentioned above, this situation may be alleviated by the use of the modified fax transmission procedure which allows binary files of any type to be transmitted. Once this facility is available, it will be possible to transfer files and process them directly on the recipient's machine.

Another useful feature of a fax machine is that it can be used to 'poll' a document from a remote machine. By setting the calling machine to 'polling mode' and calling the remote machine, any document stored on the called machine is then automatically sent to the calling machine. This can be used as the basis of a simple information retrieval system in which the called machine becomes a computer system with a fax modem.

More versatile retrieval systems can be realised by providing some sort of user interface by which the user can communicate with a remote database and select the information that is of interest to him. One method is to use an IVR (interactive voice response) dialogue in which the remote computer plays a series of recorded voice announcements. The user is expected to respond by pressing keys on his TouchTone telephone keypad which sends digits to the remote application in the form of DTMF (dual-tone multi-frequency) tones. Similar techniques can be used to develop fax mailbox or combined voice and fax mailbox services. Speech recognition may also be used in such interfaces but may be more expensive to implement.

Two other technologies that are currently being developed are OMR (optical mark recognition) and OCR (optical character recognition). In this case, the user would complete a form by filling in boxes or adding alphanumeric characters and fax the form to the remote database. The form would be interpreted at the remote system by OCR techniques and the information requested would be sent to the user by return or at a later time. The advantage of this technique, as in the case of IVR dialogues, is that the user requires no special equipment, apart from a standard telephone and fax machine.

There is also much interest in converting fax documents into EDI (electronic data interchange) messages and vice versa. In a typical application, a company can send an EDI order form through a server which converts the form into a fax document that can be received by another business which does not have EDI facilities. The recipient can then fill in the form and send it back to the originator. Here it can be converted back to an EDI format for processing as any other EDI message.

6.4.7   Teleworking by fax

A fax machine is obviously a useful tool in a teleworking environment as it provides a convenient way of transmitting documents between the teleworker, the parent organisation and the customer. The use of fax modems and suitable software in PCs can be used to automatically send and receive faxes at predetermined times and this offers considerable time savings and convenience in terms of document management. However, many of the other enhanced fax applications described above could also be used as an integral part of a teleworking environment. Consider, for example, a generic application in which a number of home-based operators are used to process customer enquiries or orders. When these are received by the parent organisation, details can be captured on a form which is then faxed to a database. When a particular operator becomes available for work, the operator rings the database access number and retrieves the forms that have been allocated to that worker. The information in the database could, for example, be accessed by means of an IVR dialogue. Once the form has been processed, the results can be sent back to the parent company or direct to the customer. The main problem with fax in the context of some applications is that received documents cannot be easily processed by the recipient. However, as mentioned earlier, the extensions to the fax transmission method to allow the transfer of binary files could open a wide range of new applications.

6.5 MOBILE SYSTEMS

Mobile systems are those which allow tetherless connection through the use of radio to replace the 'fixed wire'. There exists a large range of such networks each giving a level of communication and mobility aimed at a certain sector of the subscriber market. In the following sections we aim to cover the most important mobile systems which have most widespread use.

6.5.1 Cellular radio

In the UK there are two national cellular radio operators, Cellnet and Vodafone, both operating the TACS (Total Access Communication System) standard in the 900 MHz band. They both opened service in 1985 and, after seeing very rapid subscriber growth, had a total established subscriber base of some 1.4 million in December 1992. In the USA the growth has been equally spectacular, rising from 200 000 in 1985 to about 10 million in December 1992. However, the major difference is that instead of national operators there are hundreds of systems operating in Metropolitan and Rural Service Areas (MSAs and RSAs). They all use the AMPS (American Mobile Phone System) standard from which the UK TACS system has been derived; however, AMPS and TACS systems are not compatible (i.e. phones from one system will not operate on the other).

Throughout Europe there are a bewildering range of different national systems; most countries operate at least one cellular system, which are generally not compatible. As they are based on different technologies, 'roaming' (e.g. using your UK TACS phone in Germany) is not generally possible—although there are some exceptions, e.g. the Nordic countries use a common NMT (Nordic Mobile Telephone) system and roaming is then possible.

6.5.1.1 Cellular radio principles

Taking as an example the TACS system, two radio channels with bandwidths of 25 kHz are needed to support the 'go' and 'return' parts of the transmission. The spectrums allocation made to Cellnet and Vodafone by the Department of Trade and Industry allow them to have about 500 go and return channels each. It can therefore be readily seen that it is not possible to assign a unique frequency, or channel, to each subscriber and that some reusing of the frequencies is needed.

Frequency reuse is achieved by allocating a proportion of the available spectrum to each base-site and then limiting the area covered by those sites, to

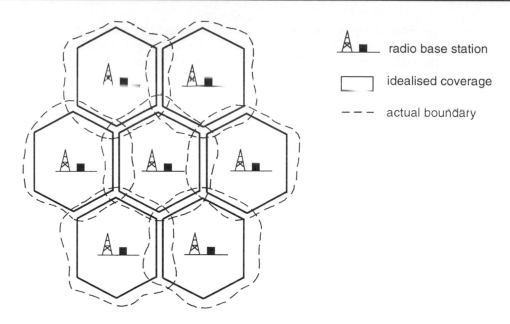

Figure 6.11   Cell layout for the TACS system

form cells. Regular patterns of these cells (see Figure 6.11) are then used to cover the required area, and provided the minimum distance between cells using the same frequency is adequate the mutual interference will be acceptable and so too will be the speech quality. In the UK each operator has about 1000 cells and channels are reused many times. Each radio base-site is connected to a mobile switching centre, which stores the current mobile location and routes calls accordingly.

6.5.1.2   System features

The main feature of any cellular system is that it allows calls to be made from and to (provided the mobile is switched on) the mobile phone anywhere within the 'coverage area'. Coverage area maps are usually produced by the network operator on a regular basis to reflect the current status of their network (i.e. with regard to roll-out of new cells).

As the AMPS and TACS systems are very similar they support very similar features. The voice transmission is based on simple frequency modulation and it is reasonably easy to eavesdrop. However, to hear a whole mobile call, which is likely to move from cell to cell and hence be allocated new radio frequencies as it progresses, would be very much more difficult. For those who need extra security some cellular operators are now offering the option to buy voice scramblers for cellular phones.

Other services that are on offer include call diversion, conference calls, call transfer, selective call barring and voice bank facilities. The latter is now widely used in the UK for incoming calls to the mobile where the mobile is switched off. The caller is automatically directed to the subscriber's voice mail-box where he deposits his message and then the mobile user will be automatically paged. The mobile user can then simply retrieve the voice mail message at a time he chooses through some simple key sequences on his phone.

Both AMPS and TACS support voice band data through the use of an external modem connected to the mobile, and specialised cellular modems are available for this purpose. It is generally accepted that rates up to 4.8 kbit/s are supported but this rate will vary with the radio conditions that apply at the time the call is made. Purpose-built fax machines are also available for connection to the cellular phone which can be powered (like the modems) from a 12 volt supply.

6.5.2 Cordless phones

Generally people are familiar with the simple analogue cordless phone they have at home which gives them a degree of mobility but probably little extra value in terms of teleworking. Digital cordless phones are now starting to appear together with telepoint use—this is dealt with under New Technologies (Chapter 6.5.5).

6.5.3 Paging

This is the most basic form of mobile communications, originally designed to provide on-site paging for hospitals, etc. Now four national systems exist in the UK operated by BT, Mercury, Aircall and Vodapage with a growing number of other regional operators. At the end of 1992 BT had about 400 000 subscribers and the other three companies about 100 000 each, giving a total of just over 700 000. In its simplest form the alerted pager will bleep, notifying the wearer to phone a pre-agreed number. More sophisticated pagers with LCD displays can receive and display simple messages.

6.5.4 Other systems

There are numerous other mobile systems which will not be discussed in any detail as their subscriber bases are much smaller than those already mentioned. Such systems include mobile satellite systems, private mobile radio systems, mobile data networks and airborne systems.

6.5.5 New technologies

6.5.5.1 Cellular systems

It was recognised in the mid-eighties that cellular mobile roaming within Europe was highly desirable and this led to the writing and agreement of the GSM (Global System Mobile) digital cellular radio systems specification. All the main countries in Europe are now committed and currently (early 1993) installing the GSM infrastructure—indeed some of the systems are just becoming operational. The roaming area will depend on commercial agreements between national operations, but in principle it will be possible to roam throughout Europe making and receiving calls. The UK operators will be Vodafone and Cellnet who operate the current TACS networks.

GSM was developed from the outset as a digital system and is almost completely compatible with the Integrated Services Digital Network (ISDN). As a result GSM customers benefit from several ISDN services such as call forwarding, call waiting, closed user groups, etc. (the latter two features to be in the GSM specification by mid 1993). Also, being digital offers other advantages. Firstly GSM can transport data directly, without the need for external modems, and more reliably. Rates up to 9.6 kbit/s are supported in both transparent and non-transparent modes. In transparent mode the bit rate will remain constant but radio errors may cause data errors (this will not always be the case as powerful error correction coding is used). In non-transparent mode, handshaking ensures that no data errors occur but at the expense of reduced throughput rate. The digital data on the radio network is converted in the GSM fixed network to standard voiceband data protocols for transmission through the PSTN. Similarly, facsimile Group 3 is fully supported by GSM.

A second advantage of GSM's digital transmission is that powerful encryption can be applied relatively simply and has therefore been included as standard in GSM. To 'break the code' would be very difficult indeed and GSM can be considered as fully secure. A third advantage for GSM is that it is more robust to radio interference, allowing frequencies to be used more often, and hence for a given bandwidth more subscribers can be supported than on TACS. It is estimated that this increases capacity by a factor of about 2.5. Although this is direct good news for the system operator, we must expect that its value will appear to the subscriber as reduced tariffs, compared with the existing analogue system, once the network matures.

GSM has been designed to work with a Subscriber Identity Module (SIM). This is a 'smart card' that is used to personalise a GSM phone (i.e. it is then the person who is traced to receive incoming calls) and give effective single-point charging. This gives a new dimension to roaming, i.e., with your SIM but without your phone.

Given that GSM is seen as a European system, it is expected that economies of scale and competition will drive mobile and service costs down to below those of existing analogue networks.

In the USA a similar, but significantly different, path is being followed. Again there is a digital system, D-AMPS (Digital-AMPS), which has much similarity to GSM but is less radical in its approach. GSM is a totally new system which requires TACS to be replaced in major frequency spectrum blocks as its usage rises and TACS usage falls. Given the large number of operators in the USA and the way in which the spectrum is allocated, this approach was not sensible. In D-AMPS it is possible in theory to remove just one AMPS channel and replace it with three D-AMPS channels, giving a similar capacity gain to GSM. The bit rates in D-AMPS are slightly lower than those of GSM so, although it can support data in the same efficient manner, 4.8 kbit/s is the maximum rate.

The evolution of D-AMPS is about the same as that of GSM, with system infrastructure currently being installed (early 1993). Due to this evolutionary approach to the roll-out of D-AMPS, dual-mode phones will be produced that can work with both AMPS and D-AMPS. Large-area roaming is also being addressed within the USA by the introduction of a backbone signalling system (IS-41). This is currently being established between many of the local operators, to bridge their effective local coverage areas.

The other 'cellular' systems that will shortly be launched in the UK are the PCN (Personal Communications Networks), Hutchison–Microtel and Mercury (a combination of the original Unitel and Mercury companies) systems. The PCN systems use the GSM standard with some minor amendments; the frequency is moved to the 1800 MHz band and only hand-held portables are specified. It is not wholly clear how this GSM technology will be 'marketed' so as to differentiate it from the GSM cellular offerings (e.g. will they push radio bypass of the BT local network?) but it is clear that the system will comprise a large number of small cells. However, the system features will be basically those of GSM, given that this is the base standard used.

6.5.5.2   Cordless phones

As with GSM, European effort has produced a pan-European standard. In the cordless case there are two standards: CT2, which is an interim European standard with products available today, and DECT (Digital European Cordless Telephone) for which products are expected in mid 1993.

The CT2 phone can be used in exactly the same way as existing analogue cordless phones but it can also be used in Telepoint systems. In a Telepoint system a local island of coverage (about 100 metres in radius) is established, for example at a petrol or railway station. In 1991 there existed four Telepoint operators in the UK but due to poor take-up of service only one remains, 'Rabbit', run by Hutchison which at the end of 1992 has some 10 000 bases but fewer subscribers than this.

The advantage of Telepoint over cellular is that of reduced tariffs but the disadvantage is its isolated and restricted coverage. This latter point can be overcome to some degree by purchasing a pager with your Telepoint phone, i.e. you can be paged anywhere in the UK and then go to your closest Telepoint site to make your call.

6.5.5.3   Paging

In alignment with European progress on cellular and cordless, the ERMES (European Radio Messaging System) has been agreed. Trials are due to start in late 1993 in several countries in Europe although roll-out plans have not yet been announced. As with GSM, the roaming capability is for the whole of Europe and that achieved for each operator will be through commercial agreement.

6.6   MOBILE PHONES

For teleworking we need mobile offices and not just simply mobile phones. Only time will tell whether the revolutionary approach of the PDA (Personal Digital Assistant), or Personal Intelligent Communicator, will achieve this goal ahead of the evolutionary approach already progressing with the cellphone. The PDA incorporates a tablet for written input, a fax terminal, a diary, and database management and access, which with an integrated mobile phone provides the Mobile Office. The first example of this product (the EO PDA) appeared in the USA in February 1993 with others (e.g. the Newton) to follow shortly. The initial cost of the EO was set at about $3000, but as with any new product, prices are predicted to fall as sales increase. These early products may well come without the mobile phone access—but later products will definitely have this feature.

On the evolutionary side we are seeing the size and cost of the cellphone decrease while its capabilities increase. On this latter point, the data and fax features of GSM (described above) are significant. TACS and AMPS cellphones are currently (1993) about 300 grams in weight and about 300 millilitres in volume, but the new generation of phones are planned to weigh about 200 grams.

It is difficult to quote exact costs, as there are numerous packages on offer in the USA and UK that trade cellphone 'up-front' cost, with the call charges, in order to accurately target various market segments. Cellphones are generally cheaper in the USA, usually in the range $100–$300 for common handheld units, with the pound price in the UK being approximately the same as the dollar price in the USA (the fairly common 1:1 dollar:pound conversion for electronic products). Typical regular charges in the USA are $15 per month subscription and $0.65 per minute for peak rate calls, and for the UK approximately £30 and £0.30 respectively (or about £17 and £0.50 for the low user tariff).

Operate times (i.e. the length of time the phone can be used before the battery needs recharging) for TACS/AMPS hand-held mobiles is product specific, with some products having different sizes of battery pack so that portability and usage time can be traded, but are approximately 12 hours standby (i.e. in receive mode) and 1 hour talk-time (noting that these are exclusive times).

Together with the development of cheaper, smaller mobiles with longer operate times, we have seen data capabilities being built into laptop PCs (i.e. integral data and fax cards) so that the next evolutionary step cannot be that far away. It should be relatively straightforward to produce a Global System Mobile PC card and then the mobile office is nearly here.

6.7 VIDEOTELEPHONY

A videophone is a telephone that allows you to see the person you are talking to, and allows them to see you. This has been a science fiction dream for many years, but with continually improving technology it is already a reality and looks set to become more widespread in the near future.

6.7.1 History

Videotelephony is not new; it was first demonstrated by AT&T in 1927, when their company president in New York spoke to then US President Herbert Hoover in Washington, although the pictures were only transmitted in one direction. The first attempt at a product launch, again by AT&T, was the Picturephone almost 40 years later. After an initial launch at the New York World's Fair in 1964, the Picturephone faded away in the mid-1970s, due to lack of use. The videotelephony marketplace has not developed since that time, until now. Only very recently, in the early 1990s, have costs of both the equipment and the transmission capacity required for videotelephony fallen to a level where it is becoming a financially viable option for business use. There are already numerous videophones on the market, and a huge worldwide R&D effort promises more and better videophones to come.

Videophones are currently pushing at the doors of the business world and are also trying to gain admission to the domestic market. If they succeed, it will become natural for teleworkers to have a videophone as part of their essential equipment.

Videotelephony cannot be considered alone, however; it has a close cousin in videoconferencing. The use of videoconferencing in business already has a proven track record. It has a small but enthusiastic, well established and growing user base. Videoconferencing shares much of the technology used in videophones, and its applications are similar. (See the case study in Chapter 4.4.)

6.7.2 Standards, networks and equipment

Current videophones fit into two groups; they are intended to work either on conventional telephone lines (the PSTN) or over a switched digital network (such as the ISDN). Videoconferencing systems are also designed to be used with a digital connection, which can be either a switched network or a leased circuit. There are widely used, internationally agreed standards for digital videophones and videoconferencing systems, but no such standards exist for PSTN videophones.

ISDN videophones come in two varieties. The first are stand-alone units which have their own display and camera, and could be described as entry-level videoconferencing terminals. The second type work on personal computers. They tend to work as applications for graphical environments such as Microsoft Windows. They appear in a window on the screen which displays the video and controls the call. A small camera is attached to the computer's monitor. The video is digitised and compressed either by external hardware or by a card that fits into the PC. This has obvious desk space savings, which can be especially important in the home environment. Both types of ISDN phones have displays which are about 16 cm across the screen diagonal.

Videoconferencing systems are larger than videophones. Even small units have displays that use 50 cm diagonal screens. Because of these larger screen sizes, videoconferencing systems need to send more data, at typically 128 to 384 kbit/s or higher. They can use lower rates (56 or 64 kbit/s) for compatibility with videophones. Typical videoconferencing suites provide one or two large monitors to show incoming pictures, and a smaller 'confidence' monitor which shows the outgoing picture. Suites such as these have a wide range of available add-on facilities: chairman control, document viewing, external VCR inputs and control of the remote camera are just a few examples. Videoconference terminals use open audio to give the impression of a face-to-face meeting, whereas videophones often use handsets to provide audio.

The quality of the video transmitted over the ISDN is good, but it may disappoint those who expect the same standard as conventional NTSC or PAL television. It is also limited compared to what can be achieved at the higher data rates such as 384 kbit/s or 2 Mbit/s which can be used for videoconferencing suites (see Thorn EMI Electronics study, Chapter 4.4.1).

Many computer-based videophones are not intended to be single applications. They form part of a larger suite of applications which are often called 'desk top conferencing'. These allow you to have a videophone conversation with another person and not only to see them, but to share data, transfer files, write on common whiteboards and examine spreadsheets together, all over the same digital network that is being used for the video.

One such system is being developed by BT and IBM in a joint venture which is known as 'Project Coco'. This is a desk top videoconferencing system for the ISDN, launched by BT as the VC 8000 multimedia communications card. There are two parts to the development: BT is responsible for the hardware, and IBM for the software. The hardware will consist of a telephone handset, camera, and two cards for slotting into a PC. On these cards a number of digital signal processing chips handle video and audio compression, huge amounts of memory for video storage are provided, and they also handle the interface to the ISDN. Initially, when a videophone call is first set up it will use all the available bandwidth, 128 kbit/s. As the call progresses, one person might want to show the other a spreadsheet with some information that he or she has been working on. The file can simply be transferred over the ISDN link that is already being used. The videophone will remain connected while this happens; the Project Coco PC videophone hardware is capable of dynamically reducing the amount of video information it transmits so that the data file can be transmitted at the same time. The system can also provide many other features. It has external audio and video connections which could be used to play video clips from a VCR, or show documents using a second camera. Access to a hard disk on the PC provides the possibility of capturing and storing video, audio and data during calls. This could form the basis of a video answering machine. As the PC is used to control the videophone it can provide 'power dialling' facilities such as directories which will remove the need to look up telephone numbers; type in a name, and the computer will find the correct number and dial it. In addition the PC does not need to be switched on to use the terminal. It can still be used for voice-only calls while the PC is turned off. The interfaces to control the hardware are being published, so anyone will be able to develop software for it. This will allow easy integration of current systems with the new videophone technology.

Project Coco provides a base for building systems that will support home-based teleworkers extremely well. Most of their communication needs for work (as well as some social interactions) can be provided over a single network, with the host PC providing an extremely flexible and versatile interface to it. The end-user price will make it half the cost of equivalent videoconferencing systems. Work is in hand to build specialised chips that will reduce the cost still further to a point that should give mass-market appeal.

There are two different analogue (PSTN) videophone technologies available at the moment. Both of these PSTN videophones have small Liquid Crystal Display (LCD) screens, about 8 cm square, and provide full colour video at a maximum rate of around 10 frames per second. The overall picture quality available with PSTN videophones is surprisingly good, but limited when compared to what can be achieved using a digital network The two types will not interwork, neither are they compatible with digital videophones or videoconferencing systems—at least, not yet. To use them, you need to know somebody else with an identical model. Marconi, however, have announced that they intend working on a bridge to allow their videophone system (M-VTS) to take part in videoconferences with equipment that uses the international standards.

Many meetings include more than two people. Similarly, in many videoconferences (over 20%, and expected to rise to 45%), more than just two sites are linked together. This is known as 'multipoint' videoconferencing. If only one (or perhaps two) people can use each terminal, as will be the case with videophones and systems like Project Coco, the need for multipoint conferences will become more acute. Currently, however, the video bridges required for multipoint videoconferencing are expensive. Costs can be expected to fall as demand increases, as it will with more videophone equipment being sold all the time. Systems are under development that will allow not just video to be provided with multipoint but entire desk top conferences to involve a number of terminals. Multipoint systems have the potential to become indispensable tools for teleworking, especially if all the facilities provided by developments like Project Coco are fully supported.

A European Videotelephone Experiment, known as the EVE-2 trial, was launched in October 1992.This is almost certainly the most extensive trial of videotelephony that has taken place worldwide. It is intended that there will be up to 250 users in each of the six countries taking part, all using ISDN videophones. There are a wide variety of videophone terminals in use in the EVE-2 trial; one of the main aims of the trial is to highlight any compatibility or interworking problems that there may be between equipment from different manufacturers or countries.

6.7.3   Applications

Videotelephony has a number of perceived advantages over more common methods of communication. In a normal office environment, you meet and talk to people during the day, both formally in meetings, and informally. Direct (face-to-face) conversations are the most effective method of communication; this is because you can build up a comprehensive view of whoever you are talking to, and fit your conversation to meet their circumstances and surroundings. There are three areas that contribute to this overall impression:

- Spoken language: Conveys factual information, as well as stresses on words and tone of voice.

- Body language: Facial expressions, gestures and general manner.

- Surroundings: The office furnishings, personal touches, the mound of work on their desk, etc.

Mail (paper or electronic), along with fax, allow precise information to be expressed. This is in the form of text, diagrams, etc. The next stage is the normal telephone and the inclusion of spoken language. This allows far more expression, so the information it conveys is more complex. Video communication (either videotelephony or videoconferencing) is the only process that can provide the complex information of body language and surroundings that make face-to-face contact so rewarding.

A different style of communication is needed for use with a videophone when compared with a telephone. In a face-to-face meeting, when someone is talking, you nod your head or use other forms of body language to show understanding. When conducting a meeting on the telephone, we have learnt to use 'acoustic nodding', i.e. showing understanding with sounds rather than actions. Communicating effectively using a telephone is an acquired skill. The natural reaction when using a videophone is to treat it as a telephone.

Unfortunately, the skills needed for videophone conversations are more like those needed for face-to-face contact. In other words, we have to learn not to show our continuing attention to a speaker with our voices, but with body language instead. It should be expected that there will be a learning curve involved when first using a videophone as we get used to using non-verbal communication in this situation.

Many people feel that it is difficult to create and maintain business relationships with people using only written media and the telephone. This is often because they have no mental image of what the other person looks like, their habits, mode of dress, etc. This is the sort of background information given about people and their reactions in a face-to-face meeting. This problem will be reduced by use of a videophone or videoconferencing. In addition, the use of a videophone has been seen to strengthen the working relationship between people who know each other, but do not meet face to face very frequently.

Many business meetings cannot easily be held over the telephone. This results in a lot of travelling in order to attend meetings. The travelling itself involves expense, and the time spent is usually unproductive. If more meetings can be held by videophone (perhaps integrated into a larger videoconference) this time and money are obviously saved (see Chapter 4.3.2).

Knowledge workers, working at home, are quite self-contained for most of their work, as long as they have all the support facilities that they require. In many cases, though, they need to visit their central base or office just to attend meetings or have discussions with their colleagues. A videophone or a desktop conferencing system allows meetings to be conducted without leaving home offices, and is especially useful for peer discussions between two people.

One of the perceived major barriers to individuals adopting teleworking is social isolation. This is due to the lack of peer contact of an informal or social nature that usually takes place at work. This contact has many forms, such as coffee breaks, chatting to someone in the corridor on the way to use the photocopier, having lunch together, or even a visit to the local pub at lunch time to celebrate someone's birthday. This social interaction adds to most people's perception and enjoyment of work, but may be missing in a teleworking environment. A videophone addresses this problem and makes contact with colleagues far more natural and valuable than just electronic mail or ordinary telephone conversations. Teleworkers need to take a proactive role in this. However, even with a videophone they have to make a decision to call, and cannot rely on bumping into someone in order to pass on office chat and gossip. Some systems have attempted to replicate this interaction, notably some work by Bellcore known as 'Cruiser'. This is essentially a desktop videophone system, but it is capable of 'cruising' around a number of offices and taking an audiovisual glance into each of them. Both people can see one another; if they want to chat they can halt the cruise. The cruise can be started either at the user's explicit command, or when the system thinks it appropriate—when the user has entered a print command, or finished reading an electronic noticeboard—any time that somebody might get up from their desk and bump into others. A fine balance must be reached, though, or such systems could become too intrusive and prevent work being done.

A related problem is 'out of sight, out of mind'. People who telework are concerned that not being in the office may reduce the number of opportunities that are available to them, perhaps for promotion or a foreign trip. Using a videophone, which is a far more natural communication method, could well help to remove this problem. In particular, if some system like 'Cruiser' was used to promote chance meeting by videophone, a team could remain far more integrated.

A videophone could be an ideal tool for giving briefings or training to teleworkers, as long as there is the facility to 'broadcast' the briefing to a number of teleworkers at a time. Presentations will carry more weight when there is a visual impact as well as the spoken word. In addition, the manager giving the briefing can watch for visual cues from the teleworkers that what is being said is being understood (see Chapter 3.5.2). Most videophone or videoconferencing products cannot provide 'broadcast' functions; they are not designed to, and to a certain extent neither are the digital networks they use. There is a need for more sophisticated facilities, like those provided by multipoint videoconferencing bridges.

Some teleworkers (for example telephone enquiry agents) may require on-line access to databases containing confidential information. Videophones can be used as an extra security measure in addition to the normal password protection. Before being given access to confidential information, a videophone call to the teleworkers' manager will confirm that it is a known user attempting to log on.

The only known use of a videophone in home teleworking is in the BT Directory Assistance Inverness teleworking experiment (Chapter 6.0). The videophone that was being used was combined with the operator's terminal; they had a single screen with a camera mounted on top of it. The videophone worked over a single ISDN B channel (at 64 kbit/s), using a BT Codec, conforming to the H.261 international standard. The video output was displayed in a window on the teleworker's PC. In this experiment the videophone was the main method of communication between the home-workers and their supervisors or managers based in the Directory Assistance Centre. It was also available for social purposes, both within the teleworking group and to chat to their office-based colleagues. It was liked by the operators and was used far more widely than the electronic mail system which was also available. To novice computer users, like the operators in this experiment, a telephone that allows you to see the person you are talking to is more readily comprehensible and accessible than a text-based electronic mail system.

There can be no doubt that the videophone is coming to the business world. It will eventually break into the domestic market as well. The question, that cannot easily be answered, is how quickly these events will take place. As an aid to teleworking, the videophone has yet to prove itself, although the initial prospects look good. There are a number of areas where the application of a videophone could be advantageous. Much of the face-to-face contact during the working day of a teleworker could, with practice, be carried out using a videophone.

6.7.4 Technical detail

Broadcast TV-quality video transmission demands a communication link with a capacity of around 140 Mbit/s. This is prohibitively expensive for videotelephony. Acceptable picture quality can be obtained using a link with much lower speeds, even as low as 14.4 kbit/s. Using low bit rates for video requires a high level of data compression (up to 2000 to 1). This in turn calls for complex coding algorithms and expensive compression hardware.

The standards used for the ISDN (as well as other digital switched networks and private circuits) have been developed by the International Telephony and Telegraphy Consultative Committee (CCITT). They are widely adhered to by equipment manufacturers in both Europe and the USA, and are the same for both videophones and videoconferencing.

The important CCITT standards are:

- H.320   The umbrella standard for narrow-band visual telephone systems: this incorporates a number of other lower level standards

- H.261   Video coding standard for data rates at multiples of 64 kbit/s up to 2 Mbit/s

- H.221   Framing standard for a 64kbit/s channel which defines how audio and video can be combined

There are also three audio coding standards:

- G.711   Telephone quality audio, 3 kHz bandwidth using 56 kbit/s

- G.722   Wideband audio, 7 kHz bandwidth at 48 or 56 kbit/s.

- G.728   Narrowband audio, 3 kHz bandwidth at 16 kbit/s.

Two other standards which are commonly mentioned are CIF and QCIF. These are picture resolutions which form part of H.261. Common Intermediate Format (CIF) uses 352 pixels (samples) per line and 288 lines per picture. QCIF gives half the resolution in each direction (176×144), or a quarter of the total pixels, hence the name Quarter CIF or QCIF.

CIF is ideal for use in videoconferencing applications where a number of people are involved at each terminal, but for single user, face-only videotelephony QCIF is often preferred. This is because it allows for more pictures per second over a limited bandwidth channel, such as one 64kbit/s ISDN channel.

In stark contrast to the digital situation, there are no internationally agreed standards for videophones on the analogue PSTN. Two systems are available at the moment; one is developed by AT&T, the other by GEC Marconi which is sold by BT in the UK, and by MCI in the USA. The two systems, although similar in concept, will not interwork, neither will they work with products conforming to the H.320 or H.261 standards. Both systems code video using their own proprietary algorithm. While at first it may seem short-sighted for new videophones not to use an algorithm that is compatible with the CCITT standards, it is for good reason. The H.261 video coding algorithm works well down to around 64 kbit/s, but is not really suitable for rates lower than this. The Marconi system uses a 14.4 kbit/s modem for transmitting the video and audio data; the AT&T videophone uses a 19.2 kbit/s unit. The Marconi system (known as the Marconi Video Telephone Standard or M-VTS) is attempting to establish itself as the de facto standard, at least in Europe.

6.8   AUDIO CONFERENCING

The term 'audioconferencing' covers a number of areas. It can refer to three-way telephone conversations (or conference-calls), or to the use of a terminal to link people into a meeting remotely.

Three way calls are available as a dial-up service using a conventional telephone. Two of the participants establish an ordinary telephone call, and then bring the third party into the conversation using a key sequence to dial them. All three parties are then connected. An alternative to user set-up conferencing is to use a pre-booked service. The network operator can use a bridge to connect together a large number of lines. In the UK this can be up to 60 callers.

Audioconferencing bridges can also be purchased for private use. These are very flexible and can be used to dial out to a number of participants, or to provide a 'chat line' service where anybody can dial in and join the conference. Most PBX switches also provide a conference call facility within the exchange, and these can often involve external calls as well. The number of people that can be involved in a single call is dependent upon the exact equipment in use. Typically up to eight people can hold an audioconference on a PBX.

Audioconferencing terminals allow a remote site to take part in a conventional meeting. A terminal that sits on the desk in the meeting room provides both a loudspeaker and a microphone. This terminal plugs into a normal telephone socket, and connects to either an ordinary phone or another audioconferencing terminal. Anything said in the meeting is heard by the remote user, and anything they say comes over the loudspeaker in the meeting room.

Audioconferencing is often seen as the poor relation of videoconferencing. Like videoconferencing it has a small but dedicated band of users in both the UK and the USA. Unlike videoconferencing, however, it can operate with conventional phone networks, and without the need for specialised customer premises equipment.

6.8.1   Applications

Audioconferencing can be used to assist teleworking in a number of ways. For example, it could provide a method for a dispersed sales force to have a weekly team meeting without having to come to a central office location. In addition a large number of employees could receive a briefing remotely, simply by dialling in to the audioconferencing bridge at a set time.

Audioconferencing can also play a role in reducing the alleged isolation of teleworkers. For example, a terminal and audioconference bridge could be provided to integrate teleworkers with the office coffee breaks. This would allow them to listen to, and take part in, the normal everyday office gossip. This interaction would help teleworkers remain part of a team, even if they do not see their colleagues each day.

6.9   EQUIPPING DISABLED TELEWORKERS

One of the groups particularly likely to benefit from telework are the disabled, as many are relatively tied to the home. There are several disabilities including epilepsy, arthritis, blindness, deafness, multiple sclerosis, amputees and psychiatric disorders. Each problem has varying degrees of seriousness which leads to an almost infinite spectrum of abilities in relation to work. Covering this diversity is beyond the scope of this book, so for the purpose of this section disabilities have been grouped into four broad categories affecting Communication, Mobility, Dexterity and movement, and Continuity and speed.

The United Nations estimate that 10% of any country's population are disabled but precise figures are difficult to obtain due to the range of impairments, the degree of affliction and a reluctance of the individuals to 'register' their disability. It is a sad reflection on 20th century society that many governments have introduced legislation to force employers to make the necessary changes in accommodation and work practices to accommodate disabled workers. However, teleworking has the potential to replace this 'big stick' with a carrot by allowing the disabled to work in their own customised environment, and to interact with employers, in the same way as able-bodied teleworkers. This provides employers with easy access to an enthusiastic and productive resource while meeting their social obligations.

6.9.1   Home environment

One of the greatest challenges for the disabled person in the traditional office job is the trip to work. Clearly, full-time telework overcomes this and even part-time telework would be of considerable benefit. Working at home enables the person to operate in a physical environment which is more tailored to their needs. For example, blind people know the layout of their homes and can control changes, unlike in an office environment where other users move things around. Similarly, the layout of shelves, filing cabinets, stationery supplies, etc. can all be arranged to suit the particular disability, e.g. low shelves for those in wheelchairs. These individual requirements can be catered for when considering the design of the home office (see Chapter

Figure 6.12   A disabled teleworker at home using a specially adapted chin switch

6.13). A further benefit is the flexibility to work hours which suit the individual, which is particularly important for those who tire quickly and need regular breaks to recover. It is difficult to accommodate this and do a good day's work when confined to rigid office hours.

6.9.2   Information technology

One of the basic tools for any teleworker is likely to be a PC or data terminal. One of the major concerns will therefore be how a disabled teleworker interacts with the machine. Fortunately, a number of suitable user interfaces and input devices exist, although few are designed specifically for the disabled. The reducing cost of high resolution, large screen PCs makes it possible to tailor the display of text, by providing large fonts for the partially sighted. Furthermore the use of graphical interfaces, such as 'windows', make it easier for people with mobility problems who find typing difficult. Input devices such as mice, tracker balls, light pens and touch-sensitive screens, as well as 'Concept' and 'Mallatron' keyboards, provide a degree of tailoring for disabilities. In the future, the use of voice interaction may provide further opportunities, particularly for the visually impaired and those with severe arthritis in the hands, wrists and arms.

6.9.3   Communications equipment

Table 6.2 lists types of communications equipment that are available for people with disabilities.

6.9.4   Communications services

Table 6.3 lists types of communications services that are available for people with disabilities.

Disabled people are already benefiting from the availability of technology and the increasing popularity of teleworking. For example, Willow Telecommuting Systems in the USA has set up WilNet, a network of home based disabled telephone enquiry agents equipped to answer calls from customers' Automatic Call Distributors (ACDs). In the UK, Abilities employs a number of disabled people providing tachograph analysis services.

These are just two examples of the opportunities that teleworking presents for the disabled. The more widespread adoption of teleworking, coupled with developing information and communications technology and services, will undoubtedly assist the disabled in securing employment using information technology.

Table 6.2

Type of equipment	Disability	Description
Telephone with an inductive coupler	Communication	provides amplification through hearing aids
Telephone with visual indicator	Communication	visual display of incoming calls for the hard of hearing
Telephone with number memory	Communication/ dexterity	provides one touch dialling
Telephone with lightweight handset	Dexterity	easier to lift,etc.
Large key telephone	Dexterity/ communication	easier to see and target
Hands-free telephone	Dexterity/ communication	no handset to hold, allows volume control for hard of hearing

Continued overleaf

Table 6.2   (continued)

Type of equipment	Disability	Description
Text telephone	Communication	provides a textual interface for people with speech difficulties
Videophone	Communication	provides opportunity for sign language and an additional communications channel for those with hearing and sight impairment
Fujitsu DTC	Communication	allows freehand drawing, writing etc. via ISDN using light pen

Table 6.3

Type of service	Disability	Description
Telephone/text	Communication	E.g. Typetalk in the UK which translates text from text phones to audio and vice versa
Electronic telephone	Communication	Transfers to a PC via modem or on CD ROM
Electronic mail	Communication	Electronic messaging, ideal for those with hearing and speech difficulties

6.10   SATELLITE AND GLOBAL COMMUNICATIONS—LAND, SEA AND AIR

There is a new family of devices that can contain all the information you will ever need and lets you keep in touch with anyone, anywhere in the world, at any time. They are called 'Personal Communicators'. You can scribble notes to yourself, translate them into computer text then exchange faxes, electronic mail, voice mail and computer files, and manage your time. It's a personal messaging device and computer rolled into one which gives you the freedom to work where you like, when you like, without losing contact with your customers and colleagues.

The next time you are in range of the cellphone system or you plug into a

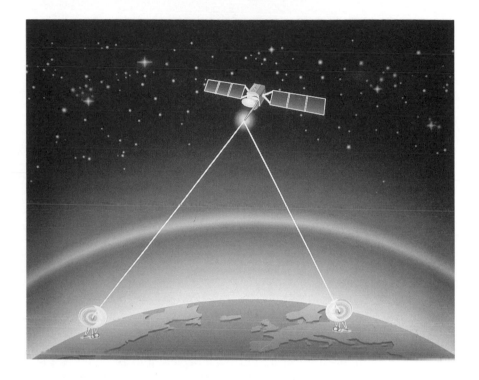

Figure 6.13   Satellites and global communications

phone wall socket, all your messages are transferred to you and any you have prepared are sent to their destinations. You can also connect to any computer, network or service in the world, providing you are prepared to pay for it and have authority.

If you want to be really remote, beyond the land-based or cellular networks, you can use a satellite. These were originally set up for maritime use but they can also be used on land. There are different global services offered depending on with whom and with what you want to communicate. The coverage is limited to the chain of four ocean regions, as shown in Figure 6.14, which include all the continents excluding the poles.

Inmarsat-Aero provides the BT-developed Skyphone service, which uses a voice Codec to offer voice communications from aircraft. The transceiver system on the aeroplane automatically changes to the correct ocean region and repoints the antenna, allowing phone calls to continue uninterrupted.

Inmarsat-M provides digital encoded voice—not telephone quality but much better than marine radio and data. The system terminal consists of an antenna, a transceiver, a phone and a socket for a data terminal (personal computer). It is a transportable system that can fit into a briefcase. You need to aim the antenna at the appropriate satellite when setting up the system and repoint it if you change regions. It is an ideal system for mobile journalists and business people, on land or sea.

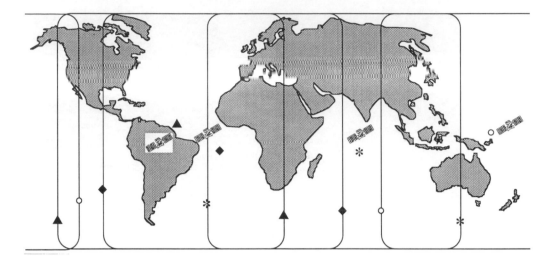

Figure 6.14   The satellite coverage

The Inmarsat-C messaging system is based on digital technology, which means that anything that can be coded into digital data—for example text or numerical information—can be sent and received as messages over the system. The system does not support voice communications. A wide range of communications services is possible on the terminal, depending on the equipment connected at each end of the communications link. Figure 6.15 shows a general arrangement of the Inmarsat communications system. As an example, the terminal may consist of an Inmarsat-C ship earth station (SES), also known as a transceiver, with a personal computer connected.

The Inmarsat-C SES omnidirectional antenna has no moving parts, but can transmit and receive signals from the satellites anywhere within its horizon, even in strong seas. The C antenna differs from the much larger Inmarsat-A directional antenna, which constantly moves to counter the motion of the vessel/vehicle and therefore requires considerably more elaborate electronics and power sources.

The SES sends and receives messages via the Inmarsat satellite system at a data signalling rate of 600 bit/s, to an Inmarsat-C coast earth station (CES), and then over land-based networks to the required destination. The role of the CES is to act as a gateway between the Inmarsat-C system and the land-based, national or international networks: telex, public data networks (such as BT's 'Global Network Services'), public switched data (PSDNs or X.25), public switched telephone (PSTNs) or private networks. In addition it can pass data to another mobile SES terminal. The types of communications traffic that the SES can pass are store-and-forward messaging, such as telex message transfer, electronic mail and mobile-to-mobile messages, all of which can be sent and received. In addition a message-to-fax service is offered, which allows faxes only to be sent from the SES and not received.

If a boat or an oil rig is fitted with Inmarsat-A equipment, high quality video footage can be sent to land stations within minutes of an event being

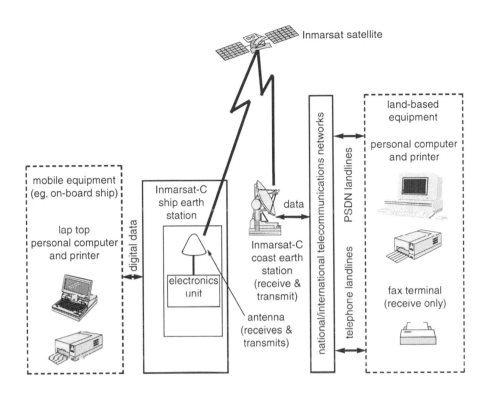

Figure 6.15   Inmarsat communication systems

recorded. This system relies partly on work done by BT in the compression of video images so that they can be sent over the Inmarsat-A chain. Experts on land can study pictures and advise on maintenance, for example, or guide people on the spot through minor surgical operations or other emergency treatments.

Inmarsat-C provides a low speed maritime service and is used as a store-and-forward system. The transceiver is about the size of a football and costs approximately £3000 ($4500). Inmarsat-A provides high speed service and can be used for full two-way voice, or video with the use of a video Codec. The transceiver is a 1-metre diameter sphere and costs between £15 000 and £25 000 ($22 500–$37 500), depending on whether it is sited on land or sea.

6.11   COMPUTER SUPPORTED COOPERATIVE WORKING

The term 'Computer Supported Cooperative Working' (CSCW) was first coined at a workshop in the USA in 1985 by a group of people discussing the way in which computer systems needed to be designed to support users in the tasks that they have to do in their daily work. It is a term that is now used to cover the study of a whole range of issues involved in providing computer support for people working together in a cooperative way. CSCW covers more than just the computer software and communications networks. It is also concerned with the sociological issues of how and why people work together and involves work in the areas of sociology and psychology to understand the 'human element' of cooperative work.

Systems used to support such cooperative work are sometimes referred to as Groupware and this term is used to describe a wide range of software products that support group working. Such products range from simple messaging and mail packages which allow users to exchange messages, through products that help schedule or run meetings, to complex systems that allow users to share documents and may even control the flow of work between people.

Groupware is not the only term used for these types of software and many of the major players have their own favourites. IBM uses the term 'Workgroup Computing', perhaps in contrast to the corporate computing which has been, and continues to be, important to its business. John Sculley of Apple has coined the term 'Interpersonal Computing', emphasising a move away from the Personal Computer environment with its personal productivity improvement software, to a networked environment supporting interpersonal as well as intercomputer communications. Microsoft's emphasis is on the Mail Enabled Applications, covering the specific segment of groupware applications that can be based on electronic mail. Others include Coordination Technology and Collaboration Technology, referring particularly to software to support the setting up and running of meetings. Group Decision Support Systems, which provide tools to enable people to analyse and handle the information needed to take decisions, can also be classed as groupware.

By these definitions, teleworking can be considered to be one aspect of CSCW and the systems used to support teleworking can be seen as a category of groupware. However, just as a group of people working together in an office using computers may not necessarily be making use of groupware, so teleworkers may be simply performing remote office working, using computer systems that support their own processes (document preparation, information retrieval, etc.) but do not actively support them in their interactions with their colleagues. So the principles being developed under CSCW need to be considered in the design of processes involving teleworkers, as much as they are needed in considering any other form of operation.

A simple way of categorising the whole range of CSCW systems is shown in Figure 6.16.

Same Time/Same Place These are systems aimed at supporting face-to-face meetings and helping with the decision process. Most products provide each participant in the meeting with their own keyboard and screen and the applications provide support for collecting and arranging information and arriving at decisions. Products in this category include GroupSystemsV from Ventana Corporation and IBM TeamFocus. VisionQuest from Collaborative Technologies Corporation has similar functionality and a complementary product is available to allow remote access to meetings.

	Same Time	**Different Time**
Different Place	Remote Meetings	Messaging
Same Place	Face-to-Face Meetings	Team Coordination

Figure 6.16   Categories of CSCW

Different Time/Same Place   These are team rooms which act as the centre for the group even if they may rarely be co-present. Support may include tools to access team information and to leave messages for other members of the group.

Same Time/Different Place   These are systems which support cross-distance meetings of two or more people at two or more sites. The system may provide either audio- or videoconferencing and there may be additional support for screen sharing or other information interchange.

A number of different conferencing products have been available for some time and are widely used in many organisations. Simple telephone conferencing can be achieved using a PBX conference bridge, separate conferencing equipment or a bureau service. The more sophisticated systems allow for hands-free operation to be provided for groups of people at two or more locations. Triton Communications' Netstar 2000 telephone handset serves the small business market in the UK with its user friendly, three-way conferencing and BT Star Services facilities.

Videoconferencing is also well established using either a corporate network or switched digital links. The equipment for videoconferencing tends to be either studio-based or 'roll about' cabinets that can be moved to ordinary conference rooms but in either case are not particularly suitable for teleworking (see Chapters 4.4 and 6.7).

For more informal collaboration and teleworking, the conferencing system needs to be integrated into the user's normal work environment, ideally within the PC or workstation. A number of systems are available which allow screen sharing so that people in two or more locations can all view the same text, data or graphics and interact with it. The Fujitsu ISDN conferencing system provides an audio link plus shared screen facilities so that participants can talk about information they can both see and manipulate. Similar facilities can be established using screen sharing products and an independent telephone connection. Available products include CarbonCopy Plus, PC Anywhere, LANsight and Timbuktu (for Macintosh). All of these could be easily used to help teleworkers share and discuss information with other remote colleagues.

The combination of videophone with screen sharing facilities can provide even better remote collaboration. BT is currently collaborating with IBM and Motorola to produce a card for a PC which will enable video communication plus information sharing over a dial-up ISDN connection. Similar products will also become available from other manufacturers bringing full featured collaboration to the desktop.

Different Time/Different Place   These systems provide for ongoing coordination by passing messages of one form or another. The messages may be text, voice or even multimedia. Systems providing project management, scheduling and workflow could also be included in this category.

E-mail is the simplest form of messaging and has been available for some considerable time. Microsoft with Microsoft Mail and cc:mail from Lotus are probably the biggest selling and best known. Microsoft Mail in particular has a wide variety of gateways to enable interworking with other systems, so improving interconnectivity. Other mail applications have additional features that enable mail to be sorted as it arrives and in some cases to trigger other actions.

Another form of information sharing and messaging is provided by Lotus Notes. An important aspect of Notes is the way that it supports a distributed database using loosely coupled, replicated servers. Lotus Notes has a number of features that makes it very suitable for teleworking. Users can work on local copies of information and then, at regular intervals, contact a central server to exchange e-mail and to update information that has changed in either the local or remote databases.

Workflow is another important mail-enabled application. These applications define the work process in terms of how information should flow between people, with various roles, within the organisation. Each item of information can then be tracked through the organisation and, as each part of the process is completed, it is routed automatically to the next stage. Staffware, Workhorse and The Coordinator are examples of products for developing workflow applications. These systems can be adapted to support teleworkers so that they can be included in the workflow process.

6.12   CUSTOMER SERVICES

Developments in computing and communications technologies have given rise to a proliferation of services offered by modern digital communications networks. It is likely that the scope and number of services will increase in the future as 'intelligence' is added to networks. Already many telephone customers in the UK and US make use of services such as paging, voice messaging, call waiting, three-way calling, call diversion, call forwarding, and many more. A lot of these services have an impact on the working and social life of teleworkers. Good use of these services allows teleworkers to improve communication based on maximising the use of a telephone line.

Consideration is given here to the services that are 'built in' to public networks with a description of what the services offer and how they can be used by teleworkers. The majority of the services described are commonly and appropriately termed 'network services' and are available on telephone lines connected to digital exchanges. There are also 'star services', particularly in the UK where Triton supply the user friendly NetStar 2000 telephone, as they utilise the '*' key on modern push-button telephones. Other services provided by networks and described here, such as paging and voice messaging, are not dependent on connection to digital telephone exchanges.

6.12.1   Call waiting

Call waiting lets a person already engaged on a call know when another caller is trying to get through. The called party hears a bleep alerting them to an incoming call; the existing call can be put on hold while the caller is identified. If the call is urgent it can be dealt with immediately; if not the original conversation can be completed. The caller, instead of hearing the engaged tone, receives a message indicating that the network is trying to connect the call.

6.12.2   Call diversion/forwarding

Call diversion enables incoming calls to be diverted automatically to any other directly dialled number and can be set up, and cancelled, at any time using the keypad of the phone. US telephone users can also use 'Select Forward' which allows the forwarding of calls from up to six specific phone numbers to a single number.

6.12.3   Three-way calling

Three-way calling, as its name suggests, brings three people together in one call. Using special codes, two calls can be set up simultaneously from one telephone, allowing a three-way discussion to take place.

6.12.4   Call barring/call block

Call barring, or call block as it is known in the US, is used to block some or all outgoing or incoming calls. For outgoing calls it is possible to bar only certain types of call such as long distance or international numbers. The US version of this service, call block, allows the blocking of calls from up to six phone numbers selected by the user of the service.

6.12.5   Charge advice

Charge advice, which is available in the UK, is used to find out how much a call, or a series of calls, has cost. Dialling a special code before or during the call causes the exchange to ring back, on completion of the call, with details of the call's cost.

6.12.6   Reminder call

This service, which is available in the UK, is used to set up a call at a specified time to act as a reminder of an important event.

6.12.7   Code dialling/speed calling

Code calling allows frequently used numbers to be called by dialling only one or two digits rather than the complete numbers. Also, when a dialled number is engaged, a short code can be used to automatically re-dial the number. Many modern phones have these capabilities built in and therefore do not need to make use of the services offered by the network. An additional service that is available in the US, called Return Call, allows automatic dialling of the phone number of the party who last called.

6.12.8   Calling line identity (CLI)/Caller ID

This lets the called party see the number of the calling line before answering the phone. At the time of writing, CLI/Caller ID is available in the USA although it is banned in certain states. Trials of CLI have taken place in the UK but it is not commercially available. CLI/Caller ID also facilitates several other services such as distinctive ringing, ring back on busy, return last call, and call tracing.

6.12.9   Priority call

This service is available in the US and identifies important callers with a special ring or tone. Up to six numbers can be selected for this.

In addition to the above network services there are others, also provided by the network, that are also relevant to teleworkers. These services such as paging and messaging are not constrained by connection to digital telephone exchanges.

6.12.10   Paging

The basic concept behind paging is the ability to be contacted by colleagues, clients, etc., anywhere and at any time. There are different types of pager, such as tone pagers which alert the carrier of the pager using a variety of tones, number pagers which receive and store numerical messages, and message pagers which receive and store fully worded messages.

6.12.11   Voice messaging

Voice messaging services let callers leave messages for people who are on the move or otherwise not available. It is possible to link the voice messaging service to a pager for immediate indication of incoming messages.

6.12.12   Application to teleworking

A teleworker's phone line is often the primary means of communication with colleagues, managers, and customers. The importance of this communication, more often than not, means that teleworkers obtain an additional phone line, particularly if there are other people at home. The teleworker is then free to customise phone-based communication using a combination of products and services, including those provided by the network, to meet his or her specific needs. The basic reason for using each service varies across many types of teleworkers but the exact set of services used depends on the individual requirements of the teleworker.

For example, call waiting ensures that incoming calls are always brought to the attention of the teleworker, thus reducing the chance of missing important calls. If the teleworker works at several locations, calls can be diverted or forwarded to the most appropriate place; this may be to the nearest telephone, a voice messaging service, an answering machine, or to a colleague. Of course, teleworkers who also have a company office may need to find a way of taking calls or messages that come in to their office phone. This could be through remote interrogation of an answering machine, call forwarding, voice messaging, paging, and so on. Many PBXs offer advanced facilities but they are not always available to remotely based workers. Voice messaging linked to a paging service is particularly useful to teleworkers who are constantly on the move.

Reducing interruptions is an important aspect of teleworking and the telephone can be a significant source of interruptions. Control of telephone interruptions can be done in several ways, the most extreme of which is to unplug the telephone from its socket; call barring or blocking has much the same effect and is not the most 'friendly' method. It is more desirable from both the teleworker's and the caller's point of view to have messages taken by either an answering machine or other messaging service. The Priority Call or CLI/Caller ID services, if available, could be used to identify important calls, such as from the teleworker's manager or customers, with other calls being ignored and left to an answering machine.

For the teleworker who becomes engrossed in the work, to the extent that he or she loses track of time, the Reminder Call service can be used to signal a meeting, the need to pick up the children, or even simply to stop working and take some time for leisure.

The other network services described, such as Code Dialling/Speed Calling, Return Last Call, and Charge Advice, are concerned with the use of the telephone for outgoing calls by the teleworker. Pressing one or two buttons rather than 10 for regularly called numbers simply speeds up the use of the telephone. It may be useful for the teleworker to know how much a call has cost, using the Charge Advice service, and thus note the business and private use of a single line or allocate call costs between clients.

Use of three-way calling means that a three way conversation can be held, allowing decisions to be reached in one call rather than iterations of several one-to-one calls.

6.13   DESIGNING A HOME WORKING ENVIRONMENT

Most homes are not designed for teleworking and current innovations in building design are accentuating the trend towards smaller housing. Some types of housing are more suited to telework, for example, detached and semi-detached houses that may not be over-occupied and have the possibility of extension or the conversion of a garage into an office. Town houses have more restraints on expansion, especially where roof space cannot be converted and where the garage is located remotely. Small 'starter homes' and flats or apartments are the least suitable for teleworking as extendability has been ignored in design and they tend to be densely occupied.

A separate room is often seen as being the ideal for teleworking. However most teleworkers don't have a separate room and have to use multipurpose rooms. Although having a separate room for working does have many advantages, some teleworkers can adequately cope in a room used for other purposes. However, a separate room does enable one to create the image and trappings of an office which can be more conducive to working and provides a good physical separation between home and work.

In choosing a suitable room for teleworking you should consider the following:

- Use by other family members during work time
- Space for furniture and equipment
- Space for visitors
- Access
- Daylight
- Artificial lighting
- Temperature
- Humidity
- Ventilation
- Sources of intermittent noise

- Provision of power and telephone sockets
- Security
- Safety

Separation of work space from the home is important psychologically, as it reduces the tendency of the teleworker to become a 'workaholic'. Having a workplace in the home can make it more difficult to stop thinking about work during family time, and similarly during work time it can be difficult to stop thinking about the house work or the children. Some ways of creating psychological boundaries between work and family life are:

- Working in a spare room
- Using screens between the work area and the rest of the room
- Creating the feel of an office
- Switching off all work equipment when finished
- Tidying away all work papers and materials
- Hiding all work equipment from view
- Going for a walk before and after work time

Most office furniture would not be suited for the home and so appropriate home-office furniture needs to be carefully selected and purchased. Furniture used by teleworkers should be ergonomically designed and conform with appropriate standards (e.g. EC or State legislation). Employers should bear some, or all, of the cost to ensure that good quality furniture is bought. The main characteristics of teleworking furniture to consider are:

- Sufficient desk top space
- Sufficient storage space for equipment and materials
- Compact
- Robust
- Hides and protects equipment
- Lockable
- Includes cable management
- Attractive appearance to fit with room decor
- No sharp edges or corners

Figure 6.17 shows a piece of teleworking furniture designed for a Telephone Enquiry Agent (e.g. a Directory Assistance operator). The unit includes most of the features outlined above.

Good ergonomically designed seating is of vital importance to teleworkers since around 90% of working time may be spent in the sitting position. Seating may also be required for visitors (e.g. managers, clients). It is important that

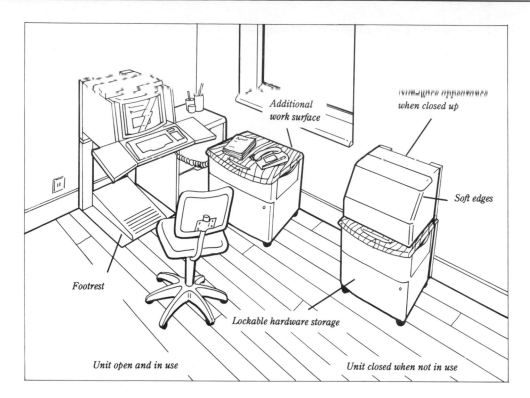

Figure 6.17

seating provides an upright work-like posture that will encourage work rather than a reclined posture that may discourage work and be very uncomfortable or even harmful for the teleworker.

Turning a domestic space into a teleworking environment is not always easy due to the variation in domestic interiors and in the lifestyles of potential teleworkers. A suggested approach is outlined below, based upon experience of setting up teleworking spaces.

Imagine you need to design a teleworking environment for a manager who teleworks part-time and needs to meet clients occasionally. You could create a questionnaire, based upon the checklists outlined above, which explores their home environment, lifestyle and aspirations of what the teleworking space could be like. You will also need to know the approximate layouts and dimensions of the rooms being considered as well as the equipment that will be used and the dimensions of suitable furniture products. Simple room layouts can be produced on graph paper and paper cut-outs of the furniture pieces produced to the same scale. By arranging the cut-outs of the furniture on the room plans, various layouts can be tried.

Figure 6.18 shows a living/dining room that is to be rearranged to accommodate a teleworking space for a manager. The room has two lights and accommodates seating and a dining table. There are two doors, one leading

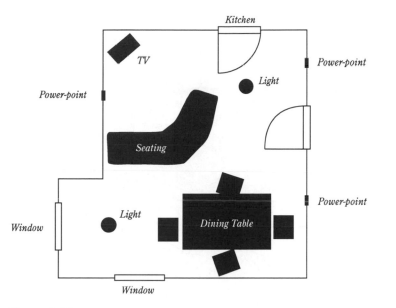

Figure 6.18

to the kitchen and the other to the hallway. There are two windows, one overlooking a busy road. By rearranging the paper cut-outs of existing and new (teleworking) furniture, the layout shown in Figure 6.19 might be chosen. This is a very simple but effective way of generating room layouts.

The work area has been located away from the doors and positioned such

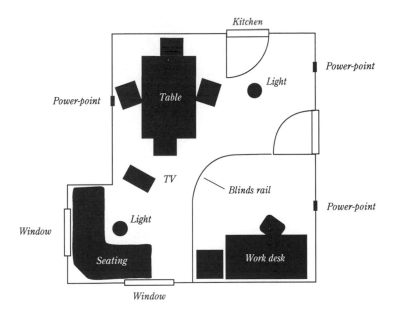

Figure 6.19

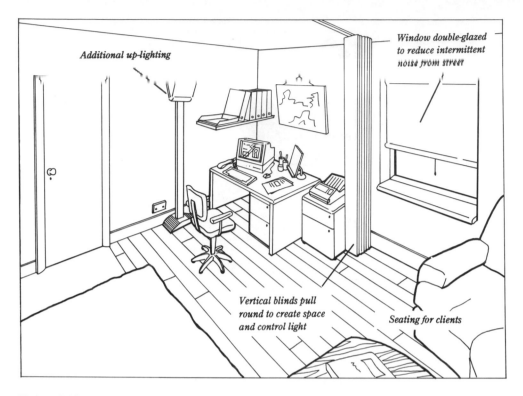

Additional up-lighting

Window double-glazed
to reduce intermittent
noise from street

Vertical blinds pull
round to create space
and control light

Seating for clients

Figure 6.20

that neither window should cause reflections on the PC screen. The desk is
located near power and telephone sockets and the seating has been moved
to allow the manager to meet clients near to the work space. Vertical blinds
can be pulled round the area to separate it from the rest of the room. The
room is shown in Figure 6.20.

Another example of a teleworking environment, for a consultant who uses
a videophone to communicate with clients, is shown in Figure 6.21. It is
required in this case that all the work equipment can be moved and stored
away. Thus the screen and storage unit are easily moved. One side of the
screen has a professional look that is used as a background for the videophone
image. The other side is designed to look attractive in the home.

With such a wide diversity in home environments, teleworking jobs and
personal tastes in design, it is not appropriate to specify the exact detail of
what is best for a teleworker. Instead the teleworker should choose the
designs that are most appropriate for them.

6.14   MAINTENANCE, REPAIR AND RENEWAL

Central office based workers particularly in larger organisations, often have
the support of technicians to deal with problems and enjoy easy access to

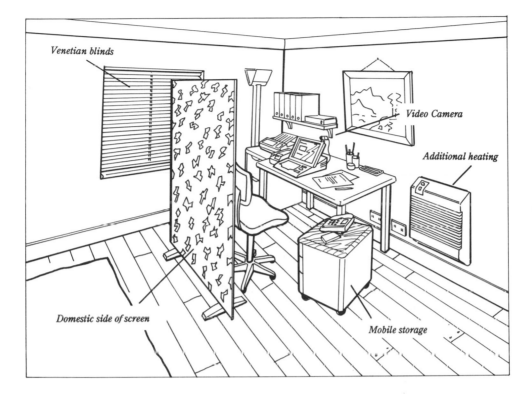

Figure 6.21

replacement equipment and spares. These are luxuries which few teleworkers enjoy, with the possible exception of those working from telecentres. One of the most important considerations for the teleworker is the availability of their equipment. In many cases the teleworker will be unable to work if key items of equipment fail. It is therefore important to plan the maintenance, repair and renewal of teleworkers' equipment to ensure adequate availability.

Availability can be considered to be a function of 'reliability' (the probability that the equipment will perform a required function) and 'maintainability'(the ease and speed with which faults may be repaired). Improved availability is achieved by improving the reliability, the maintainability or both. In order to achieve this goal it is important to consider these issues when procuring or renewing equipment.

The key factors which influence procurement decisions are shown in Figure 6.22.

There is no algorithm for successful procurement, as the relative weight associated with each of the influencing factors will vary from one application to another. For example, a teleworker who works at home part of the time and the rest at the office, with standby equipment available, will be less concerned about repair times than a full-time teleworker. It is possible to highlight the issues that require careful consideration and make some practical suggestions.

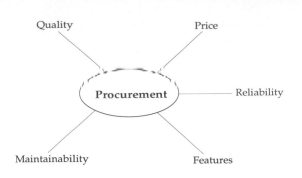

Figure 6.22 Procurement considerations

Identify key components and assess the impact of their failure This will enable you to put a value on that item, thereby enabling cost benefit analysis of various maintenance solutions.

Consider the life cycle costs, not the purchase price Equipment which is expensive to buy may be cheaper in the long run because it requires less maintenance. Similarly, items which are less reliable but cheap to repair may have low life cycle costs.

First-line support Teleworkers should expect to be asked to perform initial troubleshooting themselves. Beyond this, first-line support may be provided by a 'helpline' supported by the vendor, a third party or the teleworker's employer. Alternatively, field service personnel may be provided through the teleworker's employer. Many companies now outsource equipment maintenance so it may be possible to extend the contract to cover teleworkers.

Second-line support Second-line support is workshop maintenance provided by the teleworker's employer or through a personal maintenance contract in the case of self-employed teleworkers. Workshop repairs are likely to take several days so it may be worth arranging replacement equipment during this period. This is likely to be an option with maintenance contracts.

Adequate head office equipment support Teleworkers who rely on communications to a central office are as vulnerable to equipment failure at that end as they are in their own homes. Support for the central office end may be provided in-house or on a contract basis but, regardless of how this is provided, it is essential that the teleworker is not disadvantaged. Maintenance personnel may give the problems of office colleagues priority because those colleagues are available to 'chase' the engineers whereas teleworkers are out of sight and perhaps out of mind.

Maintenance philosophy Essentially maintenance falls into two camps, planned or event driven. With planned maintenance, components are periodically changed, even when they are still functional. This may at first seem wasteful but in some instances the loss of availability and labour and parts costs associated with 'replacement on unexpected failure' exceed the costs of scheduled replacement. Event driven maintenance, as the name suggests, involves repair on failure.

Training It is important that the maintenance personnel are adequately trained and provided with comprehensive and easy-to-understand documentation. This includes the teleworker who will benefit from sufficient training to allow simple loose cable or blown fuse type faults to be picked up and resolved quickly. A basic awareness will also assist in remote diagnostics. The teleworker may have a range of equipment (PC, fax, modem, etc.) which in an office environment would be maintained by different people. It may therefore be necessary to train field engineers in this broad range of technologies or, in the case of contract labour, specify the skills required in the contract agreement.

6.14.1 Case study: the Inverness experiment

BT's Inverness teleworking experiment (Chapter 6.0) involved a number of Directory Assistance (DA) operators working at home, in some cases from remote locations in the Highlands of Scotland. When a central office worker's equipment fails that person can usually move to another desk until the equipment is fixed. When a home based teleworker's equipment fails this is not possible and the best method of getting them back 'on line' must be considered. Efficient maintenance practices and well-trained local engineers were found to be of key importance, as any reduction in the number of operators available to answer incoming enquiries would quickly degrade the level of service.

Early on in the experiment, it became apparent that a significant proportion of faults were due to either equipment or software requiring resetting, either at the teleworker's home or in the DA Centre. Calling out a local engineer each time this happened wasted time. So, the DA Centre supervisors received formal training and documentation packs on basic maintenance techniques and diagnostics. Over the course of the experiment this resulted in some 57% of faults being fixed by the supervisors. There were faults that the supervisors could not diagnose, or fix, that needed more expert attention.

The systems used in Inverness were based on UNIX PC platforms. A major advantage of such a multi-user operating system environment is the ability to log in remotely to a teleworker's machine and perform software updates, restart tasks, diagnose local error files, etc. Furthermore, distance is no object so a UNIX PC-based central fault reporting desk can be anywhere in the country; only the engineers need be local.

BT's Integrated Services Digital Network (ISDN) was used to connect the teleworkers' work environments in their homes to the DA Centre. A maintenance option called 'Total Care' provided four-hour response for each ISDN line fault. As in every teleworking programme a balance has to be struck between the costs of rapid call-out maintenance and the costs (pay and loss of work) of having idle workers.

When engineers were called out to fix a fault they would also carry out a number of Preventive Maintenance Checks. One example is cable secureness checks as the specially designed desks have equipment and cables attached to their stowable, mobile work surface.

The teleworkers were provided with a disk and screen cleaning kit to be used at least every two weeks. Faxes or printers were not used, obviating the need to carry printer heads, paper and other items.

The teleworkers had a tendency to put pot plants on the desks. This was discouraged for obvious reasons.

Resilience was not a major issue as the central call handling equipment and directory listings database, the same system as used by the central office operators, already had their own backup systems in place. Providing standby equipment in each teleworker's home would have been pro-hibitively expensive. Full duplication of each teleworker's equipment at the central office was unnecessary as teleworkers could log in to other tele-workers' central equipment if necessary.

Maintenance is an important consideration for all teleworkers and the more remote or mobile they are, the more preventive, rather than curative, precautions need to be in place. When designing an office (Chapter 6.13), planning communications diaries (Chapter 3.5.2), and when planning security systems and routines (Chapter 5), backup electronics or fast repair procedures should be included. Like beautiful new cars, elegant communi-cations systems are of no use if they won't start.

6.15   THE SHAPE OF THINGS TO COME

It is quite enlightening to reflect back on the tremendous development of technology over the last 25 years. It is now unusual to find an office without at least a computer and fax machine, while colour TV, video recorders, compact disc and computer games have all become common household items. This section considers the way in which future advances in computers and communications are likely to shape the way that people will live their lives. It uses a little imagination to extrapolate the clear trends of today into the home and office of the future.

Advances in computer technology continue at a pace. Every year our abil-ity with electronics doubles and yet the price continues to fall. Basic micro-processors, the chips of which computers are made, are now so cheap that they can be found throughout the office and home in photocopiers, tele-phones, TVs, hi-fi systems, washing machines and even door bells. Today, microprocessors that 10 years ago were the most advanced of their time come free with a tank of fuel.

The processing power of computers continues to grow at an astounding rate, while their size is getting smaller. Computers with the power of today's desktop PC would have taken up a whole room 20 years back.

Rapid advances are also underway in data storage devices. Again, the PC on the desk serves as a good example. Just think how much information can be crammed onto a PC without ever needing to tidy it up. New technologies, such as optical storage, will allow even greater mass storage, in less space, at lower cost.

The complete works of William Shakespeare can now be stored on a fraction of a single optical disc and soon there will be small storage devices that can store all the information from an individual's lifetime. If issued at birth, these devices could store medical records, education, and holiday photos, along with any other information selected by the individual, without ever needing to erase any data.

So the trends in computers are towards 'infinite' processing power and 'free' information storage. But how will this be used in the home and the office?

It is taken as given that the office will see increasing use of information technology to improve the effectiveness of all types of processes. From word processors to databases, fax machines to digital communications, technology is bound to become an important part of the working life of everyone. However, it is interesting to consider how well equipped people are to deal with this technology. An ability to confidently use technology is based on familiarity—the more a person uses technology, the less fear it holds for them. Real familiarity will come as computers find a place in people's homes.

This is already starting to happen. Some computers sit most visibly in children's bedrooms providing hours of noisy entertainment. The explosion in the market for games consoles, led by Sega and Nintendo, illustrates the potential for computer generated entertainment. Other computers are used quietly and invisibly as part of home automation. Simple computers control the cycles of washing machines and the recording functions of video recorders. Computers will also be applied to more serious information storage and processing tasks. Home computers, that are currently used as little more than enhanced typewriters, will take on the role of advanced information terminals.

However, the real power of these individual computers will only be realised when they are linked together and able to communicate with each other. Already standards are agreed for a video recorder to 'talk' to the TV. This allows the video to be instructed to record the programme that is being watched, without needing to specify the channel.

With time, more and more domestic appliances are likely to be connected together, forming a home network. This network will link to the outside world through the domestic telephone line, allowing remote access to equipment in the home and making it possible, for example, to set the video recorder from any phone, anywhere in the world.

The telephone connection will also allow domestic appliances to dial-out. An application of this facility could be a washing machine that automatically reports a breakdown to a service centre. The machine's microprocessor would run through an auto-diagnosis to determine the fault—say a burnt-out drive motor. The machine could then arrange for a replacement part to be supplied and fitted. This would speed the repair of the machine and remove the need for a costly examination by the service technician.

Also connected to the home network will be various sensors and controllers, allowing both security and environment control. The security system will both detect unauthorised persons and raise the alarm to the Police. It could also provide a deterrent function through the environment control system by automatically controlling the lights, TV and curtains to give the appearance of occupation. Heating in the home could be similarly controlled either automatically or from a distance by the home owner.

The connection of the home network into the telephone line will provide a gateway to a whole range of information and entertainment services. Information services of the future are likely to evolve from those currently available on broadcast teletext, such as news, weather and what's-on guides. The information services would, however, be interactive, allowing a choice of exactly what information is received. For example, a travel service could provide detailed route planning for a journey based on up to the moment information about traffic delays. The planned route could even be downloaded into the car's computer, so that guidance can be provided *en route*.

Other interactive services could include teleshopping, distance learning and home banking. The terminals necessary to access all these information services are likely to enter the home in disguise. They will look little different from the TVs, videos and CD players already in many homes. But within these accepted domestic items there will be terrific functionality. The trends are already evident with advanced teletext and interactive compact disc systems.

An increasing amount of entertainment is also likely to come into the home over the telephone network. Already, children who link up their hand-held computer games at school are buying modems to allow them to continue a multi-user simulation in the evening. They've found it's more fun to play against another person, rather than against the computer.

The children who are networking their computers now, will be part of the workforce in 10 years time. These are people with an apparently intuitive understanding of computers and technology. They programme video recorders with ease, while their parents remain bemused.

There is a story that a scientist at the BT Labs, fed up with not being able to set his video, developed an improved user interface in his spare time. The interface had speech recognition, allowing the scientist to directly select the programme to be recorded by name. 'Record Star Trek tonight' was all that was needed—the interface would do the rest, consulting the TV listing to determine the channel, start time and programme length. Unfortunately, the 'interface' has now grown up and left home to go to college, leaving the scientist with a row of blinking zeros on the video timer once again.

Having grown up with technology around them, children interface with machines in a different way. They are at home with the technology, so in the future the technology will have an obvious place in their homes. It will play an essential supporting role in their lives, allowing them to do what they want to do where they want to do it. These are the people who will expect their employers to allow them to use technology to work how and when it suits them. They will see the flexibility of teleworking as the accepted and expected norm, rather than an oddity.

The future developments in telecommunications are likely to parallel the advances in computers. With digitalisation and fibre optics, the ability to transmit information will continue to grow, in terms of both amount and distance. Yet the cost of transmission will continue to fall.

New developments in optical amplification and switching will open up high-speed data highways, into people's homes, as well as offices. Down these highways will flow the raw data to support the array of new information and entertainment applications in the home.

One such application is telepresence—the ability to have a conscious presence in one place while physically being in another. The videophone is the first real step towards this dream. Once this technology is combined with that of Virtual Reality, it will truly be possible to create the perception of 'being there' without needing to travel.

So, it will be feasible to sit in a home office, working alongside virtual colleagues—who work in locations throughout the country, or maybe even the world. The possibilities that this will offer are very exciting. Organisations will be able to rapidly form virtual teams to work on projects as required.

Such telepresence technology is likely to feature significantly in the design of a futuristic desk suitable for the home, office or telecentre. BT Laboratories are studying the types of technology that might be applied to such a desk. Holographic techniques could be used to create images of coworkers in the virtual office. A large, high-resolution wrap-around screen could surround the desk and onto it could be projected life-sized representations of colleagues. This would allow very natural conversations and cooperative working to occur. The social skills of face-to-face communication would still be appropriate and therefore it would not be necessary to learn a new range of skills to use the system. Technologies such as gas plasma and laser projection will soon make such large screens a practical reality. Projection of images directly onto the retina is another not too distant possibility.

The futuristic desk is also likely to have an active surface—effectively the PC display will be embedded in the desktop. Combined with pen-based input, this will allow information to be displayed and manipulated in a way that is familiar to most people through the use of paper and pen. The human–computer interface will also be enhanced by the developments in speech recognition technology. The replacement for the QWERTY keyboard may have been found!

All the trends suggest that technology will, at some stage in the future, allow almost anything to be done, anywhere. The only question remaining is 'What do you want to do'?

7

Appendices

7.1 TACIT TELEWORKING: STATISTICAL REVIEW

At present, surveys show there are *circa* 1 million UK and 4 million US tele-workers, working at home. The majority of these are self-employed but the percentage of wholly employed personnel is growing.

A UK survey by Oxford-based SW2000, in March 1992, based on major organisations employing a total of 800 000 people (being 3.6% of the total working population and over 9% of those employed by large organisations), showed that just 0.3% were full-time teleworkers. Extrapolated to the employed population (excluding self-employed) gives 66 000 employed teleworkers.

Reports on numbers were given at Telecommute '92 in Washington in October 1992. First, Paul Rupert of Rodgers and Associates, referring to a magazine survey of 100 organisations in 1992, showed that 60% had some telecommuters but these totalled just 0.25% of the workforce. Extrapolating that figure to the 120 million employed in the USA gives 300 000 wholly employed telecommuters. Secondly, Thomas Miller of LINK Resources NYC found 2.8 million telecommuters in small businesses, which would include the self-employed, and 240 000 from large organisations. LINK Resources reported in June 1993 a 22% increase in USA teleworkers, mostly in the small business sector.

The number of formal, wholly employed teleworkers in 1992 would there-fore seem to be:

- USA   240 000–300 000
- UK   60 000

Other studies show, however, that the number of formal teleworkers is the tip of a very large iceberg.

7.2   MOBILE AND SALES PERSONNEL

For decades there have been people working out of their homes and only going into central office from time to time. Prudential Assurance, London, employs 6000 home based sales persons, half their personnel, who relate to regional offices. Prudential Insurance, New York, has 28 000 sales people linked by car phones, modems and fax. Many major sales operations are staffed in this way, making for a large population of mobile workers, who keep the roads busy through the day. These sales staff, the communicators between the organisation and the customers, are mobile teleworkers, but being familiar and established figures they are often overlooked in surveys.

Sales people now save journeys they used to make to central office by teleworking, faxing or e-mailing in reports and orders, telephoning to keep in touch and, in rare cases, calling in at teleconference facilities to see and hear their colleagues at central office.

Modern organisations no longer require computer technicians and other service engineers to commute in daily to a central point. Calls are sorted on computer systems and allocated to the nearest person, who proceeds from customer to customer by telephoning central office at the end of each assignment. Even where technicians must commute daily to a depot to collect a service vehicle, they are no longer required to drive back to the centre after each task for fresh instructions. The telecommunications network and computerised journey planning systems reduce travel time and costs. Thus they might qualify as teleworkers.

Government statistics do not record how many such travellers companies employ and, due to the variation in the number which any particular industry might employ, it is difficult to estimate. It is not difficult, however, to list 10 companies like the Prudential, with large sales forces, and to extrapolate from these to assume that there are at least as many mobile teleworkers as there are telecommuters at home, thus doubling the above numbers.

7.3   PRIVILEGED CORPORATE TELEWORKERS

SW2000's March 1992 survey asked **'Of the people in central office how many sometimes work at home during normal workdays, excluding formal telecommuters?'**

63% of employers reported significant, occasional homeworking and 37% reported none.

The 63% with occasional but unofficial homeworking (tacit teleworking) were asked to head count. The results were chaotic and many respondents, mostly personnel managers, couldn't hazard any estimates. The next question was **'Is occasional homeworking officially acknowledged?'**

89.8% said it was not acknowledged. Working at home did not officially occur.

When asked if occasional homeworking was a privilege, 20% said yes and 43% said no. The 'don't knows' were higher than for any other question.

7.3.1   Watch this space

If the personnel managers cannot give clear answers, then how do we estimate the impact of informal telecommuting? Surveys of empty desks give a clue to the real numbers. IBM, DEC and other companies have studied desk space use in their own organisations.

Dr Franklin Becker and his colleagues at Cornell University, NYS College of Human Ecology, have surveyed many corporations with traditional office layouts. In one large office, on one working day, only 30% of desks were occupied and 70% unoccupied. At peak use of the desks, 30% remained unused. As a general average, Dr Becker calculated the figure of 40% unoccupied desks.

Where were all the people? Some were away sick; on average, men in the UK lose 18 days a year and women lose 9 days—assuming equal numbers in any office, an average of 13 days out of 260 days a year, or 5%. The 1993 TUC (Trades Unions Congress) findings show a reduction in the UK to an average of 8 days a year sick leave, comparable to the USA figures.

People take holidays other than bank holidays, an average of 3 weeks or 15 days, making a further 5.8%.

It would be assumed perhaps that the missing 29% were out with customers and suppliers. But is this in fact the case? How many of the missing persons were working at home?

> Visiting a major institution in North America in 1992 produced an interesting insight. The 8000 personnel were largely professional men and women, visiting sites, writing detailed and lengthy reports and working to tight deadlines under close editorship. The personnel department confidently stated that no telecommuting existed, other than customer-site working which was a known quantity.
>
> However, the Information Technology manager, working from a different building a few miles from the centre, even more confidently reported that 1000 professionals worked at home at any one time. They chose to do so to meet deadlines which they would miss if plunged into the interruptions of the central office. This officially non-teleworking organisation had a 12.5% incidence of unofficial homeworking.

If this were typical, then we could assume 16.7% of personnel were out at customers or other sites.

While this example is not typical of large offices, because of the high proportion of professionals judged on deliverables rather than on attendance, it provides an upper measure of tacit teleworking.

A review in even the most disciplined of 'attendance based' offices will reveal a significant percentage of desks are unoccupied, particularly if the senior staff desks are included. Dr Becker has found that up to 25% of space can generally be saved if the empty, unused desks are removed.

Because we cannot know the number of personnel officially out at customers, the above information does not yet allow an accurate count of unofficial homeworkers, but it does provide valuable clues. We can guess-timate that between 12.5% and 0% are home working—say 6%.

In the USA 6% of the major organisation sector converts to 2.8 million people, in addition to officially recognised teleworkers amongst the wholly employed workforce. In the UK it converts to an extra 0.5 million people.

7.3.2   Statistics and damn lies

Tangential and anecdotal evidence may exist to confirm the accuracy or otherwise of these numbers.

The survey in March 1992 found that of 118 major employers, only a small and possibly unrepresentative sample could comment on occasional home-working, but it drew a number of precise responses to Question 5: **'Of the staff in your location, within your direct knowledge, how many work at home informally: Directors, Senior and Middle Managers, Junior Managers—Days per week?'**

A Health Authority, with 1600 people in one complex, or $1600 \times 5 = 8000$ working days a week, reported 140 manager days per week worked at home, = 1.75%.

A City area authority, with 5000 in one complex or $5000 \times 5 = 25\,000$ working days a week, reported 300 manager days per week worked at home, = 1.2%.

A private, mainly clerical, corporation with 1450 people in one building or $1450 \times 5 = 7250$ working days a week, reported 98 manager days per week at home, = 1.35% (2).

An Adult Education centre, excluding lecturers, reported staff days worked at home, = 1.1%.

An oil corporation with 300 people in one building reported only senior managers worked at home, totalling 40 days a week, = 2.6%.

Extrapolating from these few reliable responses, and bearing in mind that the question actually deals only with managers in major organisations, but assuming that junior staff do not have the flexibility to work at home at all, an average of 1.6% of all employee days in the major sector (some 40% of the employed population) emerges as working at home informally.

In the UK this calculates to ($22m \times 40\% = 8.8m$ people $\times 1.6\% =$) 140 800 people working informally at home on any one day. If the same numbers apply to the USA, they indicate ($120m \times 40\% = 48m$ people $\times 1.6\% =$) 768 000 people on any one working day.

7.4   SUMMARY OF HOMEWORKING NUMBERS

On any one working day	UK	USA
Self-employed and small business sector	576 000	2 883 000
Formal, wholly employed in major organisations (0.3%)	60 000	240 000
Informal, wholly employed in major organisations (1.6%)	140 000	768 000
Mobile teleworkers in cars	60 000	240 000
Total on any one day	836 000	4 131 000
Possible size of the tacit teleworking population (6%) of major organisations	528 000	2 880 000
Less: included above and duplicated	−140 000	−768 000
Total teleworkers who work at home on some days	1 224 000	6 243 000

7.5   COUNTING TACIT TELEWORKERS

(Reproduced by permission of SW2000, Oxford 'Teleworking Pilot Project Check List', 1992.)

Survey your organisation for existing examples of teleworking at home. 50% of all jobs are possibly suitable for telecommuting. Count desks and empty desks on 10 different working days and log the results.

Compile tacit teleworking by issuing questionnaires to all personnel. As junior ranks will not want to be challenged on their home working habits because many older managers frown on it, use anonymous questionnaires, or use named questionnaires, starting at the top of the organisation, and let the results trickle down in advance of junior people having to answer the same questions.

The questions should include:

In the last twelve months how many days have you worked away from your office desk?
  At Home
  On Business Trips
  Elsewhere

In your view was the time spent?
  More efficiently
  Less efficiently

Of the days worked away from your desk what percentages were due to?
  Commuting problems

Unwell but not ill
To avoid interruptions
Family requirements
Other

Do you have office equipment at home?
Computer
Printer
Modem
Additional Phone line
Fax
Copier
Other

The responses gathered should be collated and analysed to give the following basic information:

The number of person/desk/days when desks are unoccupied.
The number of people who sometimes work at home or remotely.
Initiatives taken to equip home/remote offices.
People who adapt to remote working efficiently.
Type of tasks undertaken at home/remotely.
Distance of remote work from central office.

Use the information to consider whether:

Occasional home/remote working should be officially recognised.
Office space can be reduced.
Employers' contributions to commuting costs might be reduced.
Sufficient tacit teleworking activity exists to evaluate as a pilot project study.

7.6   STATISTICS AND TRUTH

Despite the difficulty in gathering reliable statistics on tacit or informal teleworking, the same forces which motivate formal projects affect every individual commuter and it is not unlikely that an increasing number opt to work at home or local centres on certain days. Remember the personnel manager, above, who was confident that no telecommuting existed in his organisation, until the Information Technology manager revealed that 12% telecommuted, before dismissing tacit teleworking as a factor in your offices. Count the desks.

The factors encouraging informal working at home include:

- Availability of equipment
- Travel systems breakdown
- Poor air quality
- Family illness
- Deadlines—avoiding interruptions

- Too unwell to commute but OK to work quietly
- A modern culture at work——results, not attendance
- Knowledge that senior people homework
- Confidence in own abilities to deliver
- Distance from office——saving time

The evidence that is emerging from the presently confused statistics is that many more people are teleworking than is often recognised and they are allowed to do so, despite predominantly anti-teleworking office cultures, because the results are good. Tacit teleworking shares all the economic advantages of formal teleworking systems, if the individuals have the right equipment and the right personal characteristics. The next generation of computerate (computer literate) youngsters are going to find it difficult to accept the logic of commuting daily to work when they will have the ability and capability to produce more from their desk-top computers at home.

Tacit teleworking seems to be increasing rapidly, perhaps linked to the reducing cost and availability of computers and fax machines for the home. The growth is certain to accelerate rapidly in all modern major organisations where keyboard skills and communications equipment skills are automatically expected of all employees.

7.7   THE TELEWORKING OF TELEWORKING EXPLAINED

The 23 authors and editors of this book took a lesson from their own research and teleworked the writing of this book. It required a Project Coordinator to be appointed and a deal of patience when wrestling with the infinite combinations available to editors for creating computer file references.

The electronic links spanned the British Isles and most of the USA, where the US editor and author travelled extensively across time zones, constantly dogged by a trail of phone, fax and computer messages, demanding his instant attention. The process was by no means paperless; the team have been awarded first prize by the paper manufacturing industry for the fastest consumption of copier paper and fax rolls; the garbage trucks made extra journeys to dispose of discarded drafts in recycling units.

In the UK, the editors were linked by an ISDN (Integrated Services Digital Network) over a triangle whose base was 50 miles between Ipswich and Oxford and whose apex towered 500 miles (as far as the land stretches) to Thurso in the north of Scotland. ISDN lines supplanted the need for more traditional modems to link the computers and provided a very fast transfer of files at the rate of some 500 words, or a book page, per second.

Drafts of sections of the book were printed out on numerous desktop printers in a medley of character typefaces and sizes: small modern type from sharp-sighted younger authors and traditional, large and well-spaced type from ageing, yet wise and experienced, older team members. The drafts were read and re-read, edited, commented on and returned to authors by different systems.

One editor preferred to handwrite over received faxed texts and to re-fax them back. The fact that these papers remained legible is testimony to the remarkable accuracy of facsimile machines and to the telephone lines and exchanges which transmit the electrical pulses. Another editor systemati cally worked through texts and typed out comments and alterations on a word processor, printed the edits and faxed them in pristine and legible condition to the relevant author or editor. Some texts were edited via the ISDN lines or by networking desktop computers. The 23 authors had a choice of fax, computer modems, ISDN network, or post; and being 23 individuals, they used them all.

A few round table meetings were held, necessitating road and air travel, but not until publication did all the contributors meet at the same time. The publishers sat back and waited patiently for the real work to begin as the editors promised final draft after final draft. They (the publishers) issued guidelines as to how they would like to see the text presented: standard type, double-line spaced, bright white paper; and as for the computer disk—no formatting, don't bother to try for compatibility with our machines—it won't be compatible—and specify the headings by numbers.

A few technical snags arose. One editor/author, wrestling with the whole book on one computer file, received the patently untrue and malevolent message 'CANNOT SAVE, INSUFFICIENT MEMORY TO COMPLETE THE PROCEDURE', which refused to go away, despite technical wizardry, pleas, imprecations, physical threats to the integrity of the machine's inner and outer being , incantations and what appeared to be a war dance. Repetitions were avoided by switching on the 'automatic save' option. Another time, a large piece of text was lost after being copied onto a disc for posting by mail. Fortunately the coordinator in Thurso had a copy on computer and, with effortless superiority, was able to transmit and restore the lost text, via the ISDN lines, in a few seconds.

Fax machines ran out of paper at inconvenient times. Printers ran out of ink and authors ran out of words. But all these problems were quickly resolved.

The most enduring difficulty proved to be the translation from American to English and vice-versa. Some of the mutually excluded words were familiar and some were simply a matter of spelling, but others were surprising to representatives on both sides of the pond.

Americans don't have creches they have child care facilities; their factory chimneys are smokestacks and only their homes have chimneys, to let out the smoke from the coke, which the British burn on their fires and Americans make into a soft drink. British families live in dormitory towns while Americans inhabit bedroom communities from where they join the commute which has evolved, without Royal consent, from a verb into a noun. Saloon cars are for drinking in on the railroads in America, yet for the English are the height of sobriety on the roads, which the UK Company pays for, whereas the American Corporation rarely supplies cars to employees.

Whilst Britons say whilst, Americans use while but both will wile away the time in their apartments, though the British prefer to flake out in a flat while their transatlantic cousins crash in a condominium; which a drunken Englishman might think to use for contraception on the back seat of his saloon car. Postal services employ mailmen (and women) in the USA and postmen (and women) in the UK who deliver the mail and the post respectively; both systems deliver junk-mail which Americans trash and Britons bin. Americans, who spurn the metric system, know with certainty from five years old that 2000 pounds make one ton whilst/while English engineers know, with equal certainty, there are 2240 of the same damn pounds (weight not sterling) in a good old, reliable British ton. Both are put to rights by the French, Italians and other Roman citizens with their funny tonne which is computed (on the fingers) in tens of something or other and weighs 0.984 of an English ton or 2204 pounds—-and a bit, just to confuse the Americans; who are not OK with au fait, as they are not familiar with that term. If an American takes against an Englishman he might shove him off the sidewalk, either onto the road, which both nations build, or onto a yard where the Englishman, who paves his yard with stone, would be surprised at the softness of the grass, which grows in billions of separate blades in England and trillions in the same space in America. Local Zoning is Planning Permission, color is colour, centre is center, a lift an escalator, a loft a warehouse, a boot a trunk and a trunk a suitcase. Having eliminated 95% of Webster's and the Oxford Dictionary, this book was written from a vocabulary of just 200 common words. The nations are bound together, however, by the communion of taxation, common to all mankind; yet even this oldest of all professions is the Internal Revenue Service in America but the Inland Revenue in Britain—unmistakable terms in both languages.

Despite the language problem, this book for teleworkers and telecommuters has gotten itself written and may even have brought a few more words or phrases into use, to add to the ever growing half-million words in the English dictionary. The dollar/sterling conversion was impossible as the two currencies kept dancing around for the whole year this book was in progress. An 'Ode to a Shrinking World' and to world standards in all things remains to be written.

Did teleworking work? Yes it did. Two of the editors worked full-time from their homes and most contributors wrote the majority of text in their homes, then took or mailed computer discs to an editor who added it to the draft book, held on the redoubtable Bull/Zenith MV-875LR computer. The project coordinator homogenised the multifarious discs and brought them together in one file for transmission to the editors. The publishers sat on the sidelines, knowing it would all be the same in the end to them, but, to their surprise, gratefully receiving and editing the text on computer disc, which proved to be largely compatible with their own Macintosh system running Quark Xpress 3.1 on Quadra 700s.

Numerous journeys and meetings were cut out due to the teleworking system, office spaces were free for other uses and the time taken to edit and integrate texts was reduced. The draft was delivered (almost) on time, an unusual publishing event. The US editor, whose other work took him on many long journeys during the months of writing, was able to work on the move using his Apple PowerBook computer and have his fax and calls routed via Bell Atlantic's FeatureFAX service and his calls faithfully recorded and accessed on a PhoneMate answering machine, all to arrive at his hotels at the same time as himself.

The book would have been possible to compile without electronics, telephones and communication networks, but the time spent and the work involved would have been far greater and would have spanned many more months. The editors and authors all have cause to thank the computer hard- and software industry, the telecommunications companies in the UK and USA and the desktop printer manufacturers; whose products have made the teleworking revolution possible.

Bibliography

A. Bibby (1991) *Home Is Where The Office Is* Headway, Hodder and Stoughton

D. Blythell (1978) *The Sweated Trades* Batsford Academic

S. Burch (1991) *Teleworking: A Strategic Guide for Management* Kogan Page

J.O. Cherrington (1989) *Organisational Behaviour* Allyn and Bacon

H. Cornwell (1987) *Data Theft* Macmillan

Data Communications Directory Recommendations. CCITT X.500–X.521

Data Communications Networks Message Handling System Recommendations. CCITT X.400–X.420

DEGW/BRE (1991) *The Responsible Workplace—Case Studies Report*

A. Denbigh (1992) *Telecottages—The UK Experience* ACRE

The Economist (1990) *Vital World Statistics* Hutchinson

R.D. Evans and H.J.P. Herring (1990) *Energy Use and Energy Efficiency in the UK Domestic Sector to 2010* HMSO

J Finch (1983) *Married to the Job* George Allen and Unwin

D. Fleming (1992) Step-by-step planning for your telecommuting pilot. In: *Telecommute '92* Gil Gordon Associates.

G. Gilder (1993) *Papers 1993* Seattle Discovery Institute

S. Gold (1989) *The New Hacker's Handbook* Centurion

G. Gordon (1992, 1993) *Telecommuting Review Newsletters* Gil Gordon Associates.

G. Gordon Associates (1992) *Telecommute '92 Washington* Conference Notes Gil Gordon Associates

S. Graham (1993) *Best Practice in Developing Community Teleservice Centres* CASR, University of Manchester (UK)

M. Gray (1992) *Teleworking Support Systems* BT Labs

J. M. Griffiths (1992) *ISDN Explained* 2nd edn,Wiley/BT

M. Hafer (1992) *Telecommuting: An Alternative Route to Work* Washington State Energy Office

C. Handy (1989) *The Age of Unreason* Century Hutchinson

Henley Centre for BT (1988) *Tomorrow's Workplace. Conference papers* BT/CBI

F. Herzberg *et al* (1959) *The Motivation to Work* Wiley

HMSO (1988) *National Travel Survey*

HMSO (1991) *Annual Abstract of Statistics*

HMSO (1992) *Energy Related Carbon Emmissions in Possible Future Scenarios for the United Kingdom*

N. Hodson (1992) *The Economics of Teleworking* BT Labs

N. Hodson (1992) *Teleworking Pilot Scheme Check List* SW2000

P. Hodson (1989) *The institution as a container Conference paper* SW2000

U. Huws *et al* (1990) *Telework: Towards the Elusive Office* Wiley

ICF (1991) *Privatizing Telecommunication Systems*

Inland Revenue (1992) Booklet 480

Internal Revenue Services (1992) *Tax Guide for Small Businesses (334)*

Internal Revenue Services (1992) *Travel, Entertainment and Gifts (463)*

Internal Revenue Services (1992) *Selling Your Home (553)*

Internal Revenue Services (1992) *Employees Business Expenses for form 2106*

International Labour Office (1990) *Conditions of Work Digest*

D. Jones (1993) *Videotelephony and Teleworking* BT Labs

F. Kinsman (1987) *The Telecommuters* Wiley

R.E. Kraut (1991) *Getting Together At a Distance* Bellcore Exchange

T. Kristiansen (1991) *A Window to the Future* Norwegian Telecom Research Department

W. Landreth (1986) *Out of the Inner Circle* Random House

D. Longley and M. Shain (1987) *Data and Computer Security Dictionary* Macmillan

M.H. Lyons (1990) *A Study of the Environmental Impact of Teleworking* BT Labs

A. Obholzer *Institutional Dynamics and Resistance to Change* Tavistock Clinic (Paper No 81)

A. Obholzer *A Psychoanalytic Perspective on Group and Institutional Processes* Tavistock Clinic (Paper No 100)

S.L. O'Connell (1974) *Choice and Change* Prentice Hall

OTR Group (1991) *Telecommuting: The Environmental Push & Technology Pull* OTR Group National Forum

A. Page and D. Brain (1991) *Research and Technology on Telematic Systems in Rural Areas* Office for Official Publications of the European Communities

S. Potter (1992) *Open University* Data on transport and road research, private communication

Roarke Associates (1993) *Telecommuting Offices*

L. Sergeman-Peck (1991) *Networking and Mentoring* Piatkus

D. Smith (1981) *Reliability and Maintainability in Perspective* Macmillan

J. Stanworth and C. Stanworth (1991) *Telework: The Human Resource Implications* Institute of Personnel Management

W.R. Stevens (1990) *UNIX Network Programming* Prentice Hall Software Series

C. Stoll (1989) *The Cuckoo's Egg* The Bodley Head

J. Timbs (1867) *Curiosities of London* J. Timbs

Tolleys (1989) *Tolley's Tax Cases*

Tolleys (1992) *Tax Planning for Private Residences*

Tolleys (1992) *Tax Data 1992–93*

University of California (1991) *Transportation Center Transportation Research*

D. Tucknutt and A. McGrath (1992) *A Study of Homeworking Environments* BT Labs

Wall Street Journal Europe (1993)

J. Withnell (1992) *Achieving Your Business Objectives through Teleworking* BT Labs

Index